CSI:

CRIME SCENE INVESTIGATION™

secret identity

IDW Publishing
San Diego, CA

ISBN: 1-933239-40-9
08 07 06 05   1 2 3 4 5

www.idwpublishing.com

Special Thanks to Maryann Martin and Ken Ross at CBS Consumer
Products for their invaluable assistance.

IDW Publishing is:
Ted Adams, Publisher
Chris Ryall, Editor-in-Chief
Robbie Robbins, Design Director
Kris Oprisko, Vice President
Alex Garner, Art Director
Dan Taylor, Editor
Aaron Myers, Distribution Manager
Tom B. Long, Designer
Chance Boren, Editorial Assistant
Yumiko Miyano, Business Development
Rick Privman, Business Development

CSI: Crime Scene Investigation
Created by Anthony E. Zuiker

Licensed to IDW by CBS Consumer Products

"Secret Identity"

Written by
Steven Grant

Pencils and Inks by
Gabriel Rodriguez

Colors by
Scott Keating

Painted Artwork by
Steven Perkins

Lettered by
Robbie Robbins & Tom B. Long

Book Design by
Neil Uyetake

Edited by
Chris Ryall & Alex Garner

Cover Photos by
CBS Photo/Robert Voets

chapter **one**

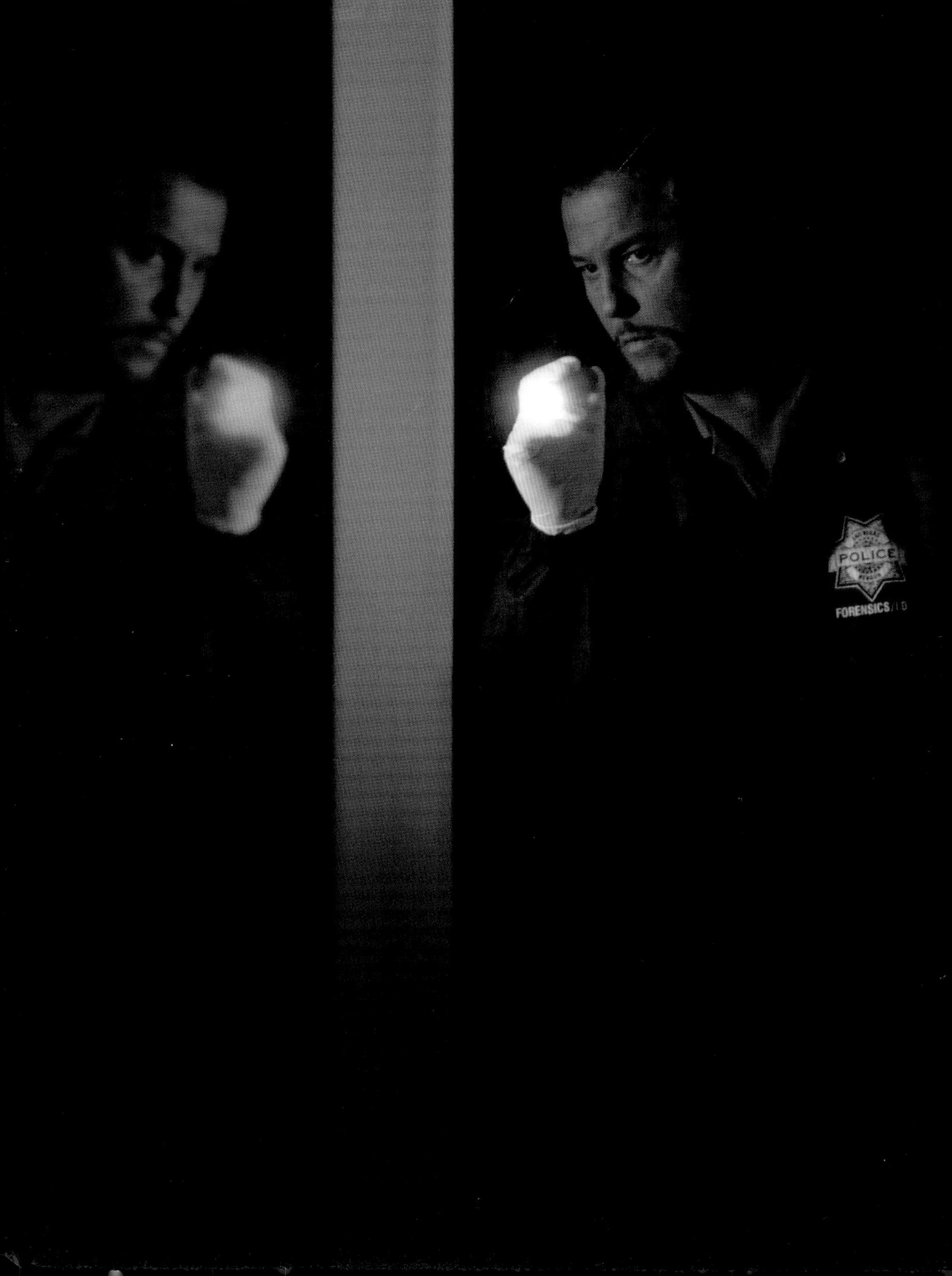
POLICE
FORENSICS/ID

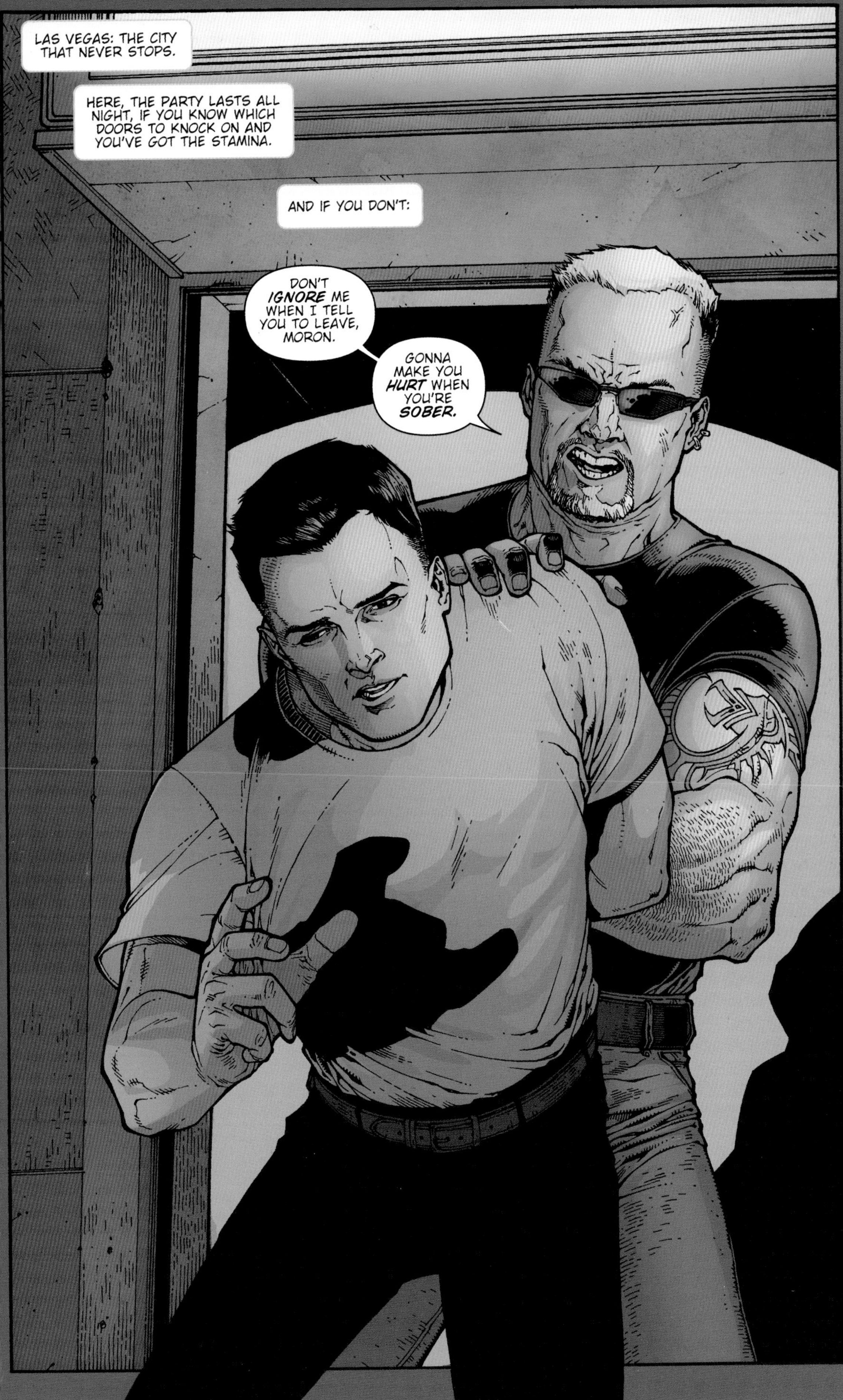
LAS VEGAS: THE CITY THAT NEVER STOPS.
HERE, THE PARTY LASTS ALL NIGHT, IF YOU KNOW WHICH DOORS TO KNOCK ON AND YOU'VE GOT THE STAMINA.
AND IF YOU DON'T:
DON'T *IGNORE* ME WHEN I TELL YOU TO LEAVE, MORON.
GONNA MAKE YOU *HURT* WHEN YOU'RE *SOBER.*

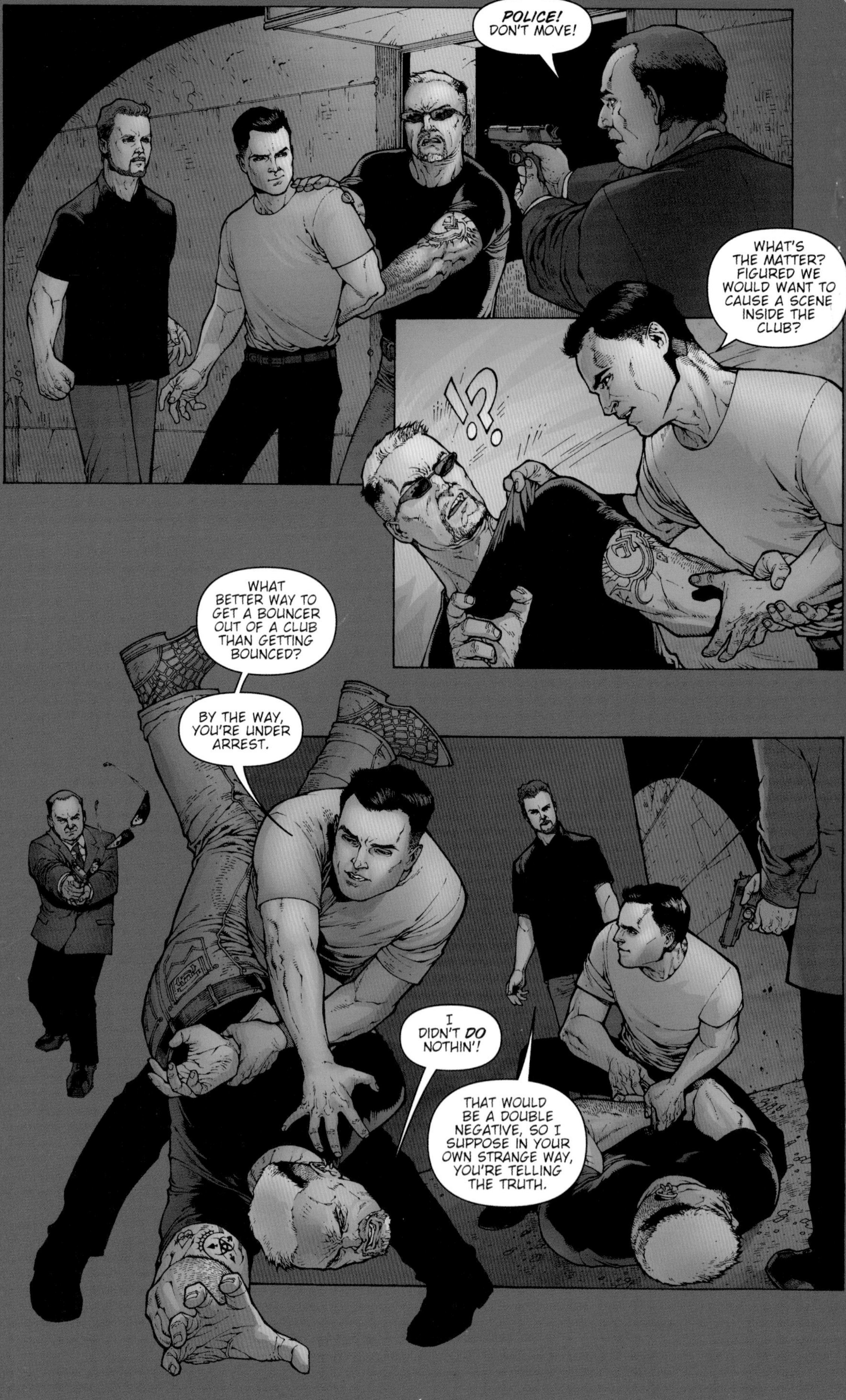

POLICE! DON'T MOVE!
WHAT'S THE MATTER? FIGURED WE WOULD WANT TO CAUSE A SCENE INSIDE THE CLUB?
!?
WHAT BETTER WAY TO GET A BOUNCER OUT OF A CLUB THAN GETTING BOUNCED?
BY THE WAY, YOU'RE UNDER ARREST.
I DIDN'T DO NOTHIN'!
THAT WOULD BE A DOUBLE NEGATIVE, SO I SUPPOSE IN YOUR OWN STRANGE WAY, YOU'RE TELLING THE TRUTH.

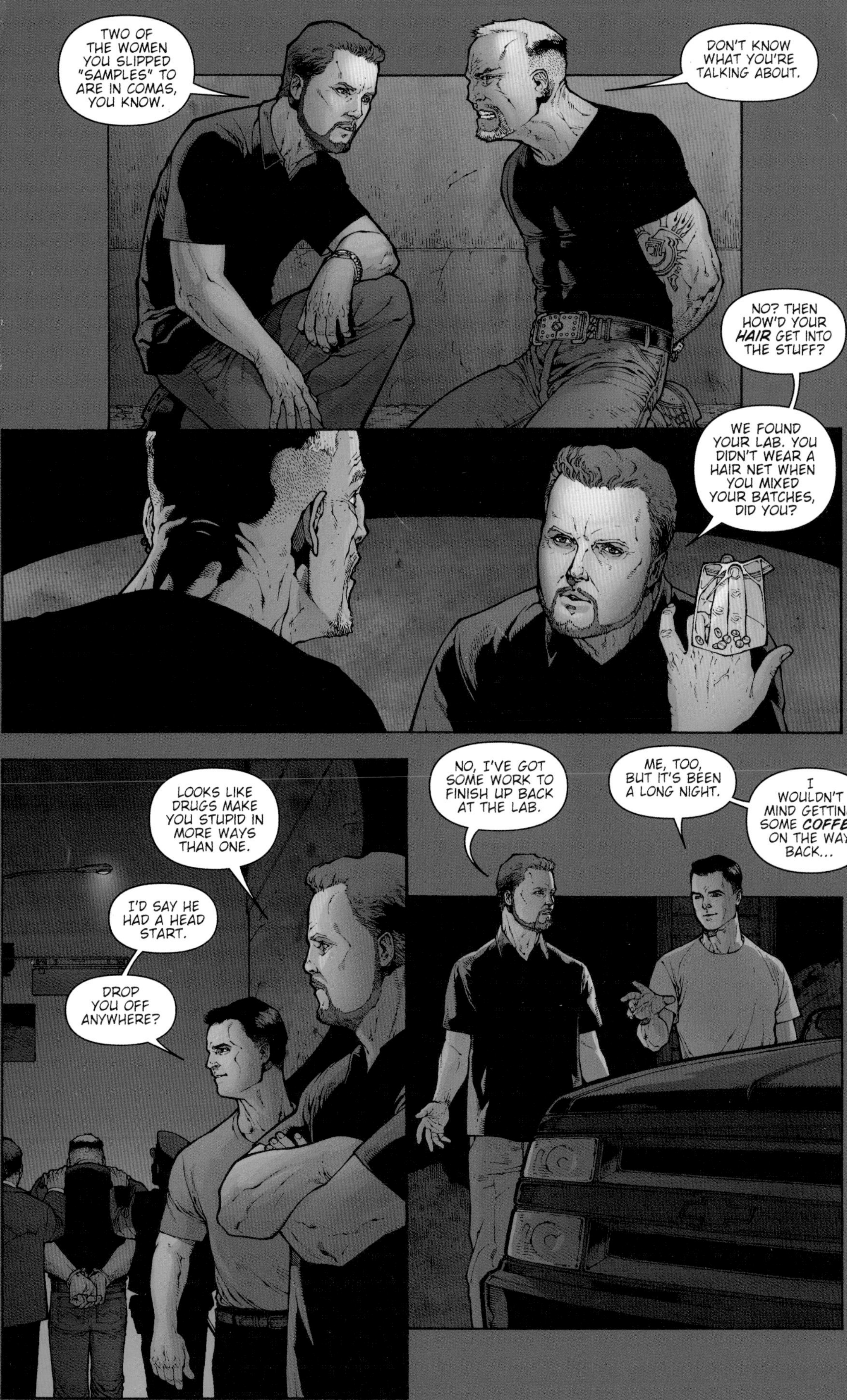

TWO OF THE WOMEN YOU SLIPPED "SAMPLES" TO ARE IN COMAS, YOU KNOW.
DON'T KNOW WHAT YOU'RE TALKING ABOUT.
NO? THEN HOW'D YOUR HAIR GET INTO THE STUFF?
WE FOUND YOUR LAB. YOU DIDN'T WEAR A HAIR NET WHEN YOU MIXED YOUR BATCHES, DID YOU?
LOOKS LIKE DRUGS MAKE YOU STUPID IN MORE WAYS THAN ONE.
I'D SAY HE HAD A HEAD START.
DROP YOU OFF ANYWHERE?
NO, I'VE GOT SOME WORK TO FINISH UP BACK AT THE LAB.
ME, TOO, BUT IT'S BEEN A LONG NIGHT.
I WOULDN'T MIND GETTING SOME COFFEE ON THE WAY BACK...

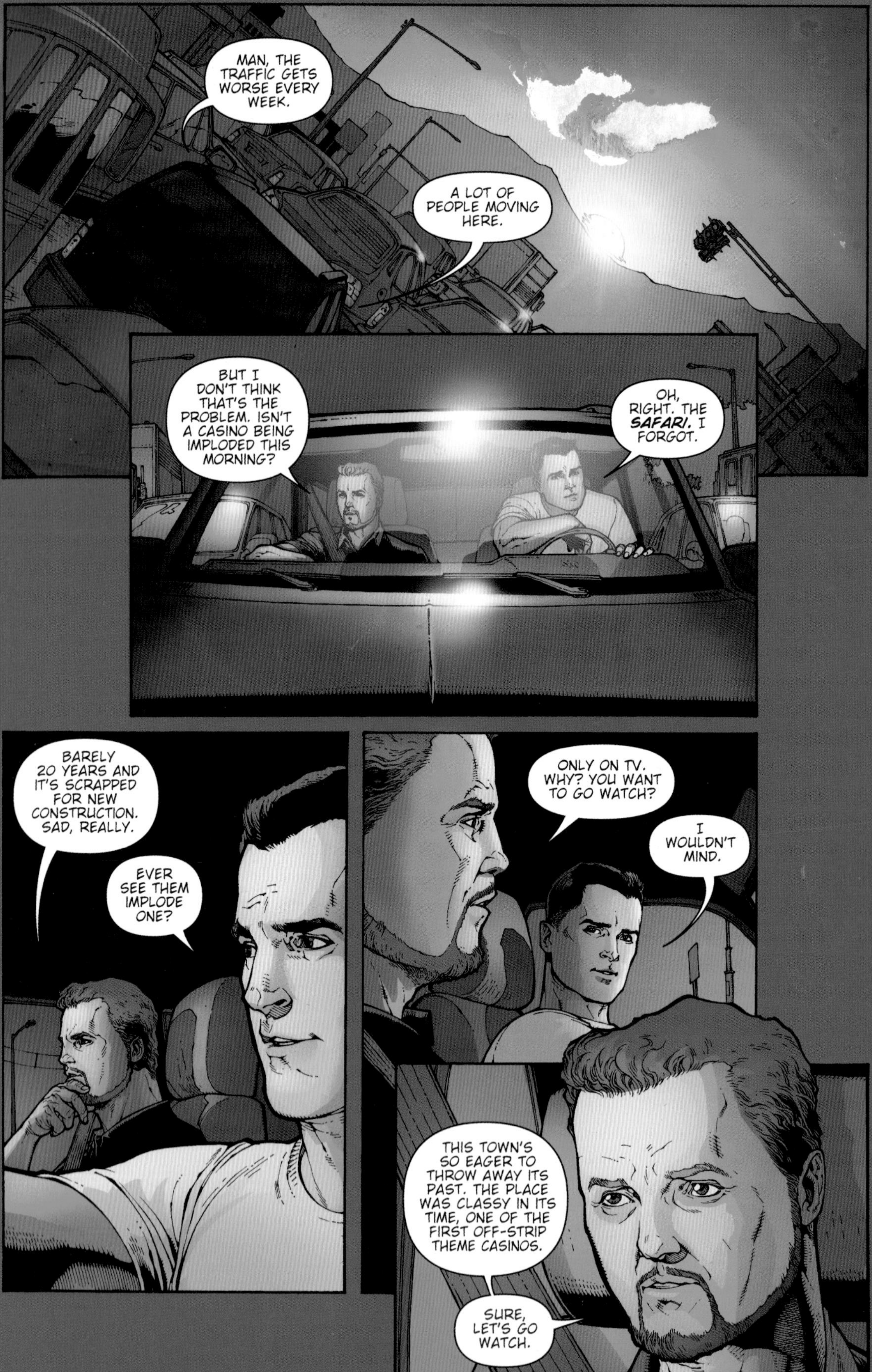
MAN, THE TRAFFIC GETS WORSE EVERY WEEK.
A LOT OF PEOPLE MOVING HERE.
BUT I DON'T THINK THAT'S THE PROBLEM. ISN'T A CASINO BEING IMPLODED THIS MORNING?
OH, RIGHT. THE *SAFARI.* I FORGOT.
BARELY 20 YEARS AND IT'S SCRAPPED FOR NEW CONSTRUCTION. SAD, REALLY.
EVER SEE THEM IMPLODE ONE?
ONLY ON TV. WHY? YOU WANT TO GO WATCH?
I WOULDN'T MIND.
THIS TOWN'S SO EAGER TO THROW AWAY ITS PAST. THE PLACE WAS CLASSY IN ITS TIME, ONE OF THE FIRST OFF-STRIP THEME CASINOS.
SURE, LET'S GO WATCH.

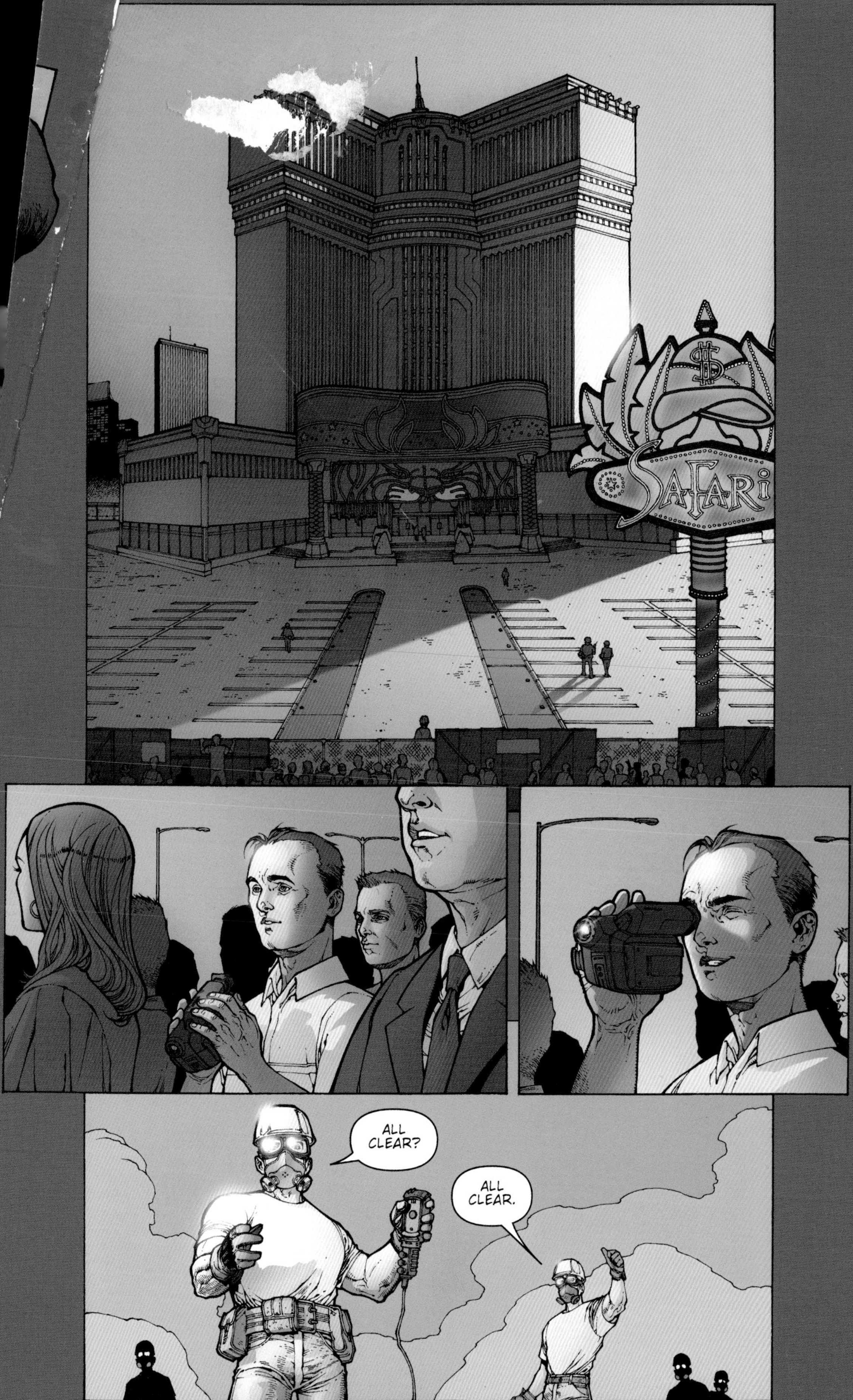
SAFARI
ALL CLEAR?
ALL CLEAR.

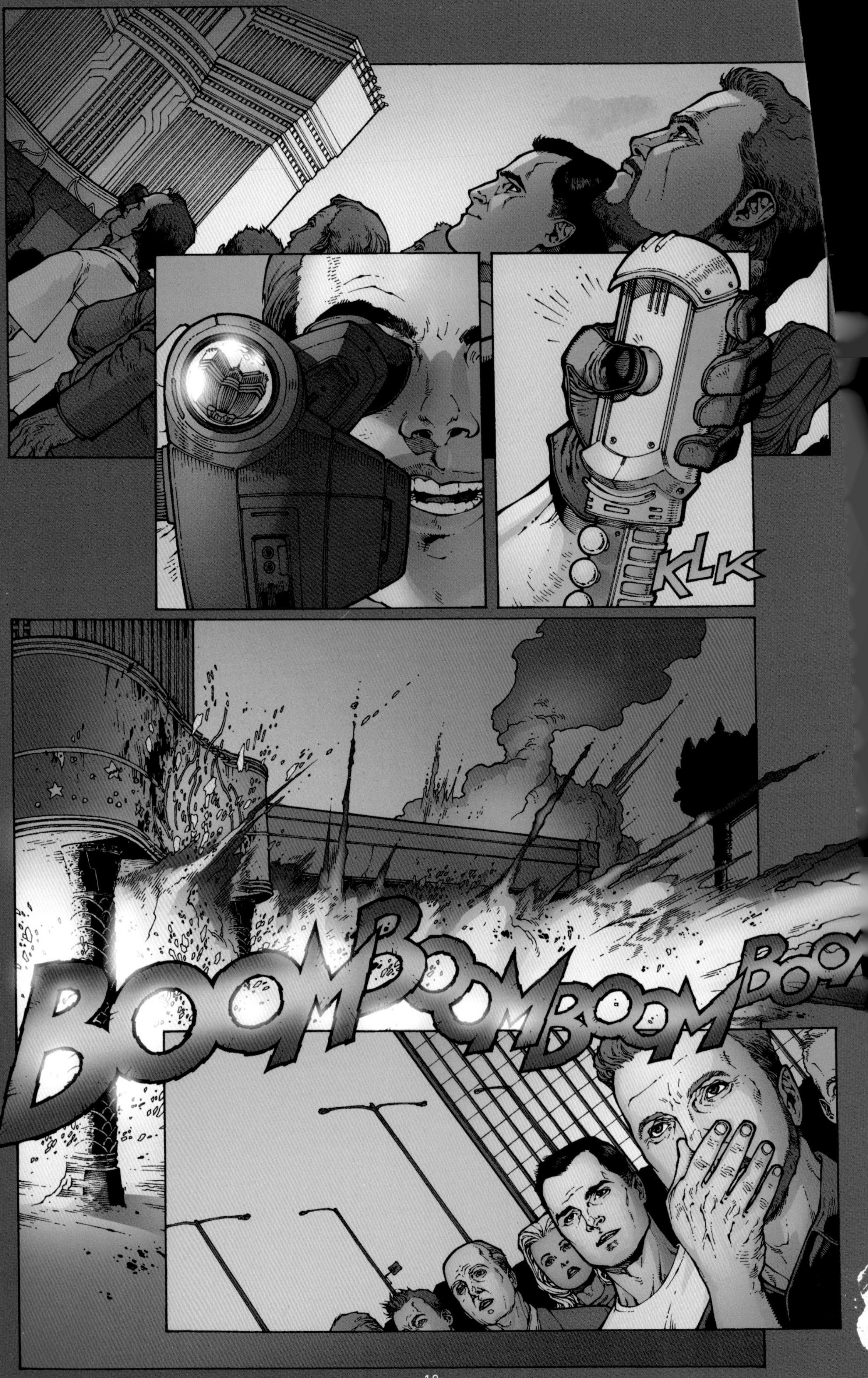
KLK
BOOMBOOMBOOMBOO

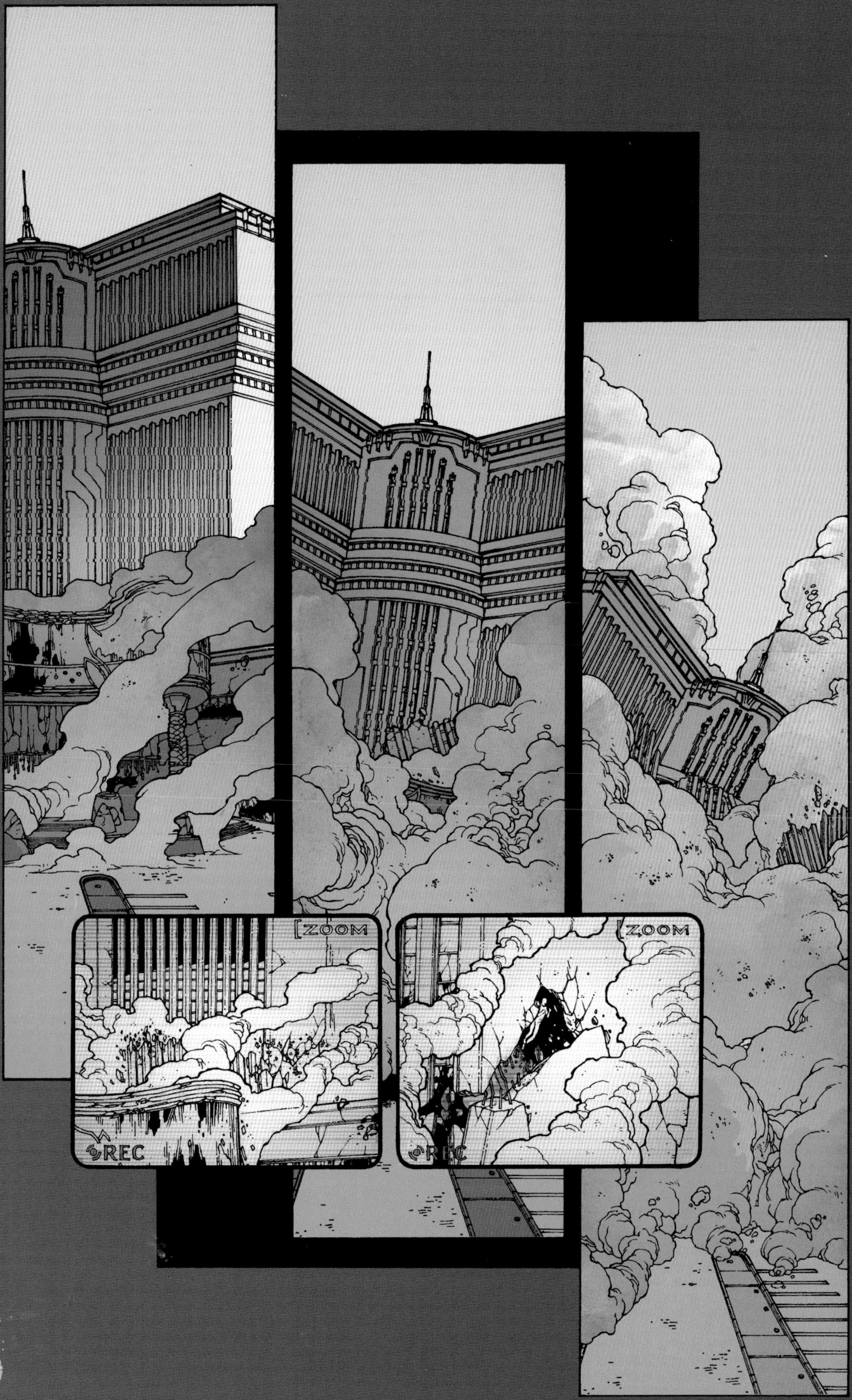
ZOOM
REC
ZOOM
REC

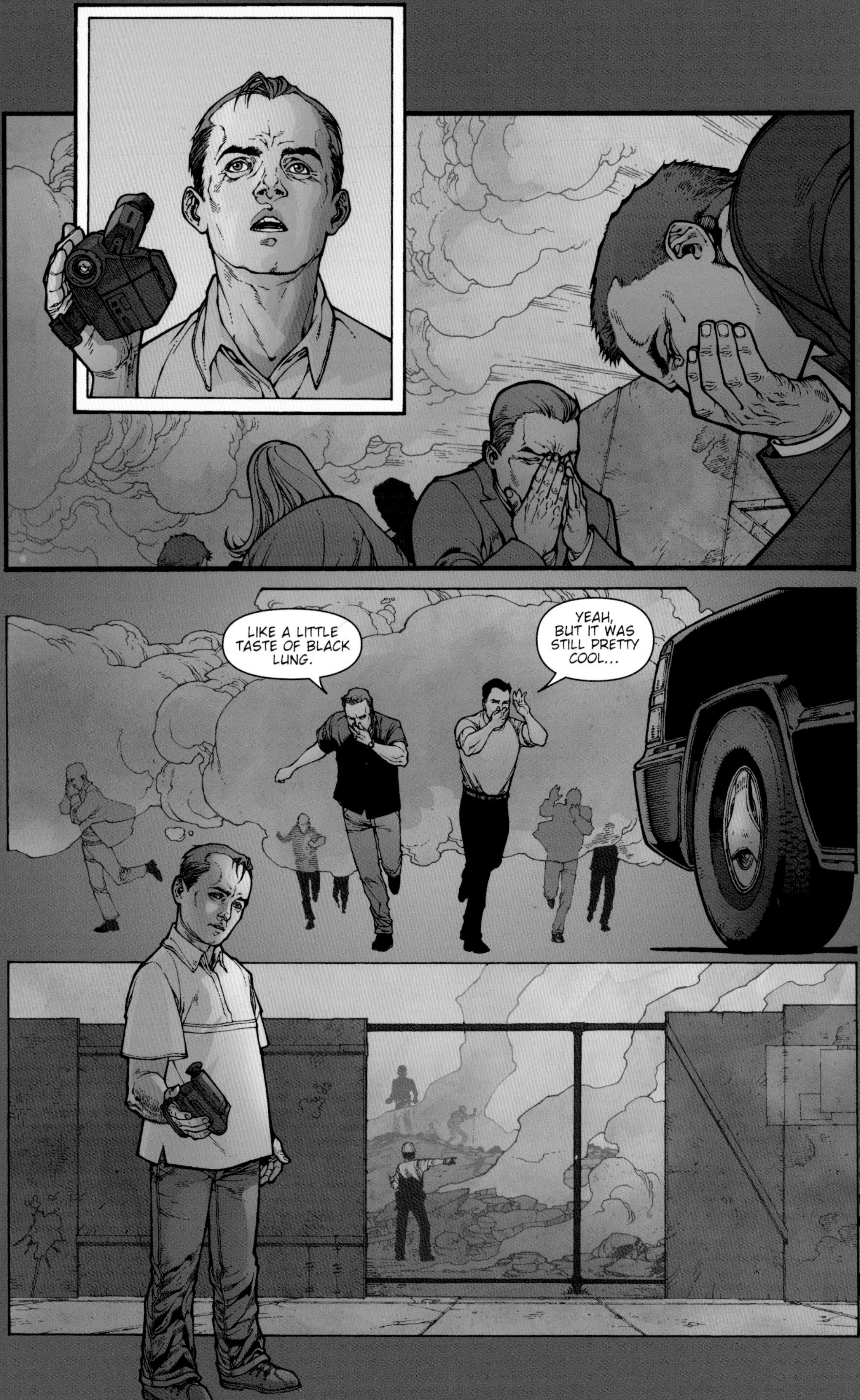
LIKE A LITTLE TASTE OF BLACK LUNG.
YEAH, BUT IT WAS STILL PRETTY COOL...

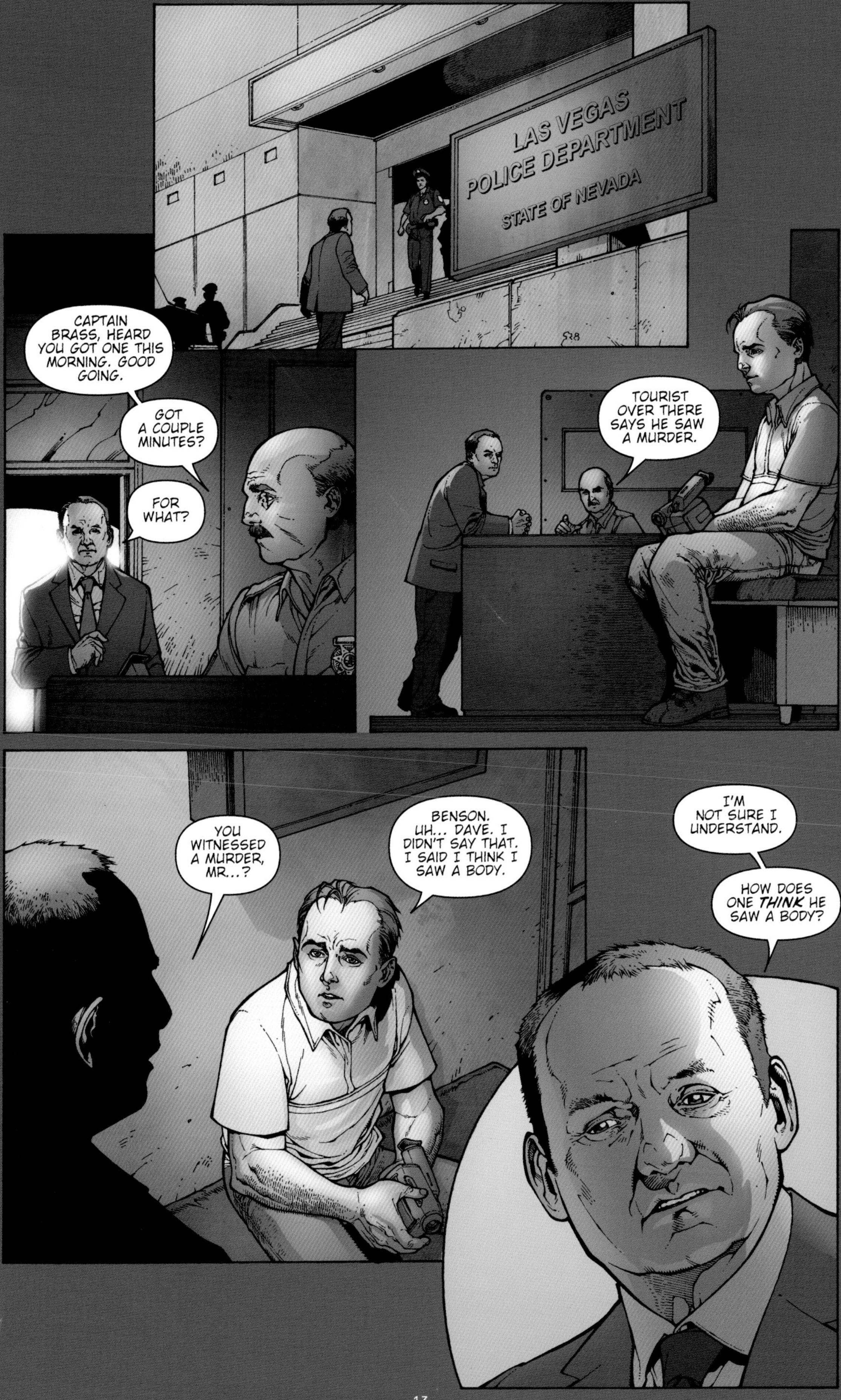
LAS VEGAS POLICE DEPARTMENT
STATE OF NEVADA
CAPTAIN BRASS, HEARD YOU GOT ONE THIS MORNING. GOOD GOING.
GOT A COUPLE MINUTES?
FOR WHAT?
TOURIST OVER THERE SAYS HE SAW A MURDER.
YOU WITNESSED A MURDER, MR...?
BENSON. UH... DAVE. I DIDN'T SAY THAT. I SAID I THINK I SAW A BODY.
I'M NOT SURE I UNDERSTAND.
HOW DOES ONE *THINK* HE SAW A BODY?

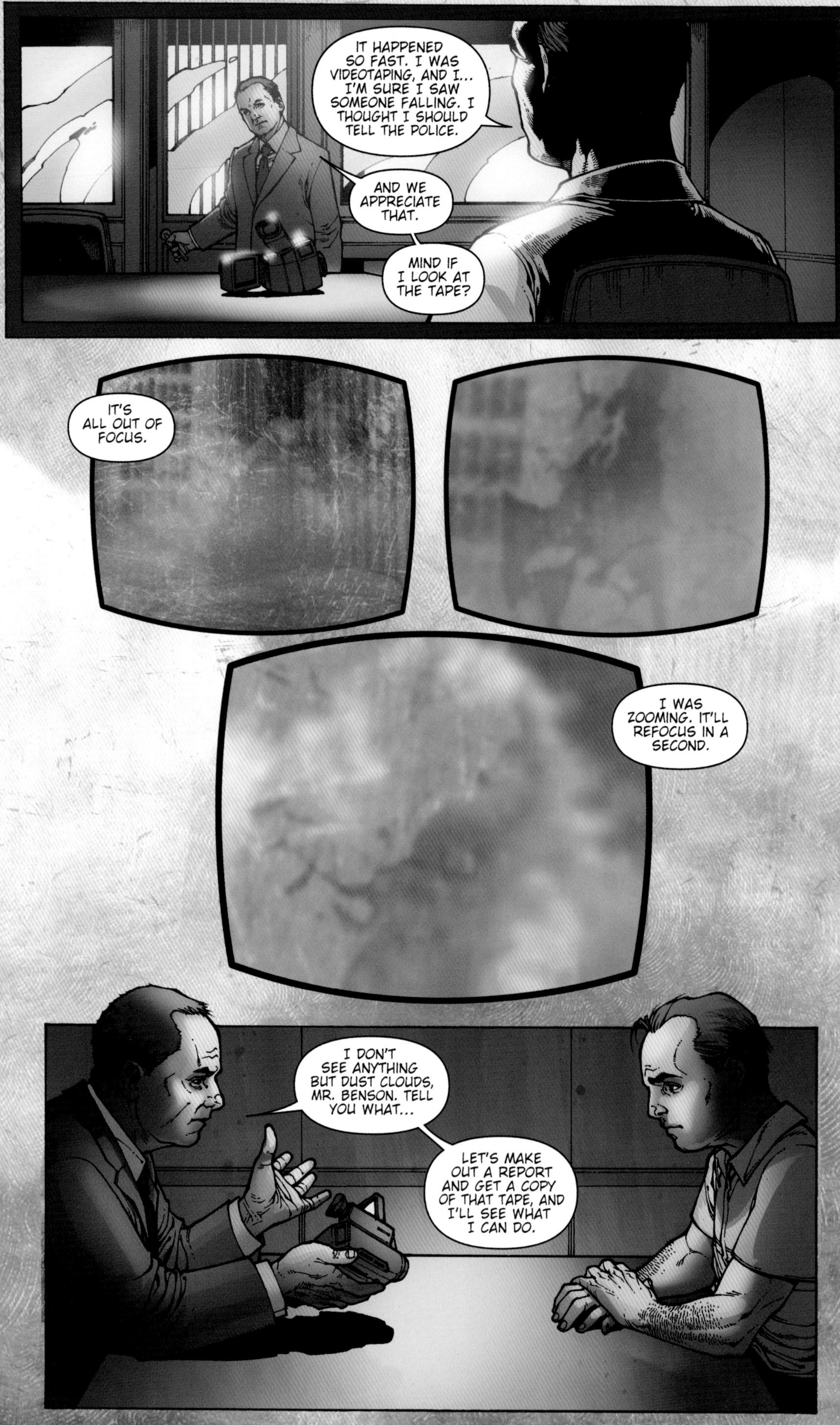
IT HAPPENED SO FAST. I WAS VIDEOTAPING, AND I... I'M SURE I SAW SOMEONE FALLING. I THOUGHT I SHOULD TELL THE POLICE.
AND WE APPRECIATE THAT.
MIND IF I LOOK AT THE TAPE?
IT'S ALL OUT OF FOCUS.
I WAS ZOOMING. IT'LL REFOCUS IN A SECOND.
I DON'T SEE ANYTHING BUT DUST CLOUDS, MR. BENSON. TELL YOU WHAT...
LET'S MAKE OUT A REPORT AND GET A COPY OF THAT TAPE, AND I'LL SEE WHAT I CAN DO.

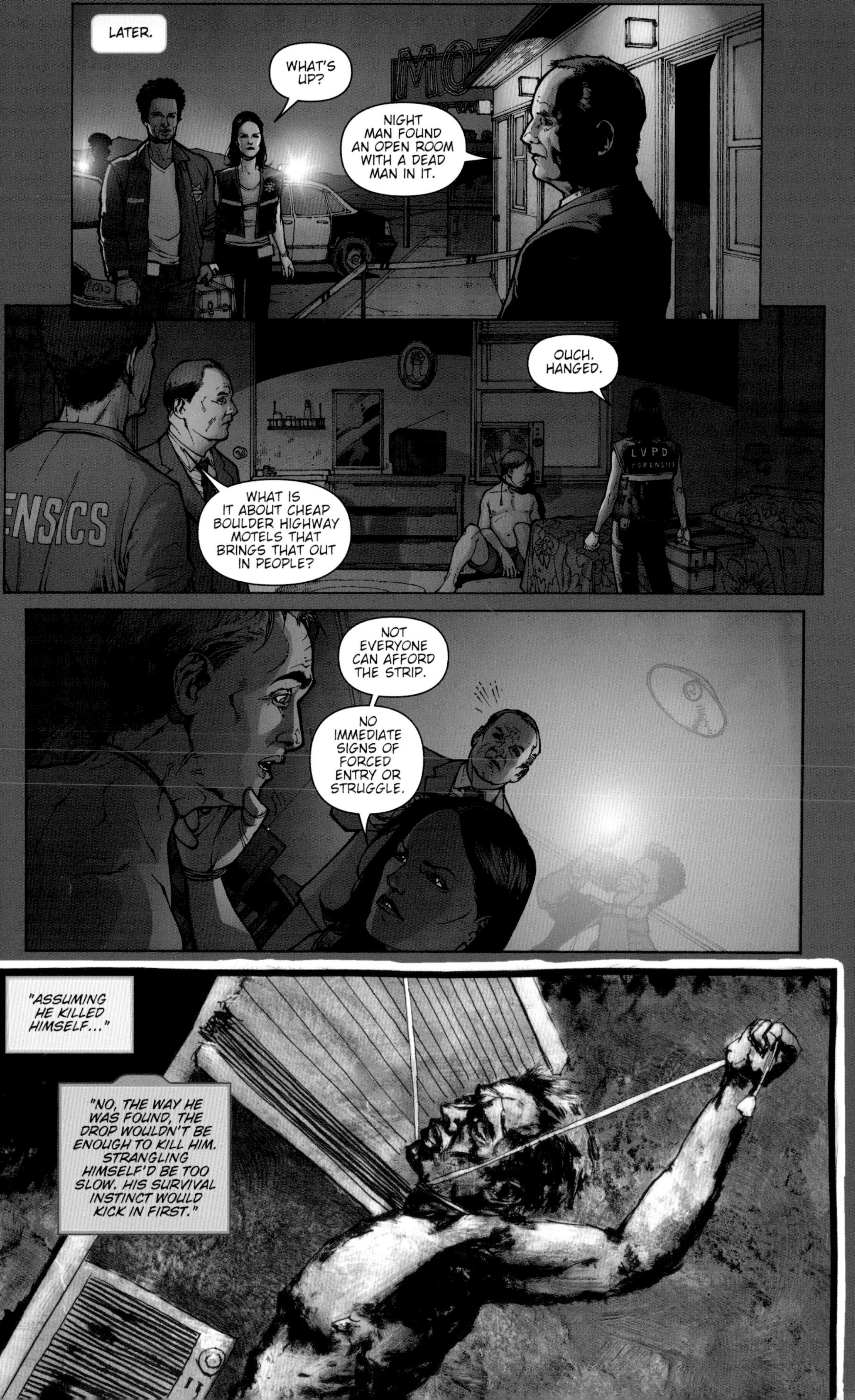
LATER.
WHAT'S UP?
NIGHT MAN FOUND AN OPEN ROOM WITH A DEAD MAN IN IT.
OUCH. HANGED.
WHAT IS IT ABOUT CHEAP BOULDER HIGHWAY MOTELS THAT BRINGS THAT OUT IN PEOPLE?
LVPD
NOT EVERYONE CAN AFFORD THE STRIP.
NO IMMEDIATE SIGNS OF FORCED ENTRY OR STRUGGLE.
"ASSUMING HE KILLED HIMSELF..."
"NO, THE WAY HE WAS FOUND, THE DROP WOULDN'T BE ENOUGH TO KILL HIM. STRANGLING HIMSELF'D BE TOO SLOW. HIS SURVIVAL INSTINCT WOULD KICK IN FIRST."

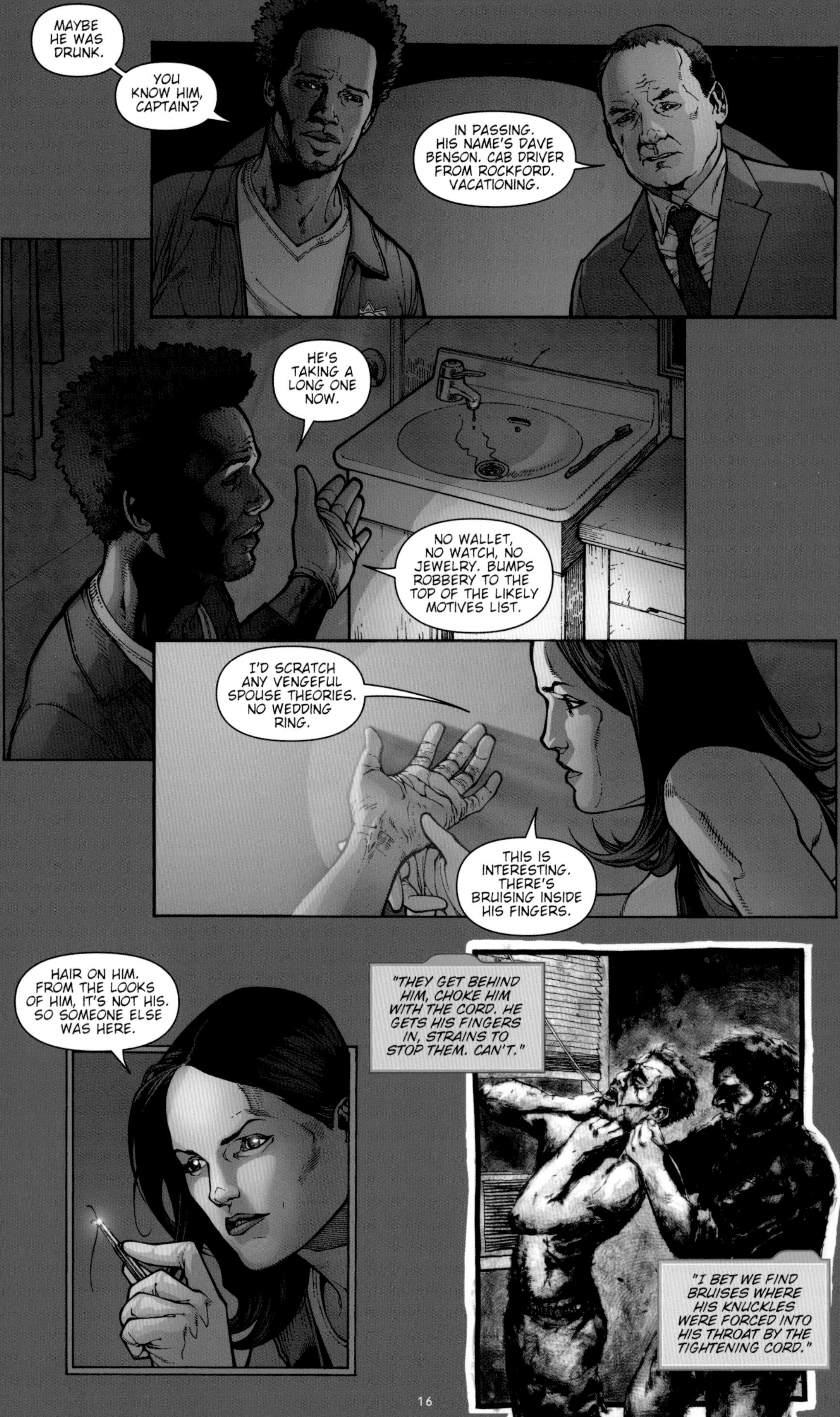
MAYBE HE WAS DRUNK.
YOU KNOW HIM, CAPTAIN?
IN PASSING. HIS NAME'S DAVE BENSON. CAB DRIVER FROM ROCKFORD. VACATIONING.
HE'S TAKING A LONG ONE NOW.
NO WALLET, NO WATCH, NO JEWELRY. BUMPS ROBBERY TO THE TOP OF THE LIKELY MOTIVES LIST.
I'D SCRATCH ANY VENGEFUL SPOUSE THEORIES. NO WEDDING RING.
THIS IS INTERESTING. THERE'S BRUISING INSIDE HIS FINGERS.
HAIR ON HIM. FROM THE LOOKS OF HIM, IT'S NOT HIS. SO SOMEONE ELSE WAS HERE.
"THEY GET BEHIND HIM, CHOKE HIM WITH THE CORD. HE GETS HIS FINGERS IN, STRAINS TO STOP THEM. CAN'T."
"I BET WE FIND BRUISES WHERE HIS KNUCKLES WERE FORCED INTO HIS THROAT BY THE TIGHTENING CORD."

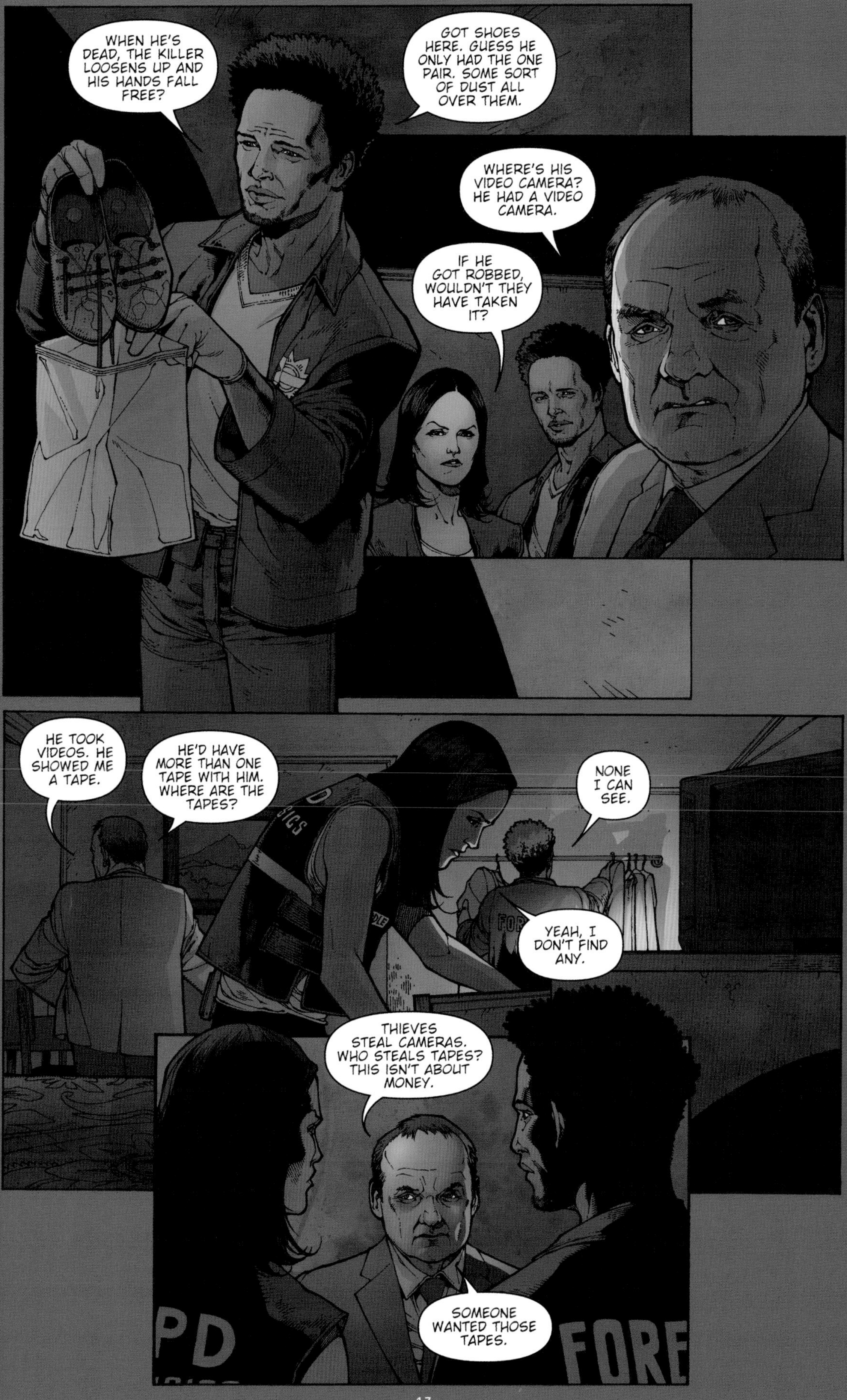
WHEN HE'S DEAD, THE KILLER LOOSENS UP AND HIS HANDS FALL FREE?
GOT SHOES HERE. GUESS HE ONLY HAD THE ONE PAIR. SOME SORT OF DUST ALL OVER THEM.
WHERE'S HIS VIDEO CAMERA? HE HAD A VIDEO CAMERA.
IF HE GOT ROBBED, WOULDN'T THEY HAVE TAKEN IT?
HE TOOK VIDEOS. HE SHOWED ME A TAPE.
HE'D HAVE MORE THAN ONE TAPE WITH HIM. WHERE ARE THE TAPES?
NONE I CAN SEE.
YEAH, I DON'T FIND ANY.
THIEVES STEAL CAMERAS. WHO STEALS TAPES? THIS ISN'T ABOUT MONEY.
SOMEONE WANTED THOSE TAPES.
PD
FORE

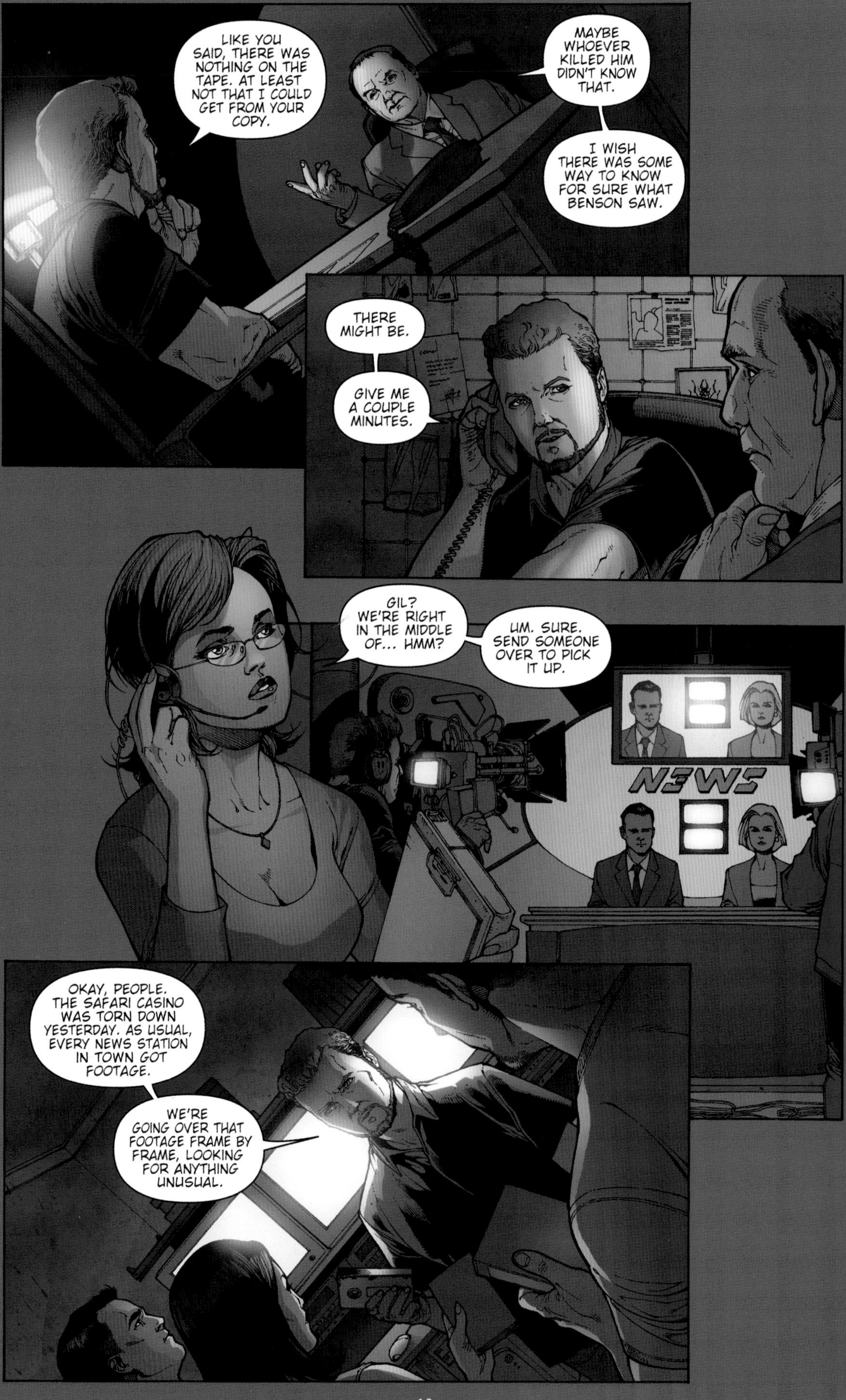
LIKE YOU SAID, THERE WAS NOTHING ON THE TAPE. AT LEAST NOT THAT I COULD GET FROM YOUR COPY.
MAYBE WHOEVER KILLED HIM DIDN'T KNOW THAT.
I WISH THERE WAS SOME WAY TO KNOW FOR SURE WHAT BENSON SAW.
THERE MIGHT BE.
GIVE ME A COUPLE MINUTES.
GIL? WE'RE RIGHT IN THE MIDDLE OF... HMM?
UM. SURE. SEND SOMEONE OVER TO PICK IT UP.
NEWS
OKAY, PEOPLE. THE SAFARI CASINO WAS TORN DOWN YESTERDAY. AS USUAL, EVERY NEWS STATION IN TOWN GOT FOOTAGE.
WE'RE GOING OVER THAT FOOTAGE FRAME BY FRAME, LOOKING FOR ANYTHING UNUSUAL.

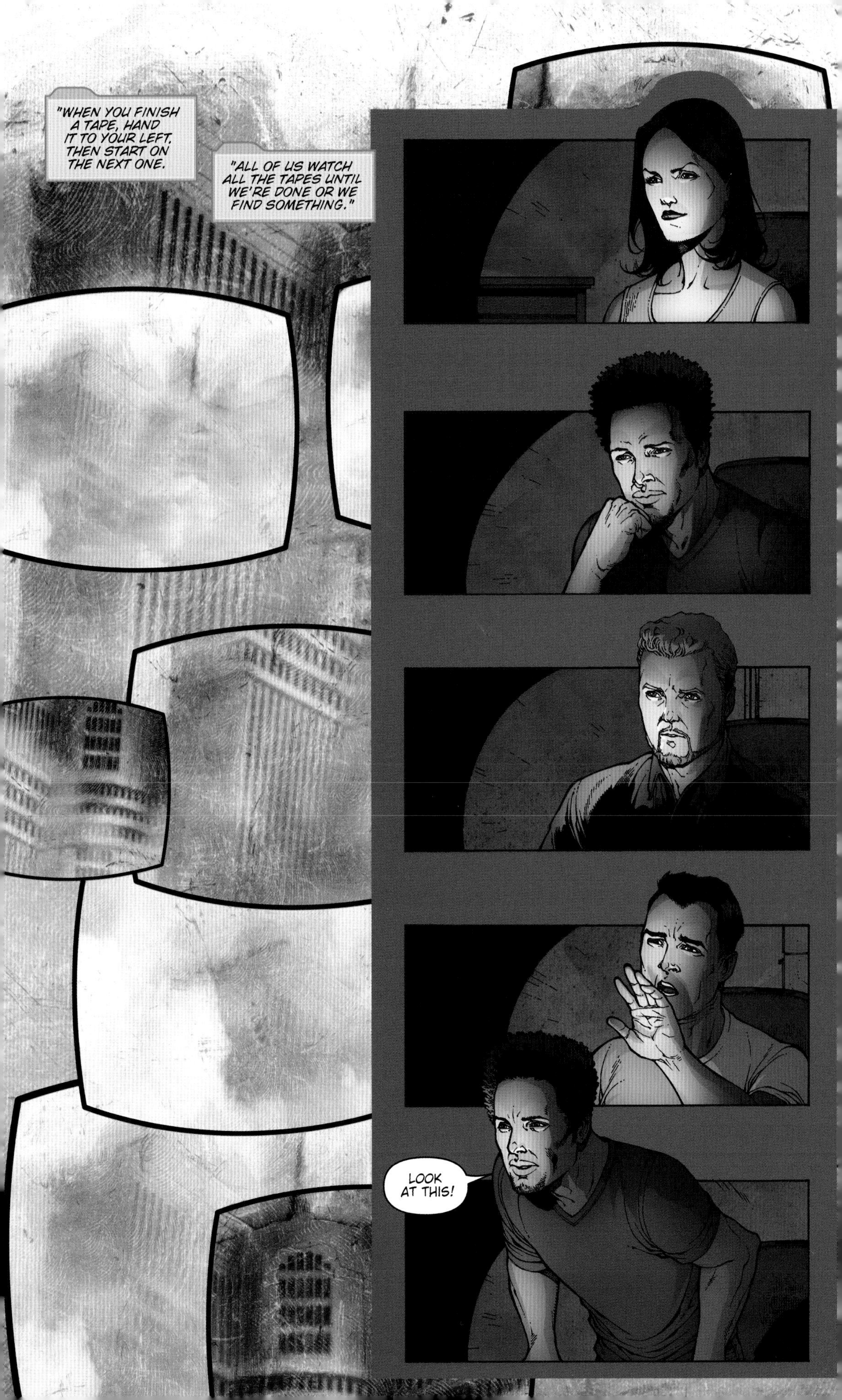
"WHEN YOU FINISH A TAPE, HAND IT TO YOUR LEFT. THEN START ON THE NEXT ONE.
"ALL OF US WATCH ALL THE TAPES UNTIL WE'RE DONE OR WE FIND SOMETHING."
LOOK AT THIS!

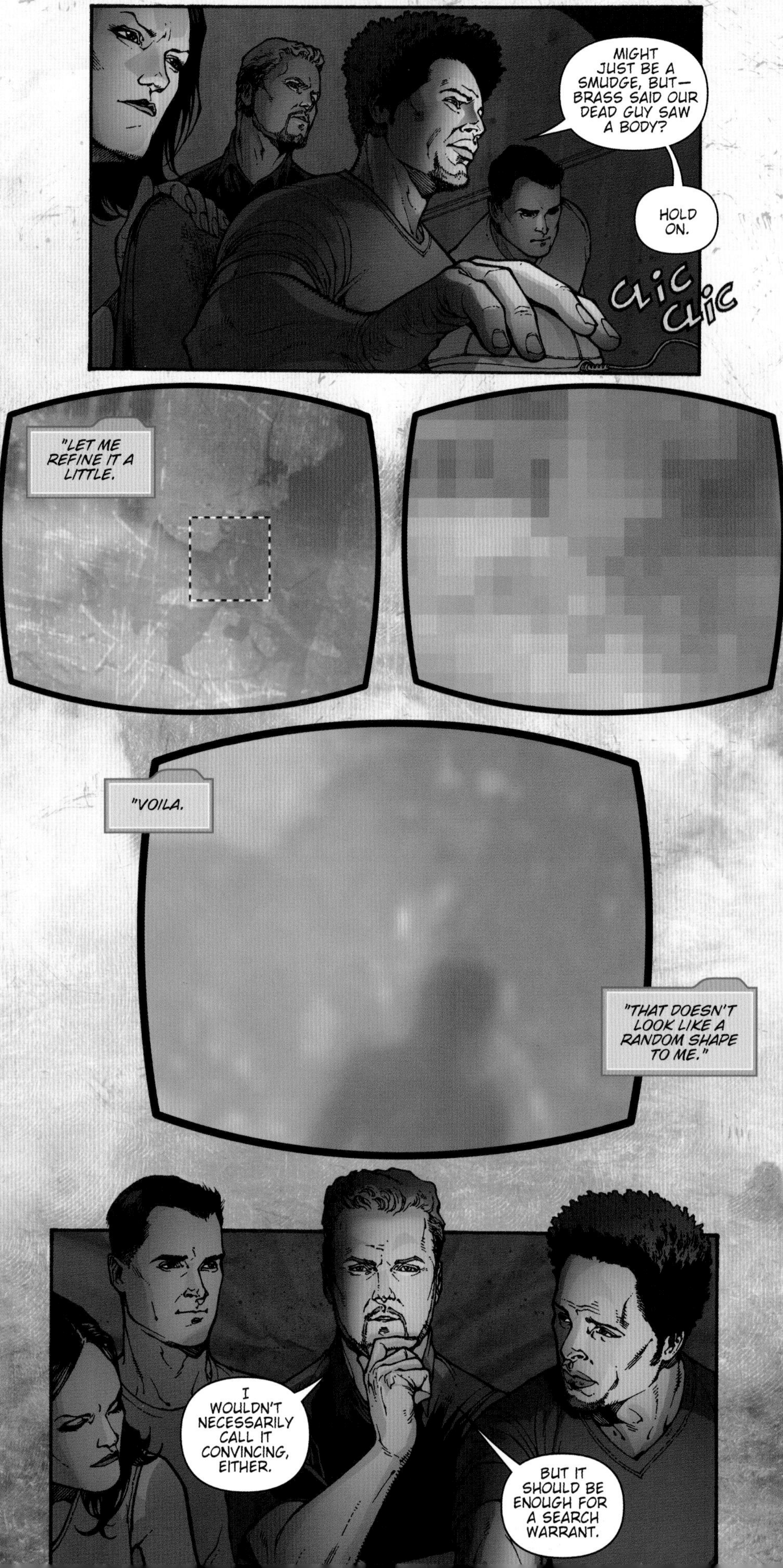

MIGHT JUST BE A SMUDGE, BUT— BRASS SAID OUR DEAD GUY SAW A BODY?
HOLD ON.
CLIC CLIC
"LET ME REFINE IT A LITTLE.
"VOILA.
"THAT DOESN'T LOOK LIKE A RANDOM SHAPE TO ME."
I WOULDN'T NECESSARILY CALL IT CONVINCING, EITHER.
BUT IT SHOULD BE ENOUGH FOR A SEARCH WARRANT.

HEY! YOU CAN'T COME IN HERE!

THIS IS A CONSTRUCTION SITE! IT'S DANGEROUS!

KEEP OUT!!!

DEMOLITION
AU...D
PERS...NLY

LVPD

I'M CAPTAIN BRASS, LVPD. I HAVE TO ASK YOU TO TELL YOUR MEN TO STOP WHAT THEY'RE DOING.

UNTIL FURTHER NOTICE, THIS IS A CRIME SCENE.

EXCUSE ME, HAS ANYTHING BEEN REMOVED FROM HERE?

SURE, LAST TWO DAYS. LANDFILL OUT ON THE EAST SIDE.

SARA, NICK, I WANT YOU TO CHECK THE LANDFILL. WARRICK AND I WILL SEARCH HERE.

IF YOU THOUGHT THIS MORNING WAS FUN, YOU'LL BE IN HEAVEN NOW. I KNOW I DON'T HAVE TO TELL YOU TO BE CAREFUL, BUT BE CAREFUL.

WOW. TOO BAD CATHERINE'S OFF WITH HER KID TODAY.

SHE'LL CRY WHEN SHE HEARS WHAT FUN SHE'S MISSING.

GRISSOM

LVPD

LVPD

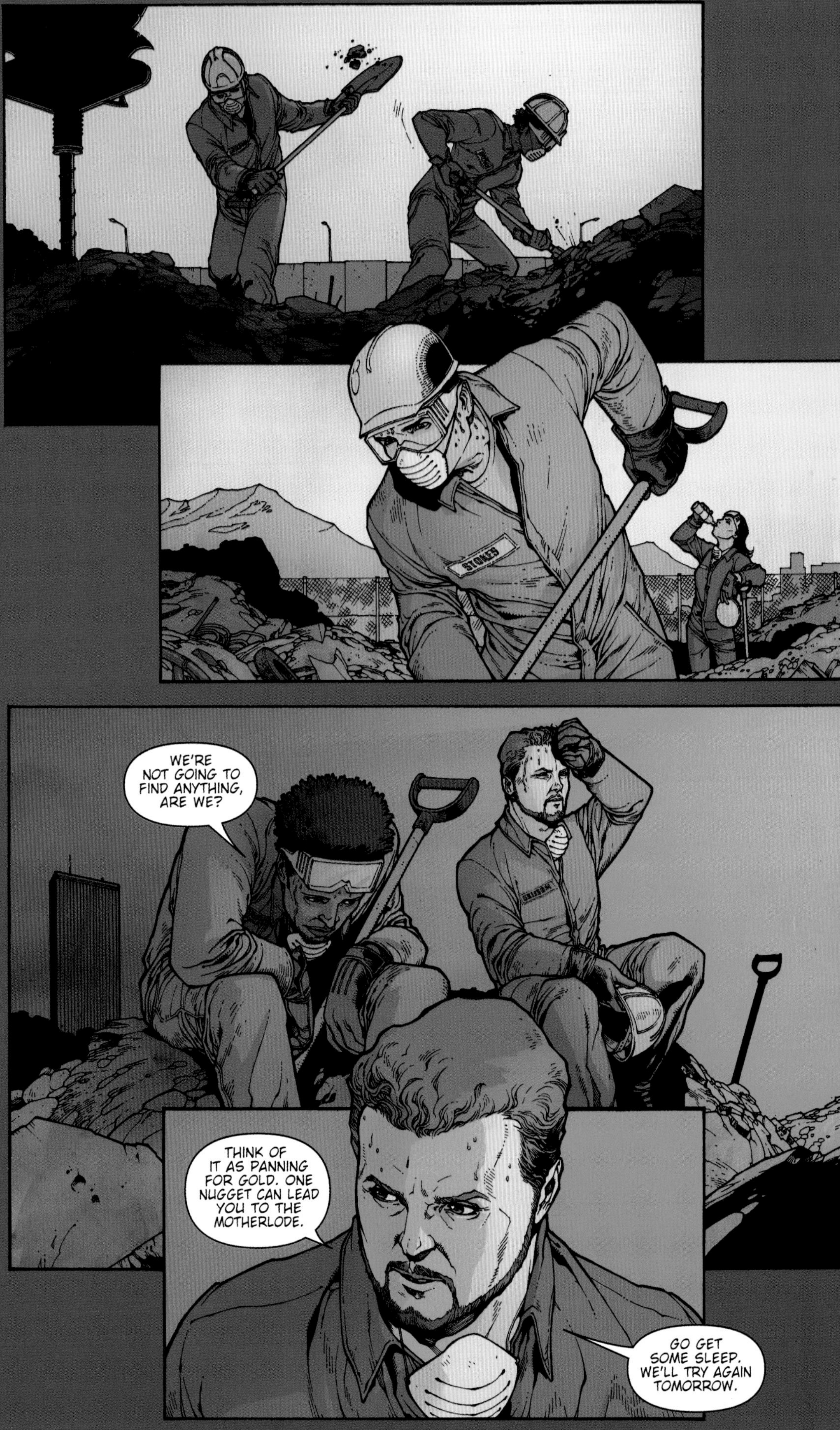
STOKES
WE'RE NOT GOING TO FIND ANYTHING, ARE WE?
THINK OF IT AS PANNING FOR GOLD. ONE NUGGET CAN LEAD YOU TO THE MOTHERLODE.
GO GET SOME SLEEP. WE'LL TRY AGAIN TOMORROW.

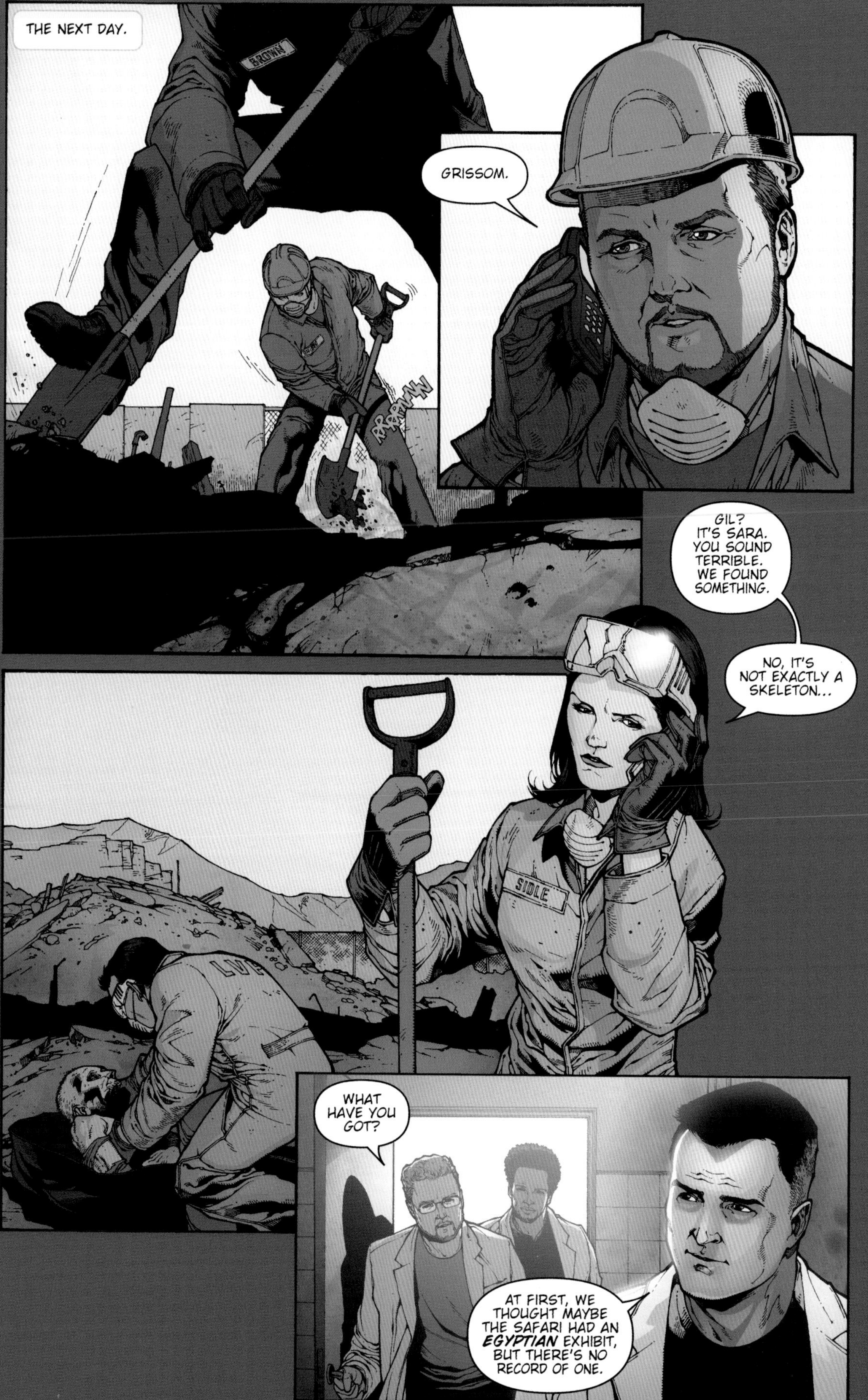
THE NEXT DAY.
BROWN
RRRRMMMN
GRISSOM.
GIL? IT'S SARA. YOU SOUND TERRIBLE. WE FOUND SOMETHING.
NO, IT'S NOT EXACTLY A SKELETON...
SIDLE
WHAT HAVE YOU GOT?
AT FIRST, WE THOUGHT MAYBE THE SAFARI HAD AN EGYPTIAN EXHIBIT, BUT THERE'S NO RECORD OF ONE.

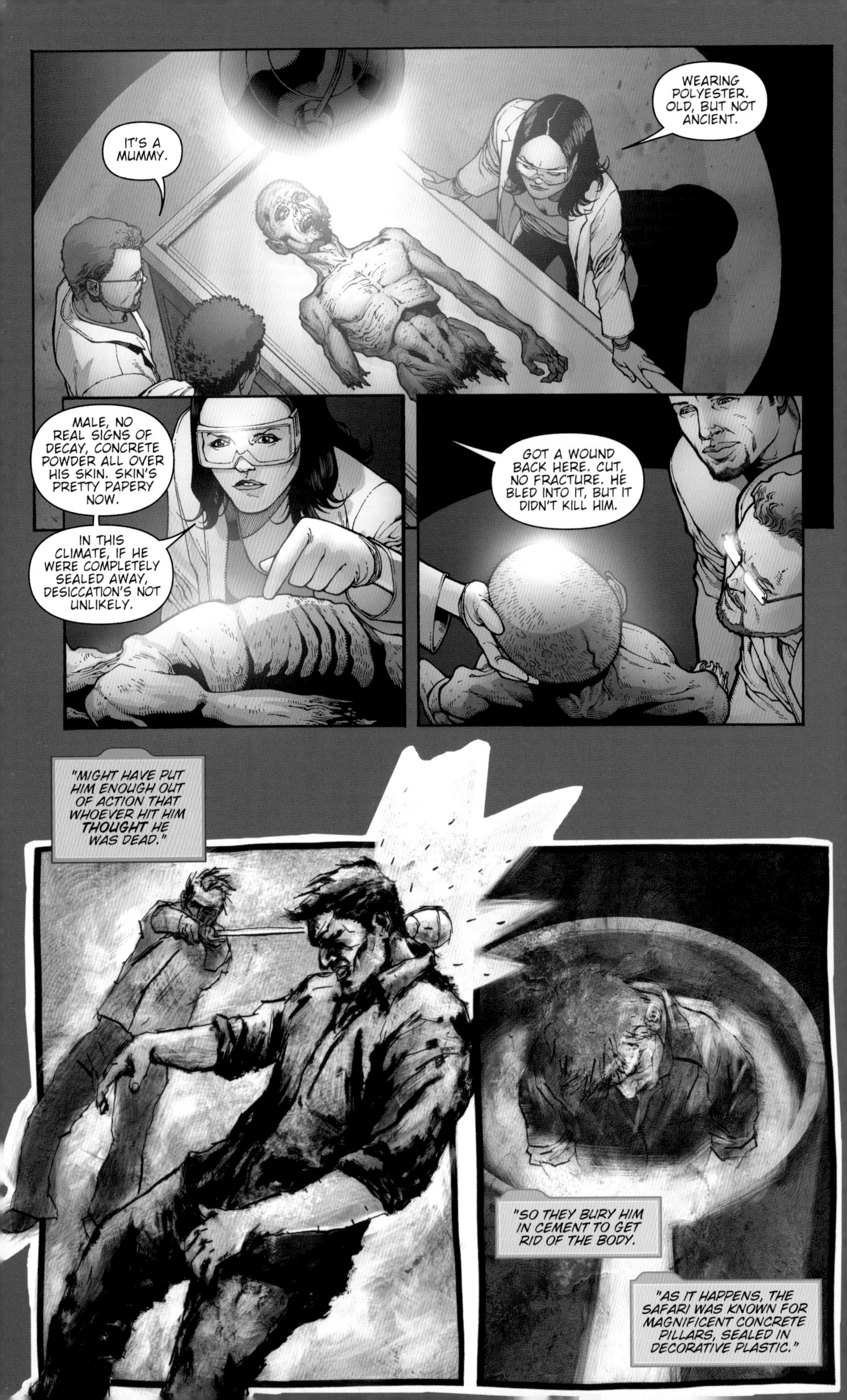
IT'S A MUMMY.
WEARING POLYESTER. OLD, BUT NOT ANCIENT.
MALE, NO REAL SIGNS OF DECAY, CONCRETE POWDER ALL OVER HIS SKIN. SKIN'S PRETTY PAPERY NOW.
IN THIS CLIMATE, IF HE WERE COMPLETELY SEALED AWAY, DESICCATION'S NOT UNLIKELY.
GOT A WOUND BACK HERE. CUT, NO FRACTURE. HE BLED INTO IT, BUT IT DIDN'T KILL HIM.
"MIGHT HAVE PUT HIM ENOUGH OUT OF ACTION THAT WHOEVER HIT HIM *THOUGHT* HE WAS DEAD."
"SO THEY BURY HIM IN CEMENT TO GET RID OF THE BODY.
"AS IT HAPPENS, THE SAFARI WAS KNOWN FOR MAGNIFICENT CONCRETE PILLARS, SEALED IN DECORATIVE PLASTIC."

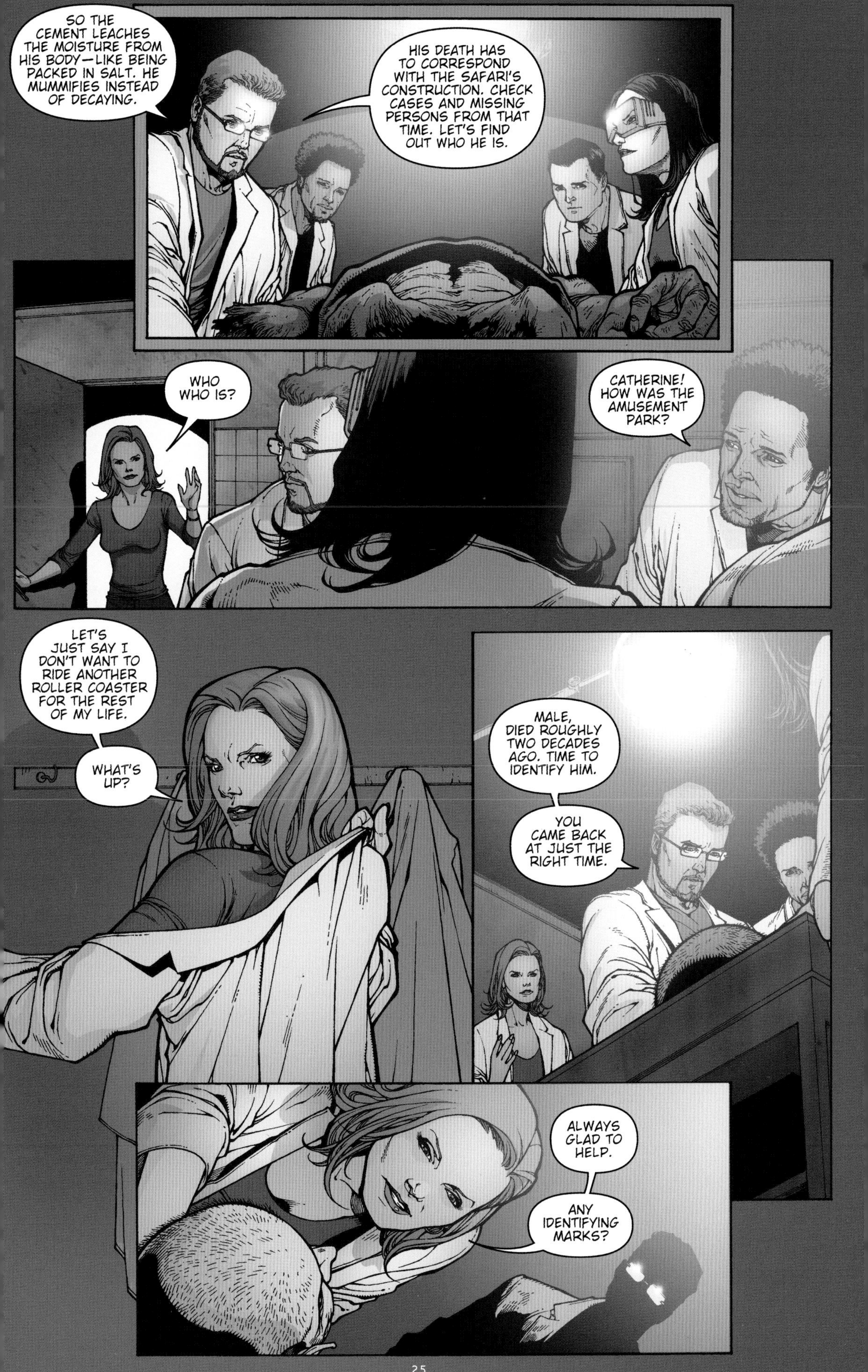
SO THE CEMENT LEACHES THE MOISTURE FROM HIS BODY—LIKE BEING PACKED IN SALT. HE MUMMIFIES INSTEAD OF DECAYING.
HIS DEATH HAS TO CORRESPOND WITH THE SAFARI'S CONSTRUCTION. CHECK CASES AND MISSING PERSONS FROM THAT TIME. LET'S FIND OUT WHO HE IS.
WHO WHO IS?
CATHERINE! HOW WAS THE AMUSEMENT PARK?
LET'S JUST SAY I DON'T WANT TO RIDE ANOTHER ROLLER COASTER FOR THE REST OF MY LIFE.
WHAT'S UP?
MALE, DIED ROUGHLY TWO DECADES AGO. TIME TO IDENTIFY HIM.
YOU CAME BACK AT JUST THE RIGHT TIME.
ALWAYS GLAD TO HELP.
ANY IDENTIFYING MARKS?

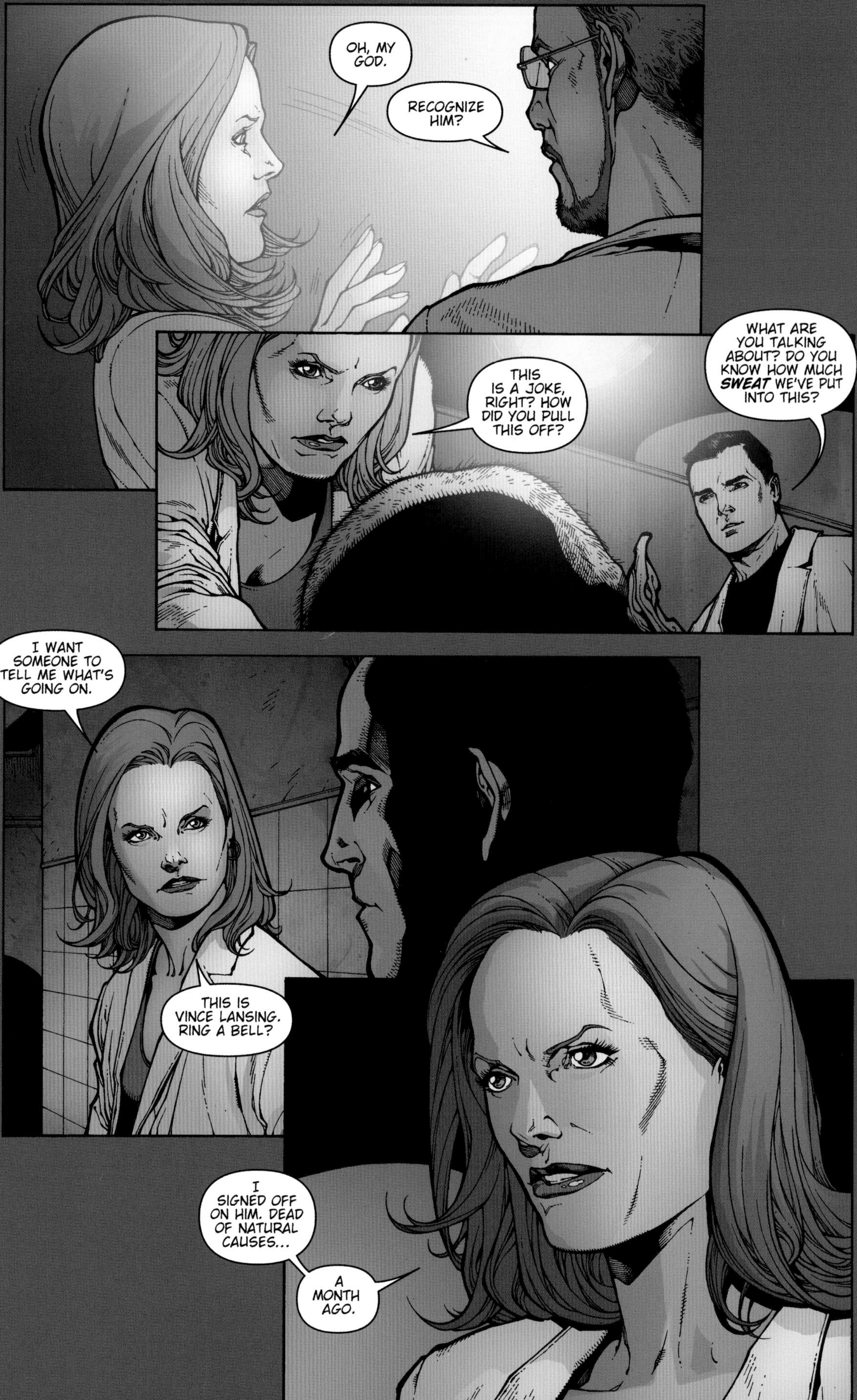
OH, MY GOD.
RECOGNIZE HIM?
THIS IS A JOKE, RIGHT? HOW DID YOU PULL THIS OFF?
WHAT ARE YOU TALKING ABOUT? DO YOU KNOW HOW MUCH **SWEAT** WE'VE PUT INTO THIS?
I WANT SOMEONE TO TELL ME WHAT'S GOING ON.
THIS IS VINCE LANSING. RING A BELL?
I SIGNED OFF ON HIM. DEAD OF NATURAL CAUSES...
A MONTH AGO.

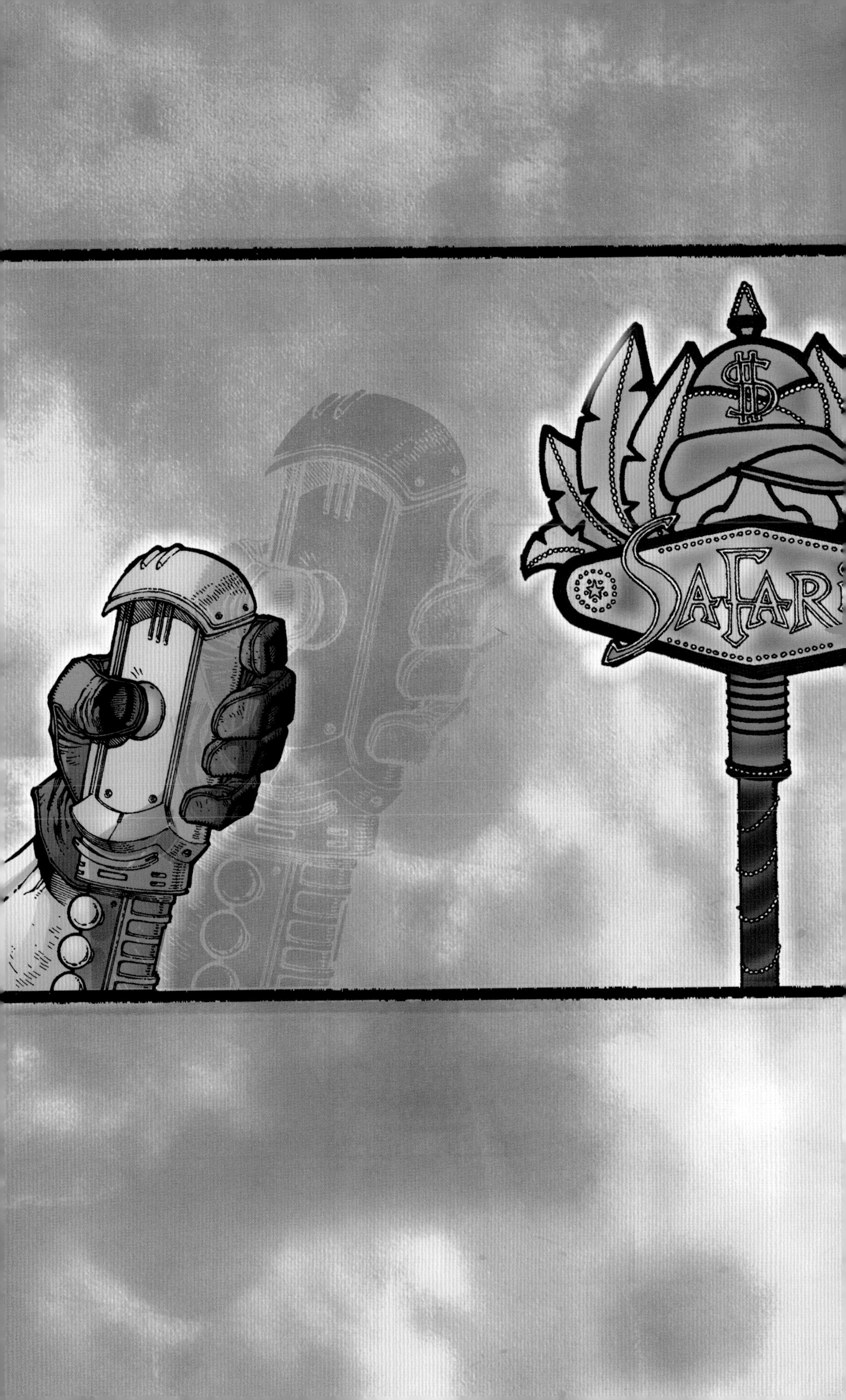
SAFAR

chapter two

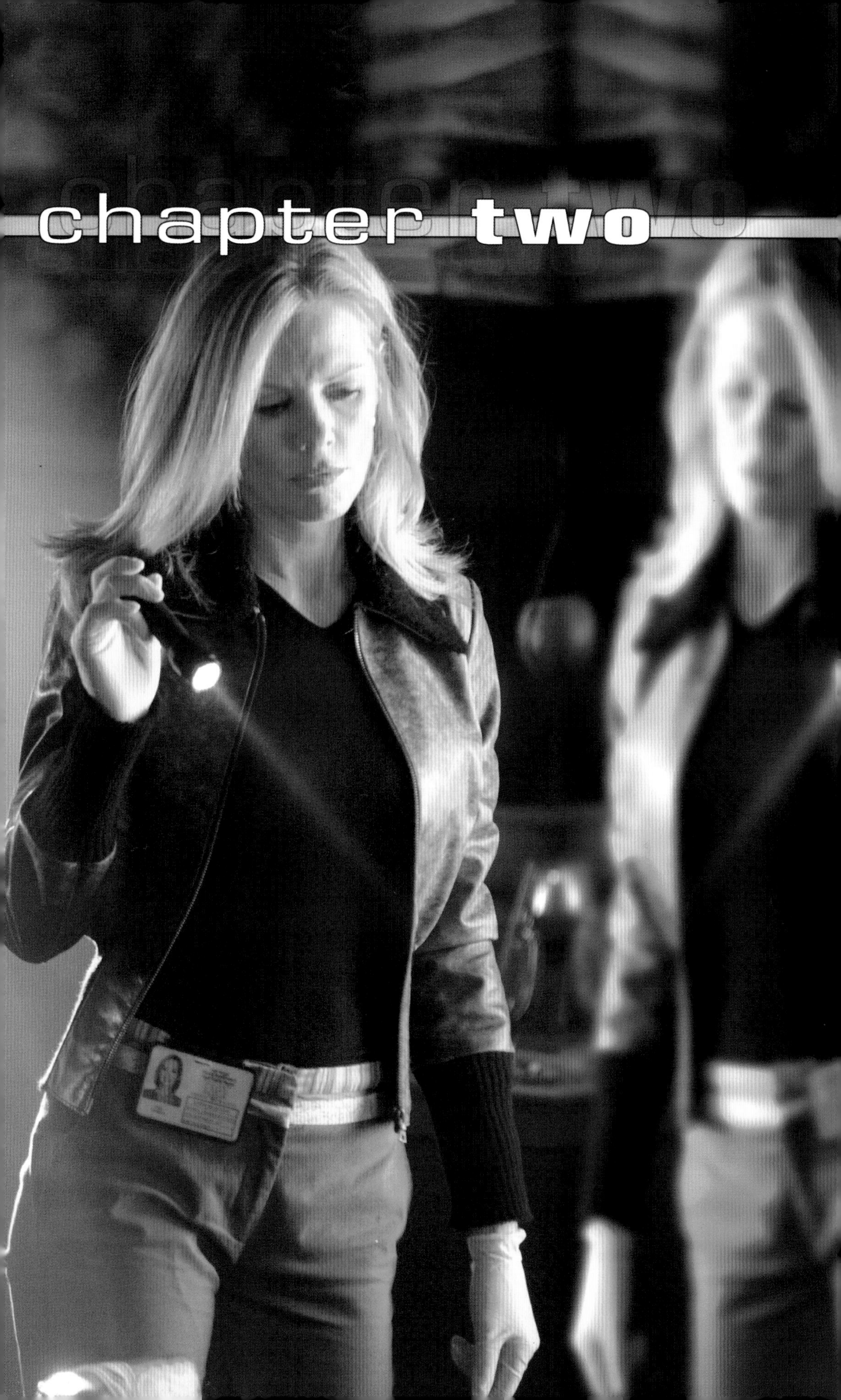

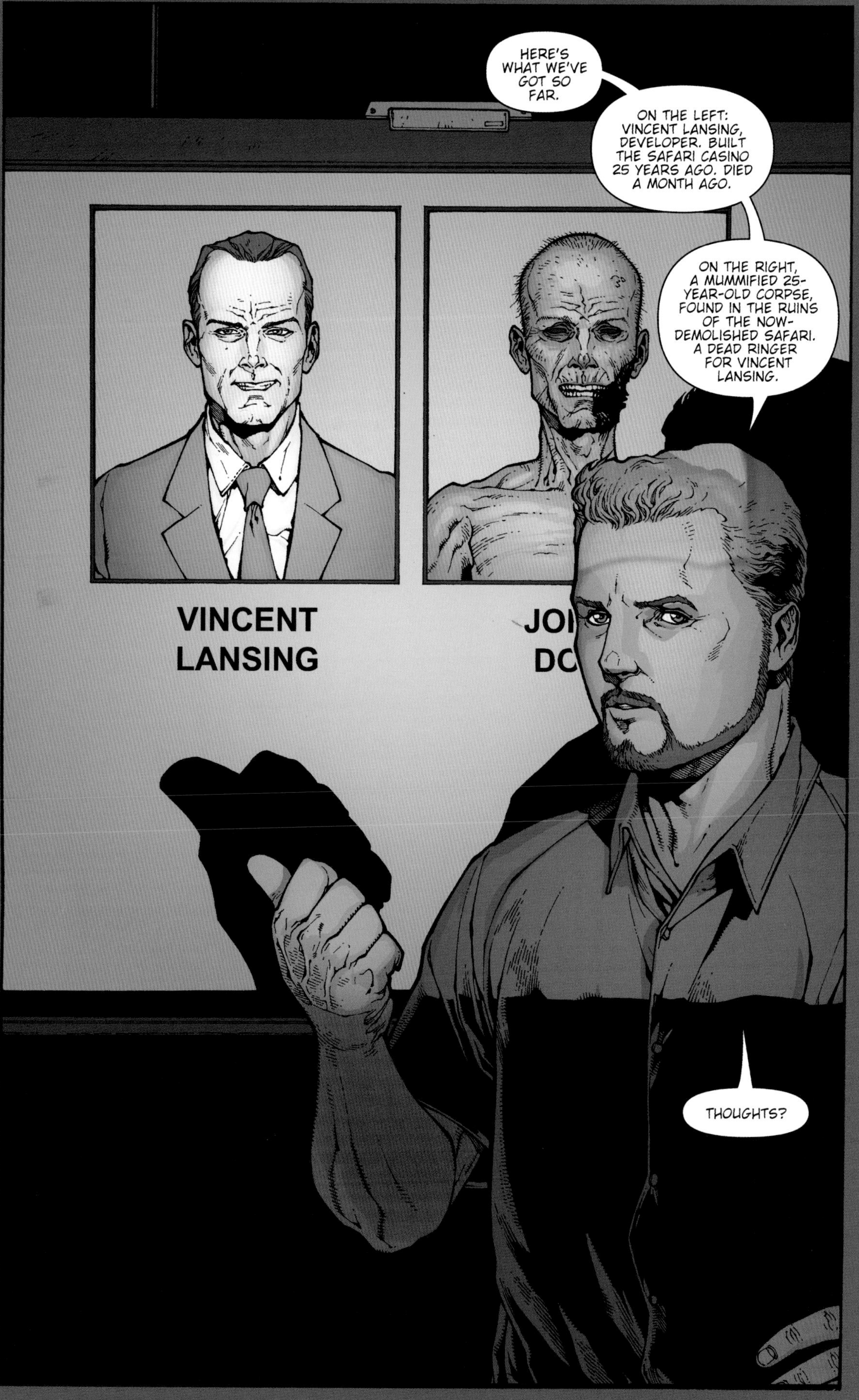
HERE'S WHAT WE'VE GOT SO FAR.
ON THE LEFT: VINCENT LANSING, DEVELOPER. BUILT THE SAFARI CASINO 25 YEARS AGO. DIED A MONTH AGO.
ON THE RIGHT, A MUMMIFIED 25-YEAR-OLD CORPSE, FOUND IN THE RUINS OF THE NOW-DEMOLISHED SAFARI. A DEAD RINGER FOR VINCENT LANSING.
VINCENT LANSING
THOUGHTS?

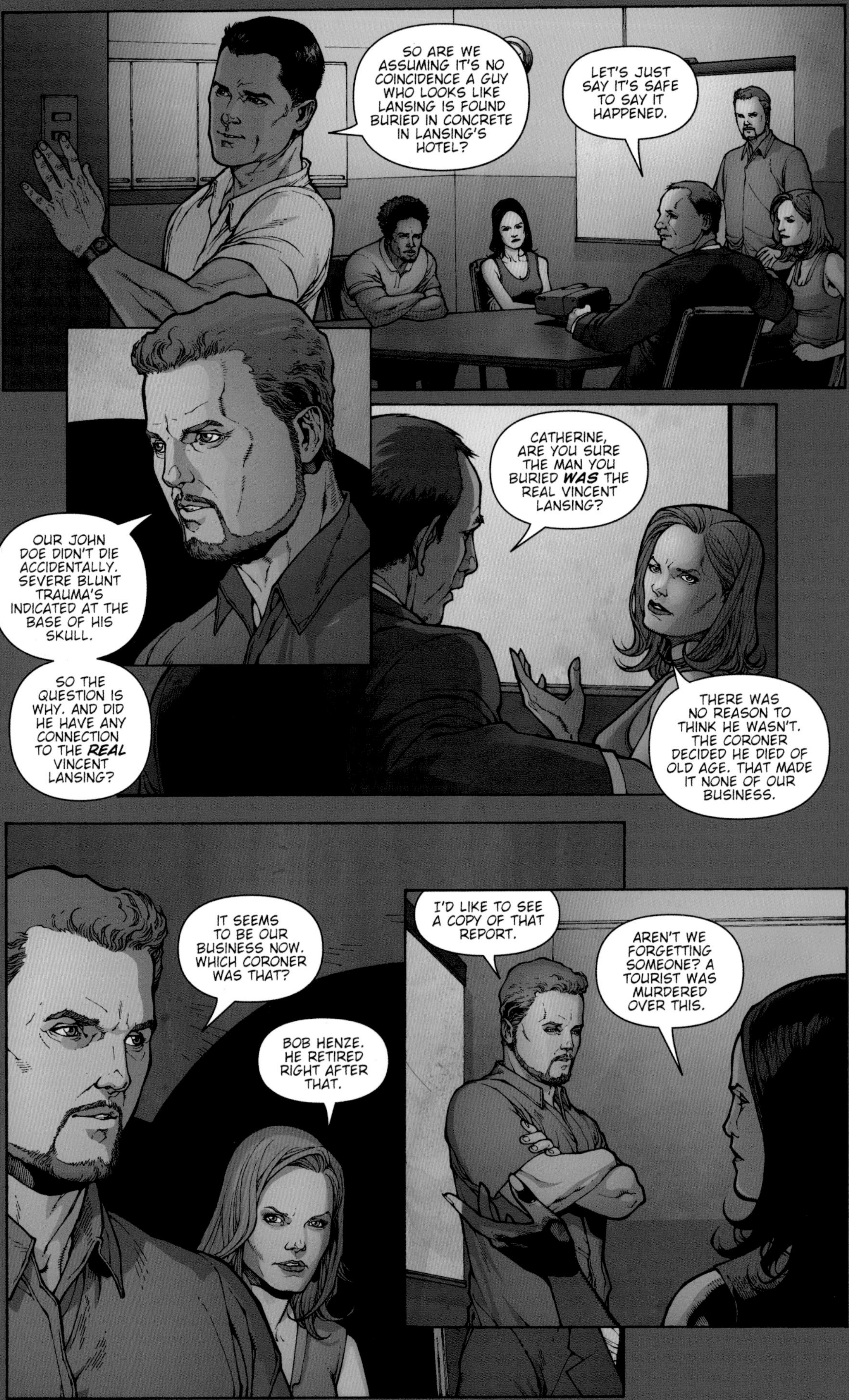
SO ARE WE ASSUMING IT'S NO COINCIDENCE A GUY WHO LOOKS LIKE LANSING IS FOUND BURIED IN CONCRETE IN LANSING'S HOTEL?
LET'S JUST SAY IT'S SAFE TO SAY IT HAPPENED.
OUR JOHN DOE DIDN'T DIE ACCIDENTALLY. SEVERE BLUNT TRAUMA'S INDICATED AT THE BASE OF HIS SKULL.
SO THE QUESTION IS WHY. AND DID HE HAVE ANY CONNECTION TO THE *REAL* VINCENT LANSING?
CATHERINE, ARE YOU SURE THE MAN YOU BURIED *WAS* THE REAL VINCENT LANSING?
THERE WAS NO REASON TO THINK HE WASN'T. THE CORONER DECIDED HE DIED OF OLD AGE. THAT MADE IT NONE OF OUR BUSINESS.
IT SEEMS TO BE OUR BUSINESS NOW. WHICH CORONER WAS THAT?
BOB HENZE. HE RETIRED RIGHT AFTER THAT.
I'D LIKE TO SEE A COPY OF THAT REPORT.
AREN'T WE FORGETTING SOMEONE? A TOURIST WAS MURDERED OVER THIS.

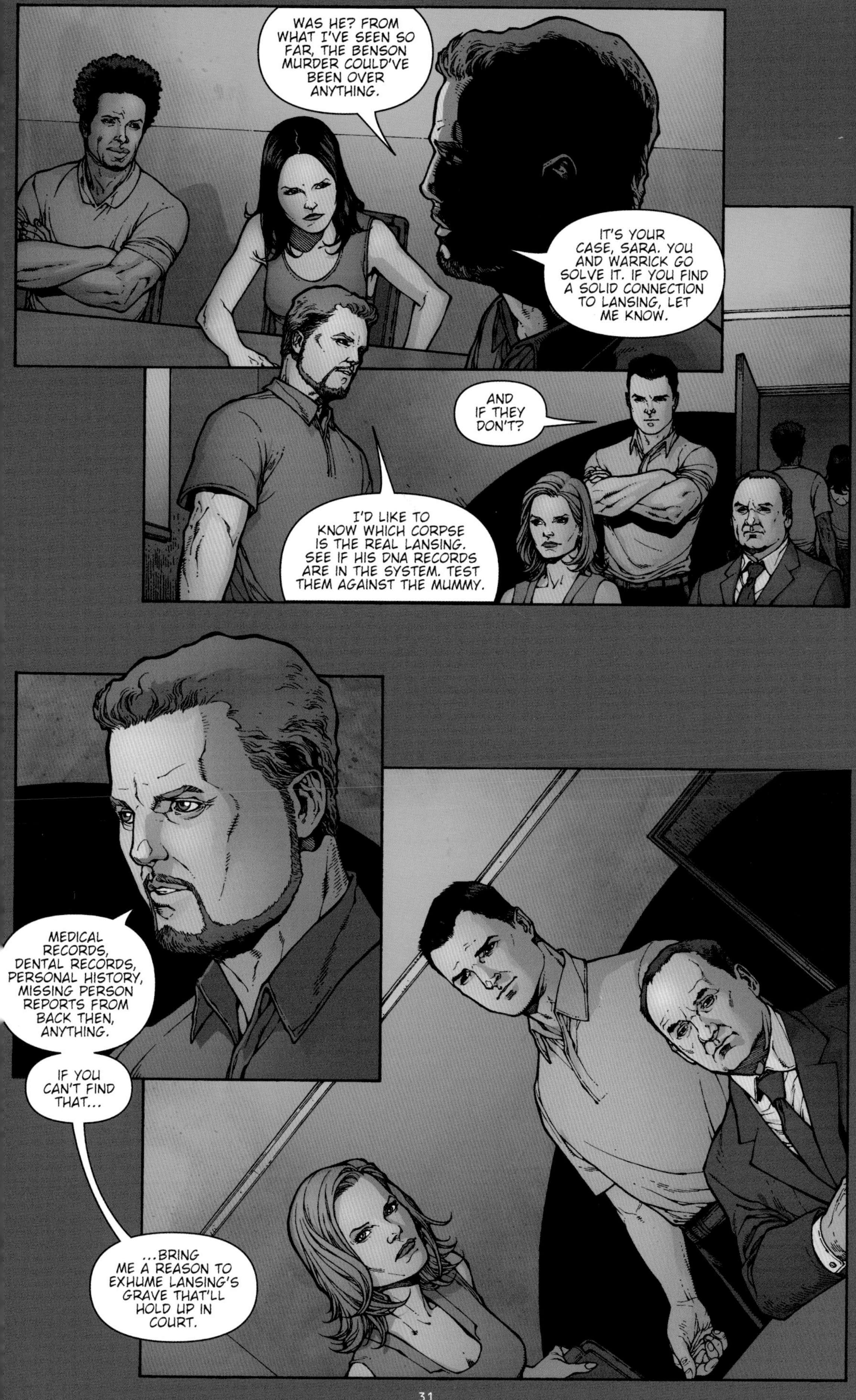

WAS HE? FROM WHAT I'VE SEEN SO FAR, THE BENSON MURDER COULD'VE BEEN OVER ANYTHING.
IT'S YOUR CASE, SARA. YOU AND WARRICK GO SOLVE IT. IF YOU FIND A SOLID CONNECTION TO LANSING, LET ME KNOW.
AND IF THEY DON'T?
I'D LIKE TO KNOW WHICH CORPSE IS THE REAL LANSING. SEE IF HIS DNA RECORDS ARE IN THE SYSTEM. TEST THEM AGAINST THE MUMMY.
MEDICAL RECORDS, DENTAL RECORDS, PERSONAL HISTORY, MISSING PERSON REPORTS FROM BACK THEN, ANYTHING.
IF YOU CAN'T FIND THAT...
...BRING ME A REASON TO EXHUME LANSING'S GRAVE THAT'LL HOLD UP IN COURT.

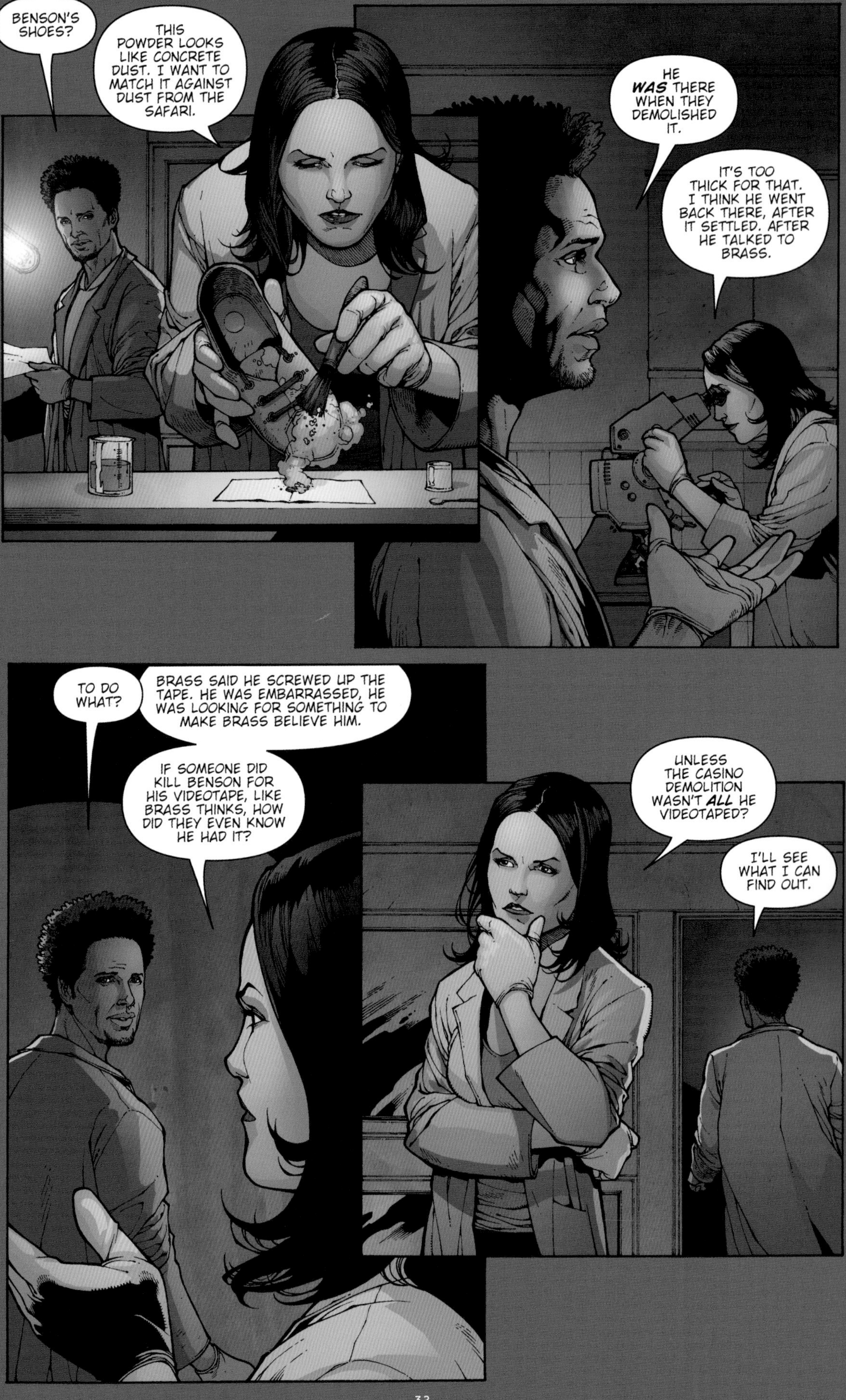
BENSON'S SHOES?
THIS POWDER LOOKS LIKE CONCRETE DUST. I WANT TO MATCH IT AGAINST DUST FROM THE SAFARI.
HE WAS THERE WHEN THEY DEMOLISHED IT.
IT'S TOO THICK FOR THAT. I THINK HE WENT BACK THERE, AFTER IT SETTLED. AFTER HE TALKED TO BRASS.
TO DO WHAT?
BRASS SAID HE SCREWED UP THE TAPE. HE WAS EMBARRASSED, HE WAS LOOKING FOR SOMETHING TO MAKE BRASS BELIEVE HIM.
IF SOMEONE DID KILL BENSON FOR HIS VIDEOTAPE, LIKE BRASS THINKS, HOW DID THEY EVEN KNOW HE HAD IT?
UNLESS THE CASINO DEMOLITION WASN'T ALL HE VIDEOTAPED?
I'LL SEE WHAT I CAN FIND OUT.

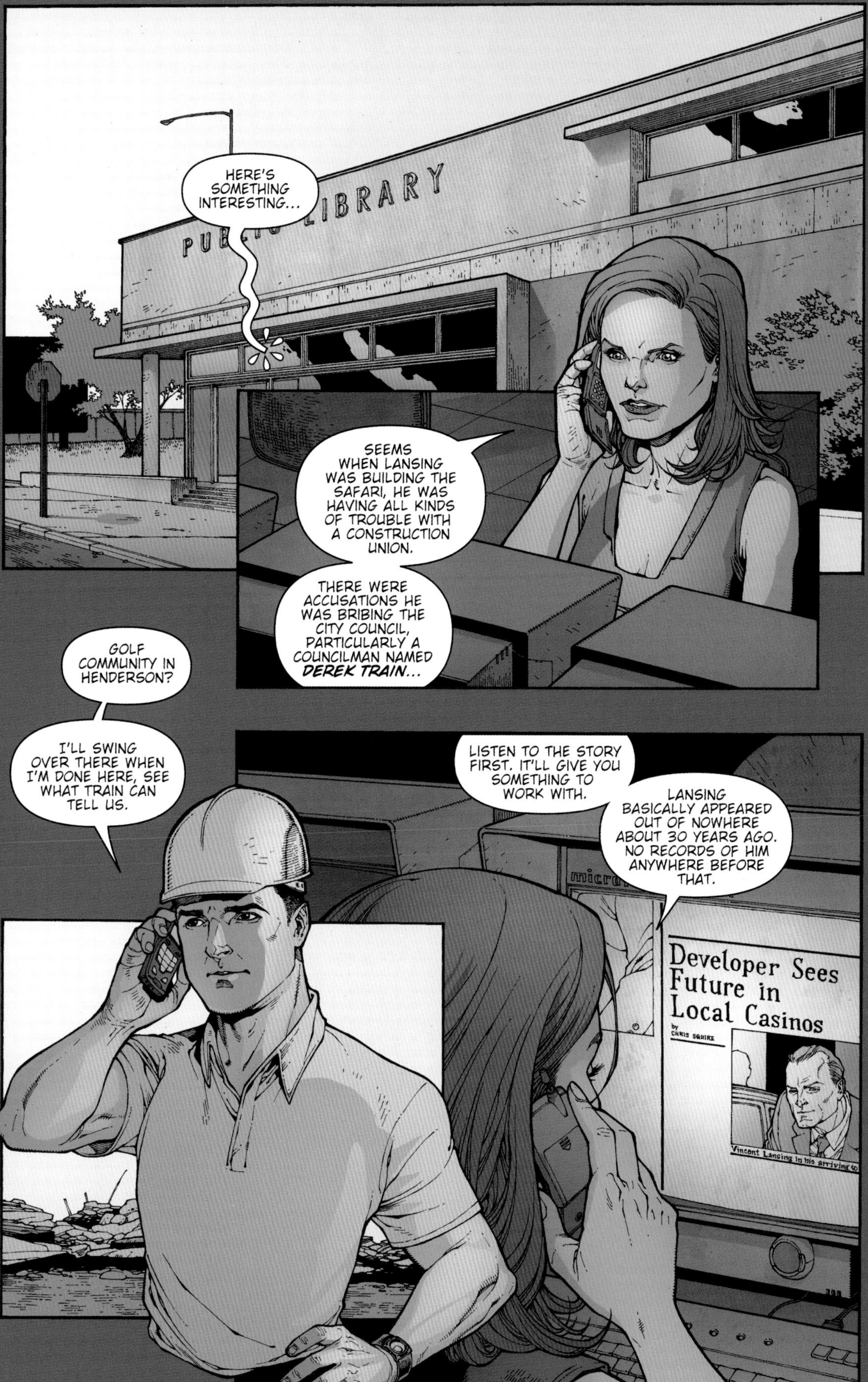
PUBLIC LIBRARY
HERE'S SOMETHING INTERESTING...
SEEMS WHEN LANSING WAS BUILDING THE SAFARI, HE WAS HAVING ALL KINDS OF TROUBLE WITH A CONSTRUCTION UNION.
THERE WERE ACCUSATIONS HE WAS BRIBING THE CITY COUNCIL, PARTICULARLY A COUNCILMAN NAMED ***DEREK TRAIN***...
GOLF COMMUNITY IN HENDERSON?
I'LL SWING OVER THERE WHEN I'M DONE HERE, SEE WHAT TRAIN CAN TELL US.
LISTEN TO THE STORY FIRST. IT'LL GIVE YOU SOMETHING TO WORK WITH.
LANSING BASICALLY APPEARED OUT OF NOWHERE ABOUT 30 YEARS AGO. NO RECORDS OF HIM ANYWHERE BEFORE THAT.
Developer Sees Future in Local Casinos
by CHRIS SQUIRE
Vincent Lansing in his arriving to

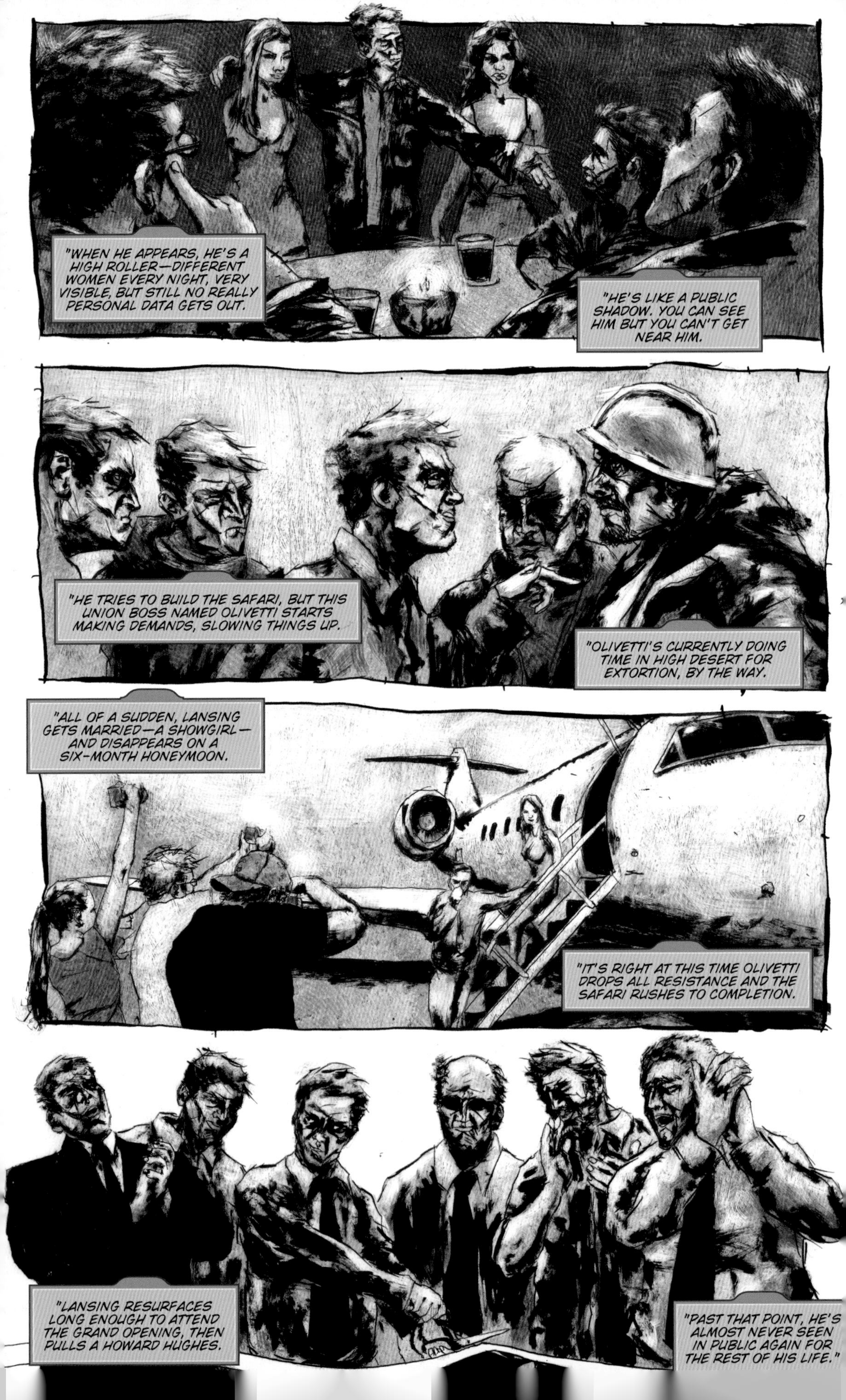
"WHEN HE APPEARS, HE'S A HIGH ROLLER—DIFFERENT WOMEN EVERY NIGHT, VERY VISIBLE, BUT STILL NO REALLY PERSONAL DATA GETS OUT.
"HE'S LIKE A PUBLIC SHADOW. YOU CAN SEE HIM BUT YOU CAN'T GET NEAR HIM.
"HE TRIES TO BUILD THE SAFARI, BUT THIS UNION BOSS NAMED OLIVETTI STARTS MAKING DEMANDS, SLOWING THINGS UP.
"OLIVETTI'S CURRENTLY DOING TIME IN HIGH DESERT FOR EXTORTION, BY THE WAY.
"ALL OF A SUDDEN, LANSING GETS MARRIED—A SHOWGIRL—AND DISAPPEARS ON A SIX-MONTH HONEYMOON.
"IT'S RIGHT AT THIS TIME OLIVETTI DROPS ALL RESISTANCE AND THE SAFARI RUSHES TO COMPLETION.
"LANSING RESURFACES LONG ENOUGH TO ATTEND THE GRAND OPENING, THEN PULLS A HOWARD HUGHES.
"PAST THAT POINT, HE'S ALMOST NEVER SEEN IN PUBLIC AGAIN FOR THE REST OF HIS LIFE."

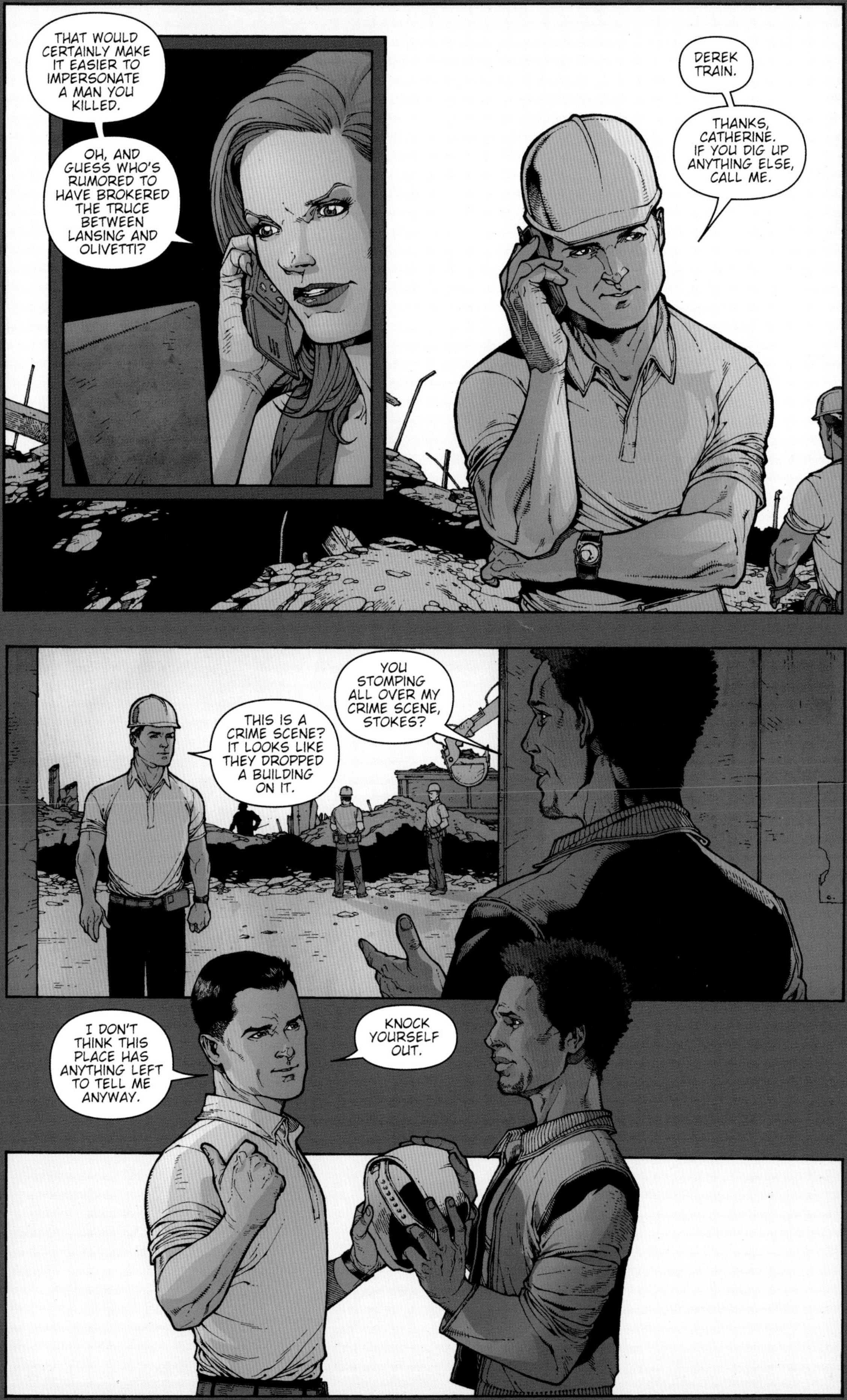
THAT WOULD CERTAINLY MAKE IT EASIER TO IMPERSONATE A MAN YOU KILLED.
OH, AND GUESS WHO'S RUMORED TO HAVE BROKERED THE TRUCE BETWEEN LANSING AND OLIVETTI?
DEREK TRAIN.
THANKS, CATHERINE. IF YOU DIG UP ANYTHING ELSE, CALL ME.
YOU STOMPING ALL OVER MY CRIME SCENE, STOKES?
THIS IS A CRIME SCENE? IT LOOKS LIKE THEY DROPPED A BUILDING ON IT.
I DON'T THINK THIS PLACE HAS ANYTHING LEFT TO TELL ME ANYWAY.
KNOCK YOURSELF OUT.

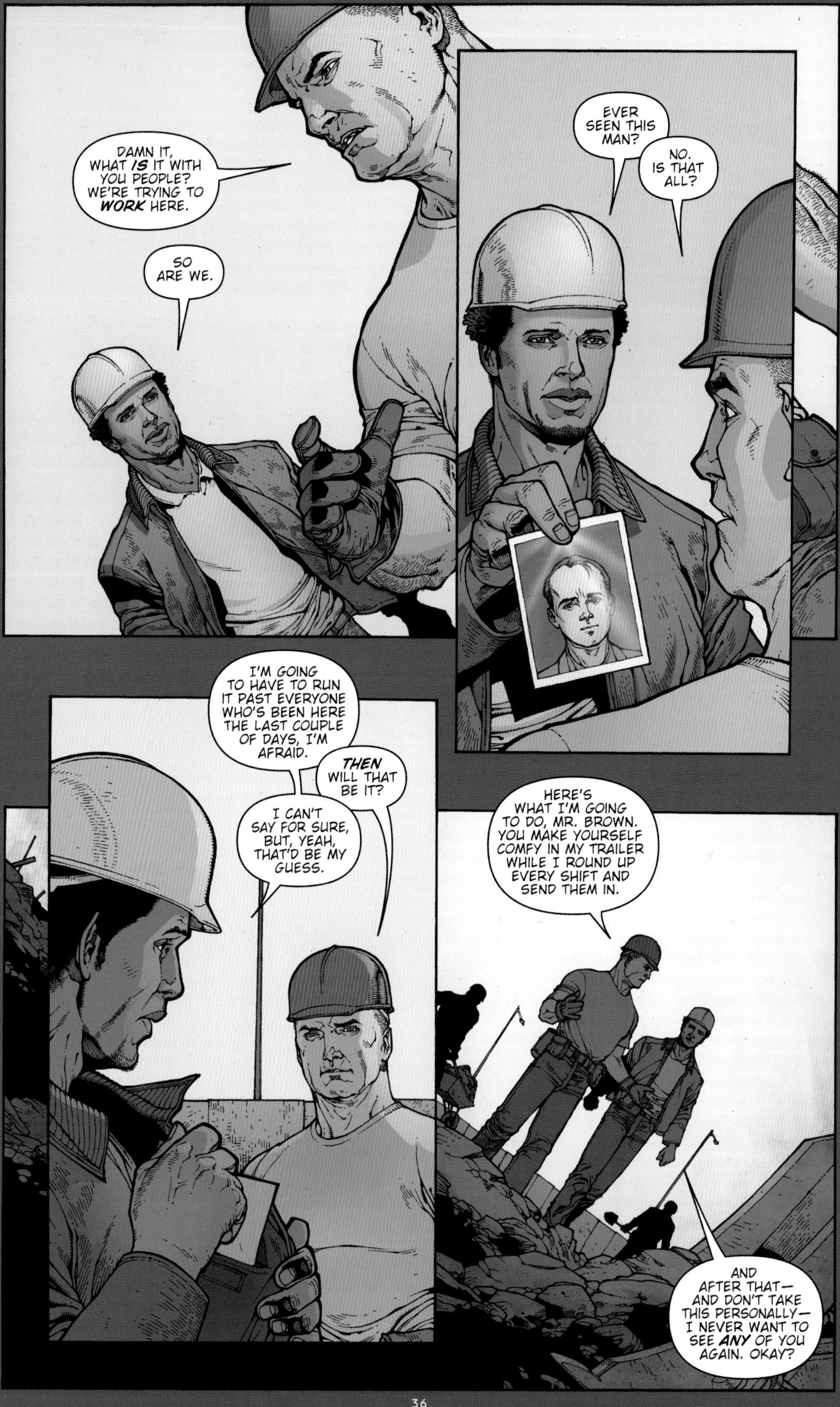
DAMN IT, WHAT *IS* IT WITH YOU PEOPLE? WE'RE TRYING TO **WORK** HERE.
SO ARE WE.
EVER SEEN THIS MAN?
NO. IS THAT ALL?
I'M GOING TO HAVE TO RUN IT PAST EVERYONE WHO'S BEEN HERE THE LAST COUPLE OF DAYS, I'M AFRAID.
THEN WILL THAT BE IT?
I CAN'T SAY FOR SURE, BUT, YEAH, THAT'D BE MY GUESS.
HERE'S WHAT I'M GOING TO DO, MR. BROWN. YOU MAKE YOURSELF COMFY IN MY TRAILER WHILE I ROUND UP EVERY SHIFT AND SEND THEM IN.
AND AFTER THAT— AND DON'T TAKE THIS PERSONALLY— I NEVER WANT TO SEE *ANY* OF YOU AGAIN. OKAY?

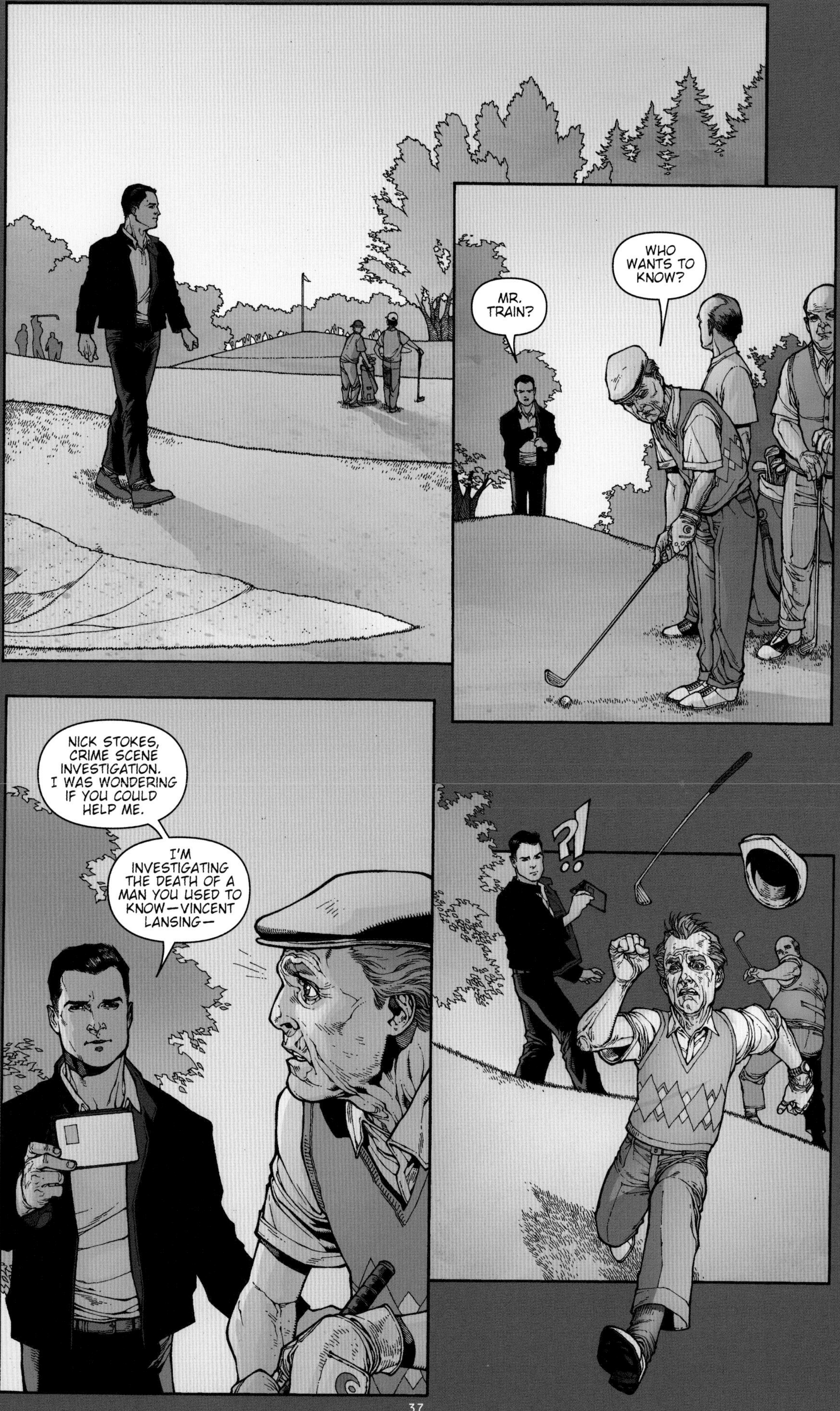
MR. TRAIN?
WHO WANTS TO KNOW?
NICK STOKES, CRIME SCENE INVESTIGATION. I WAS WONDERING IF YOU COULD HELP ME.
I'M INVESTIGATING THE DEATH OF A MAN YOU USED TO KNOW—VINCENT LANSING—
?!

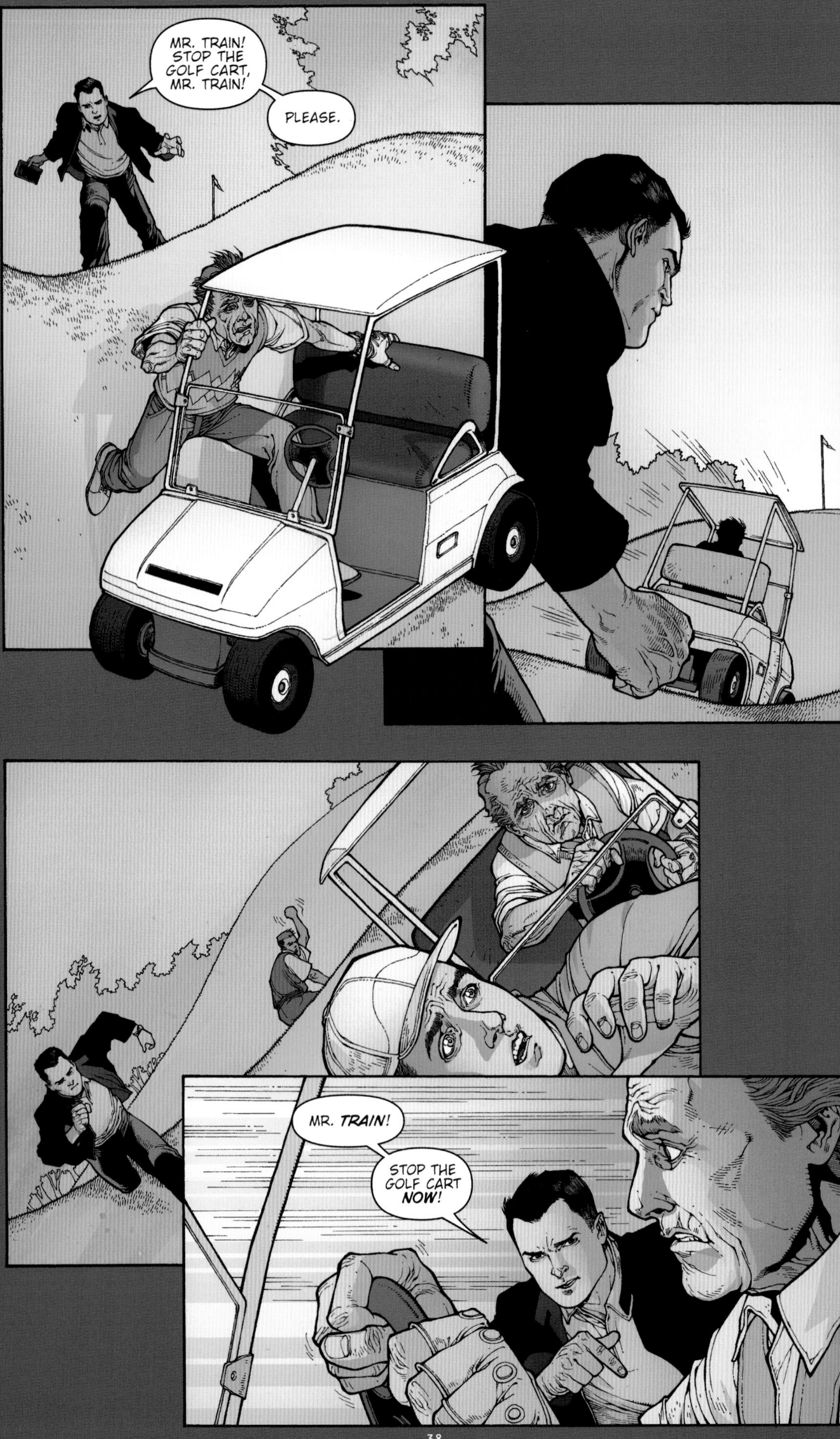
MR. TRAIN! STOP THE GOLF CART, MR. TRAIN!
PLEASE.
MR. *TRAIN*!
STOP THE GOLF CART *NOW*!

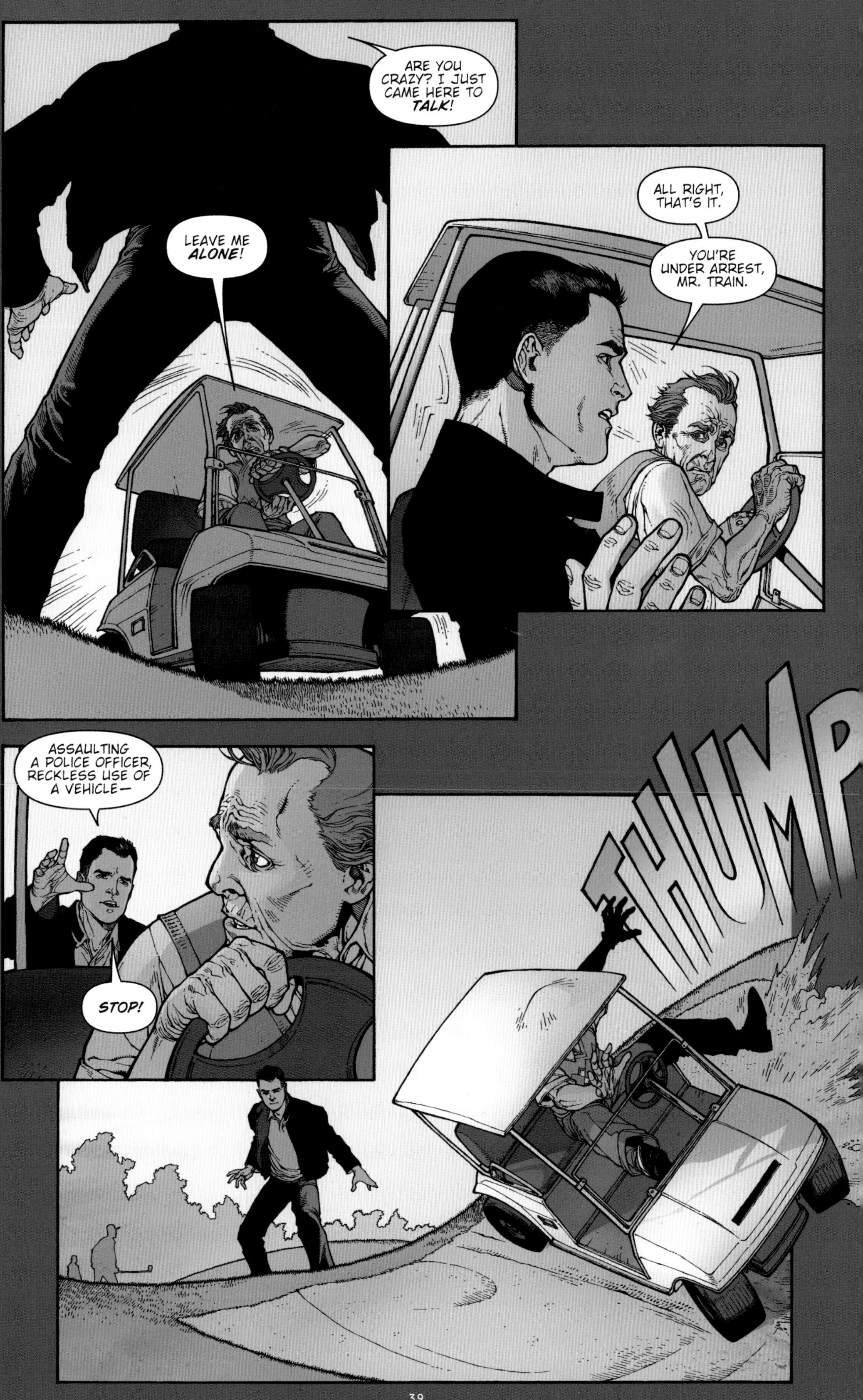

ARE YOU CRAZY? I JUST CAME HERE TO TALK!
LEAVE ME ALONE!
ALL RIGHT, THAT'S IT.
YOU'RE UNDER ARREST, MR. TRAIN.
ASSAULTING A POLICE OFFICER, RECKLESS USE OF A VEHICLE—
STOP!
THUMP

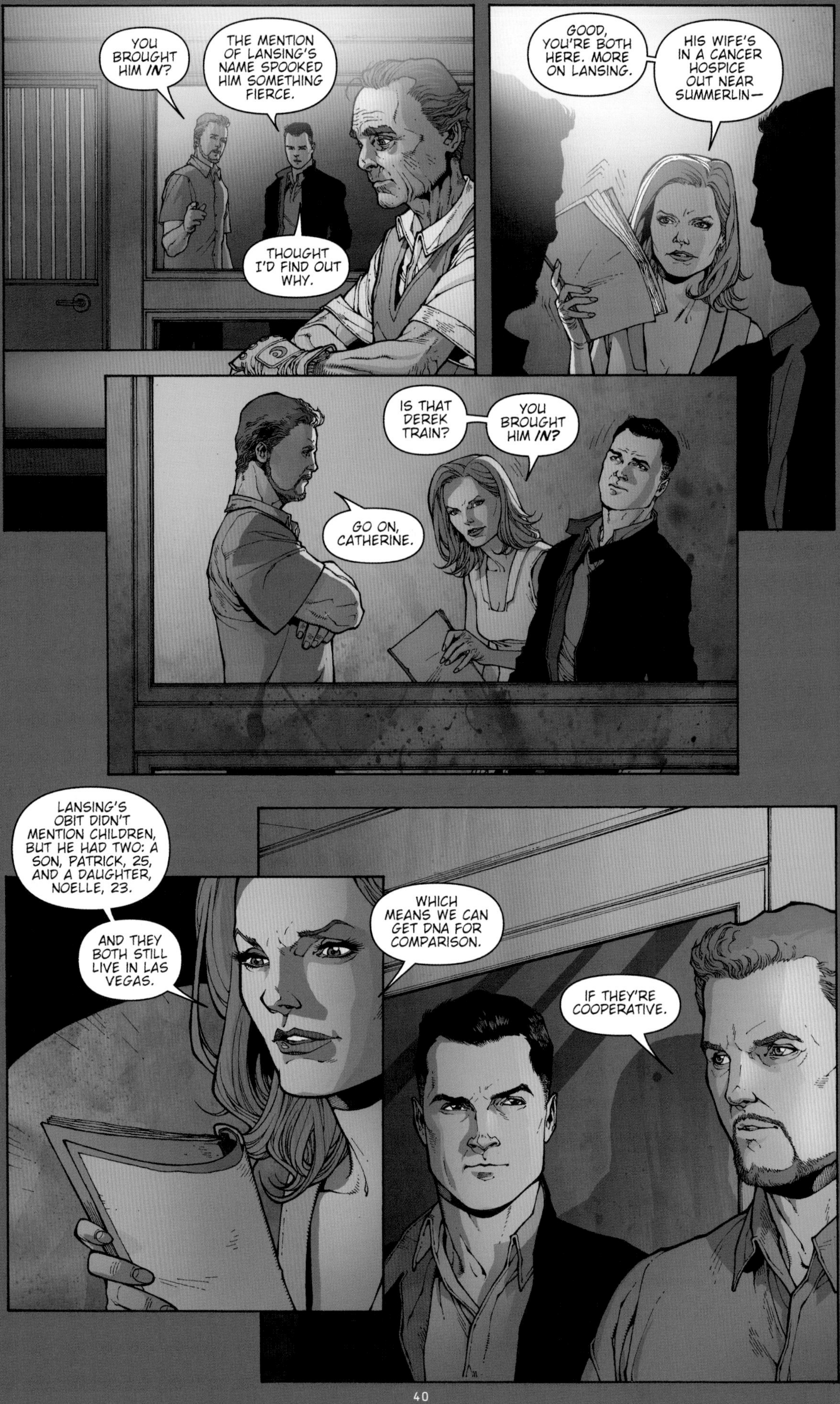
YOU BROUGHT HIM *IN*?
THE MENTION OF LANSING'S NAME SPOOKED HIM SOMETHING FIERCE.
THOUGHT I'D FIND OUT WHY.
GOOD, YOU'RE BOTH HERE. MORE ON LANSING.
HIS WIFE'S IN A CANCER HOSPICE OUT NEAR SUMMERLIN—
IS THAT DEREK TRAIN?
YOU BROUGHT HIM *IN?*
GO ON, CATHERINE.
LANSING'S OBIT DIDN'T MENTION CHILDREN, BUT HE HAD TWO: A SON, PATRICK, 25, AND A DAUGHTER, NOELLE, 23.
AND THEY BOTH STILL LIVE IN LAS VEGAS.
WHICH MEANS WE CAN GET DNA FOR COMPARISON.
IF THEY'RE COOPERATIVE.

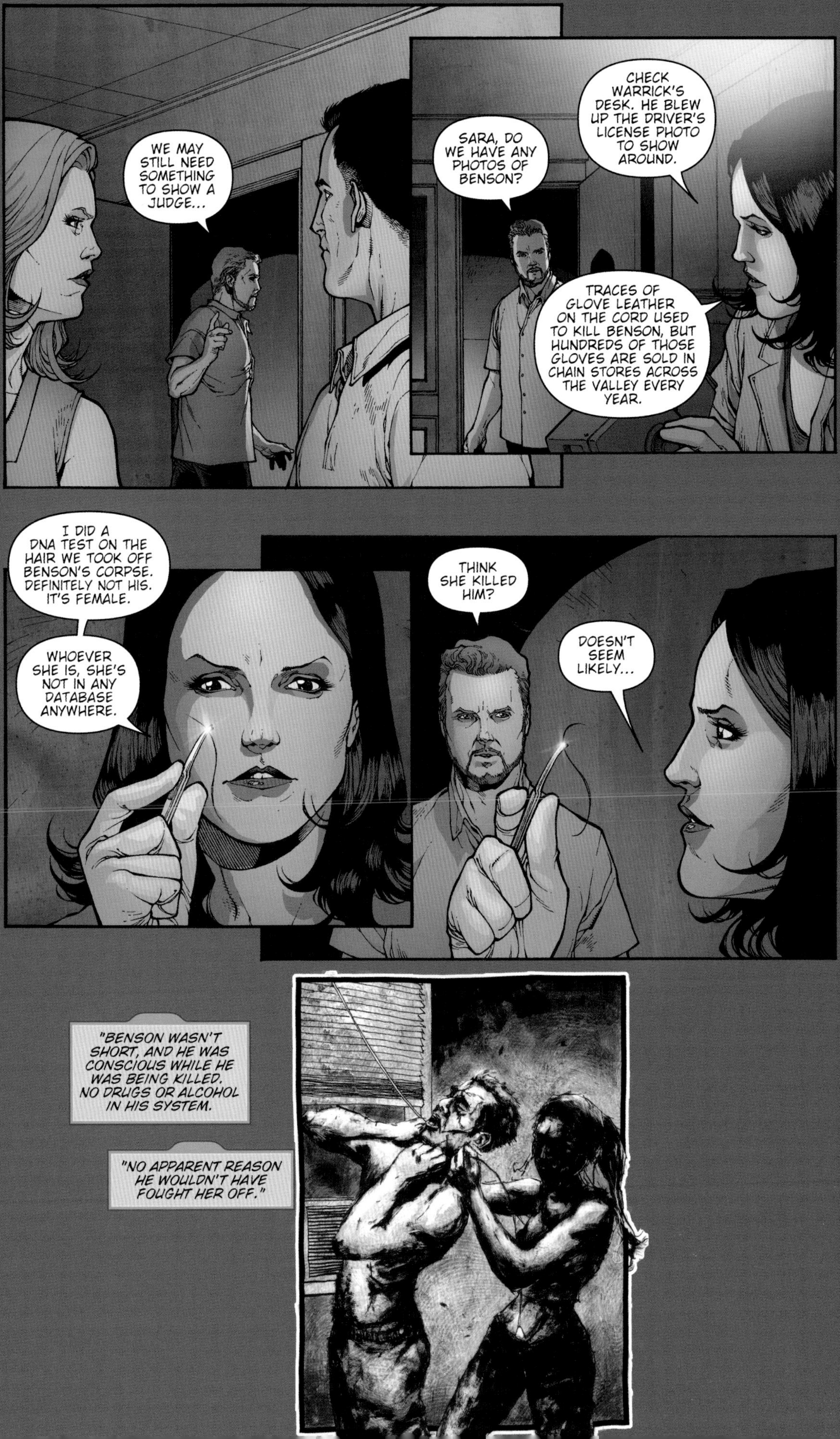
WE MAY STILL NEED SOMETHING TO SHOW A JUDGE...
SARA, DO WE HAVE ANY PHOTOS OF BENSON?
CHECK WARRICK'S DESK. HE BLEW UP THE DRIVER'S LICENSE PHOTO TO SHOW AROUND.
TRACES OF GLOVE LEATHER ON THE CORD USED TO KILL BENSON, BUT HUNDREDS OF THOSE GLOVES ARE SOLD IN CHAIN STORES ACROSS THE VALLEY EVERY YEAR.
I DID A DNA TEST ON THE HAIR WE TOOK OFF BENSON'S CORPSE. DEFINITELY NOT HIS. IT'S FEMALE.
WHOEVER SHE IS, SHE'S NOT IN ANY DATABASE ANYWHERE.
THINK SHE KILLED HIM?
DOESN'T SEEM LIKELY...
"BENSON WASN'T SHORT, AND HE WAS CONSCIOUS WHILE HE WAS BEING KILLED. NO DRUGS OR ALCOHOL IN HIS SYSTEM.
"NO APPARENT REASON HE WOULDN'T HAVE FOUGHT HER OFF."

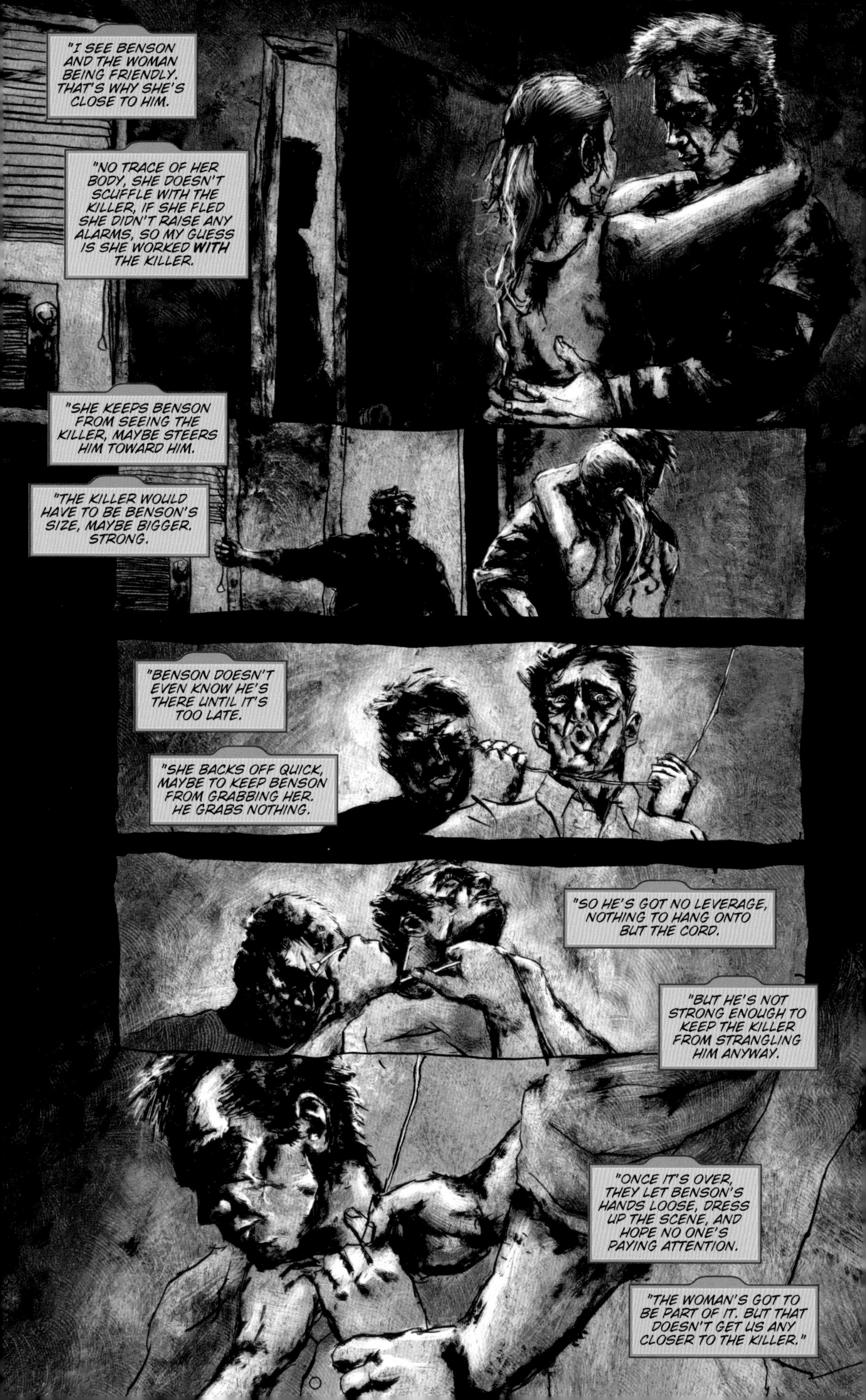
"I SEE BENSON AND THE WOMAN BEING FRIENDLY. THAT'S WHY SHE'S CLOSE TO HIM.
"NO TRACE OF HER BODY, SHE DOESN'T SCUFFLE WITH THE KILLER, IF SHE FLED SHE DIDN'T RAISE ANY ALARMS, SO MY GUESS IS SHE WORKED **WITH** THE KILLER.
"SHE KEEPS BENSON FROM SEEING THE KILLER, MAYBE STEERS HIM TOWARD HIM.
"THE KILLER WOULD HAVE TO BE BENSON'S SIZE, MAYBE BIGGER. STRONG.
"BENSON DOESN'T EVEN KNOW HE'S THERE UNTIL IT'S TOO LATE.
"SHE BACKS OFF QUICK, MAYBE TO KEEP BENSON FROM GRABBING HER. HE GRABS NOTHING.
"SO HE'S GOT NO LEVERAGE, NOTHING TO HANG ONTO BUT THE CORD.
"BUT HE'S NOT STRONG ENOUGH TO KEEP THE KILLER FROM STRANGLING HIM ANYWAY.
"ONCE IT'S OVER, THEY LET BENSON'S HANDS LOOSE, DRESS UP THE SCENE, AND HOPE NO ONE'S PAYING ATTENTION.
"THE WOMAN'S GOT TO BE PART OF IT. BUT THAT DOESN'T GET US ANY CLOSER TO THE KILLER."

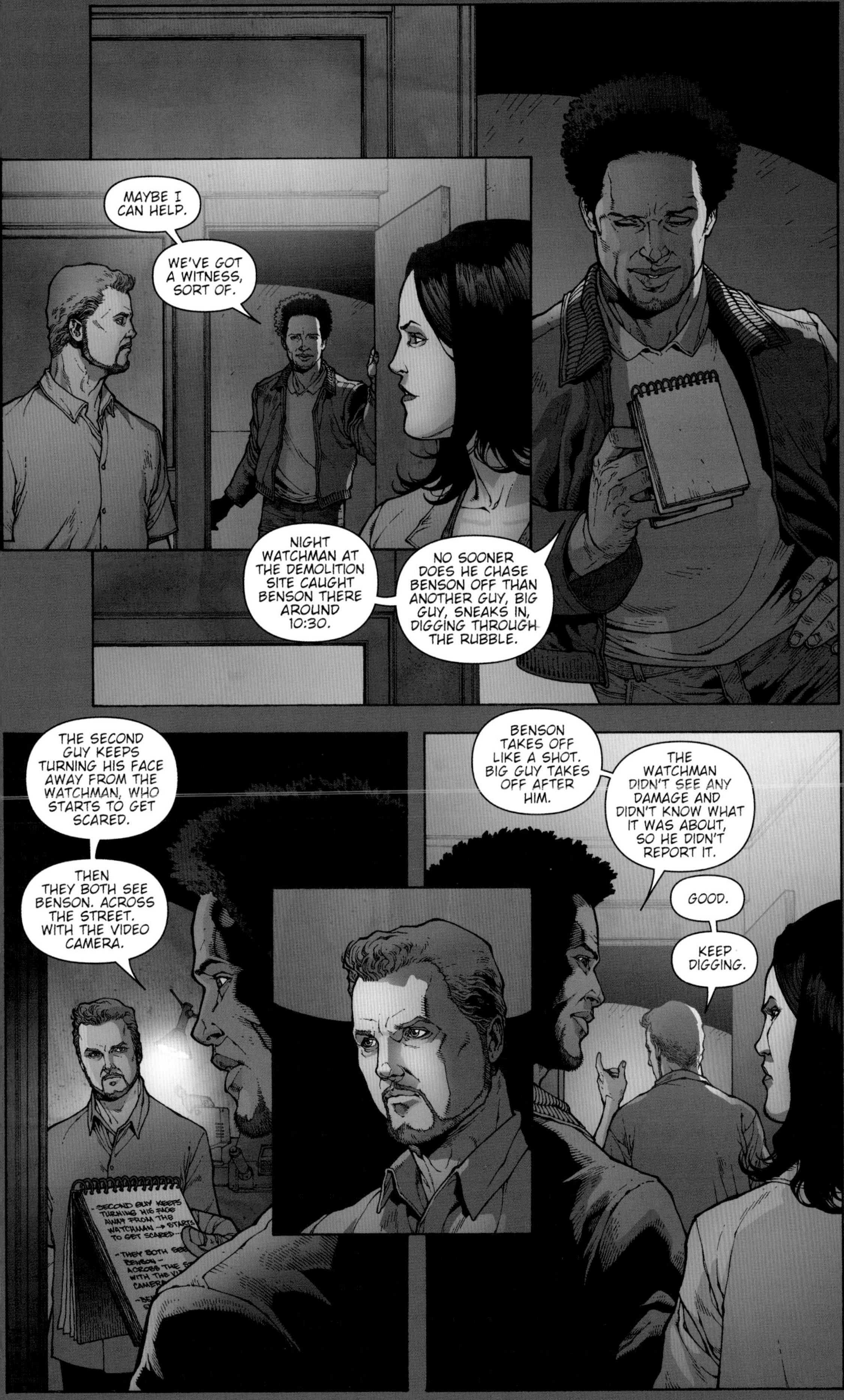
MAYBE I CAN HELP.
WE'VE GOT A WITNESS, SORT OF.
NIGHT WATCHMAN AT THE DEMOLITION SITE CAUGHT BENSON THERE AROUND 10:30.
NO SOONER DOES HE CHASE BENSON OFF THAN ANOTHER GUY, BIG GUY, SNEAKS IN, DIGGING THROUGH THE RUBBLE.
THE SECOND GUY KEEPS TURNING HIS FACE AWAY FROM THE WATCHMAN, WHO STARTS TO GET SCARED.
THEN THEY BOTH SEE BENSON. ACROSS THE STREET. WITH THE VIDEO CAMERA.
BENSON TAKES OFF LIKE A SHOT. BIG GUY TAKES OFF AFTER HIM.
THE WATCHMAN DIDN'T SEE ANY DAMAGE AND DIDN'T KNOW WHAT IT WAS ABOUT, SO HE DIDN'T REPORT IT.
GOOD.
KEEP DIGGING.

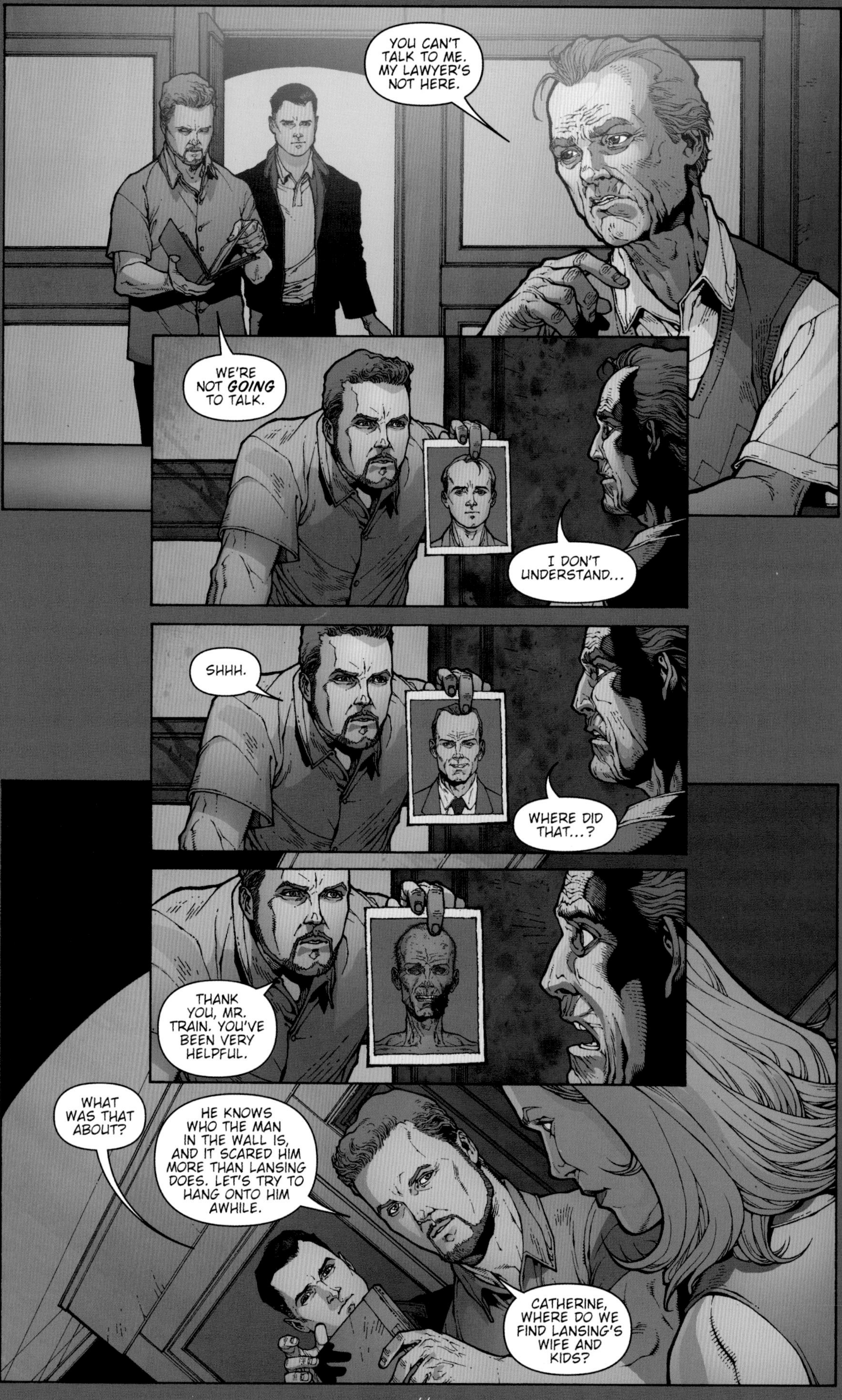
YOU CAN'T TALK TO ME. MY LAWYER'S NOT HERE.
WE'RE NOT GOING TO TALK.
I DON'T UNDERSTAND...
SHHH.
WHERE DID THAT...?
THANK YOU, MR. TRAIN. YOU'VE BEEN VERY HELPFUL.
WHAT WAS THAT ABOUT?
HE KNOWS WHO THE MAN IN THE WALL IS, AND IT SCARED HIM MORE THAN LANSING DOES. LET'S TRY TO HANG ONTO HIM AWHILE.
CATHERINE, WHERE DO WE FIND LANSING'S WIFE AND KIDS?

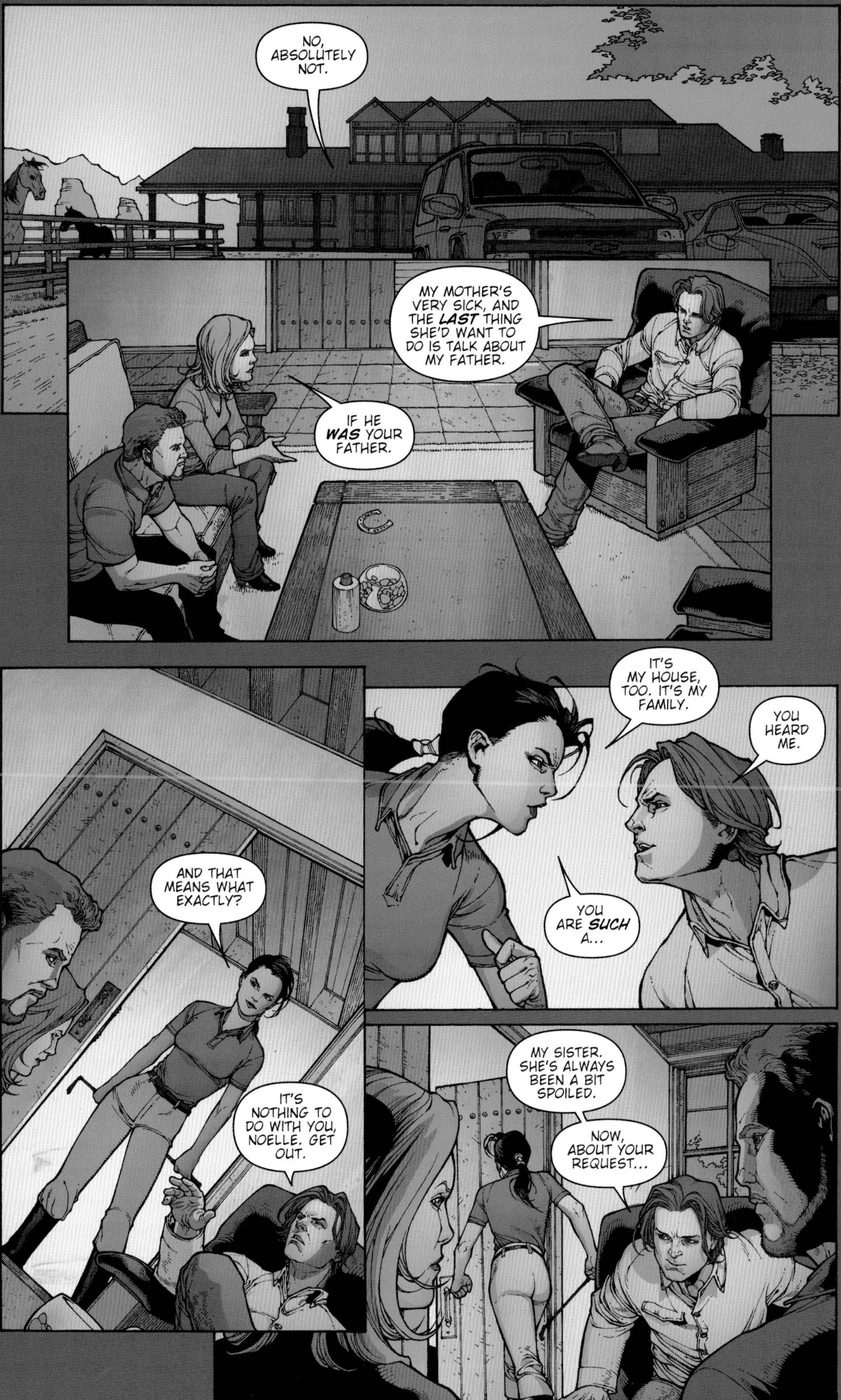
NO, ABSOLUTELY NOT.
MY MOTHER'S VERY SICK, AND THE LAST THING SHE'D WANT TO DO IS TALK ABOUT MY FATHER.
IF HE WAS YOUR FATHER.
AND THAT MEANS WHAT EXACTLY?
IT'S NOTHING TO DO WITH YOU, NOELLE. GET OUT.
IT'S MY HOUSE, TOO. IT'S MY FAMILY.
YOU HEARD ME.
YOU ARE SUCH A...
MY SISTER. SHE'S ALWAYS BEEN A BIT SPOILED.
NOW, ABOUT YOUR REQUEST...

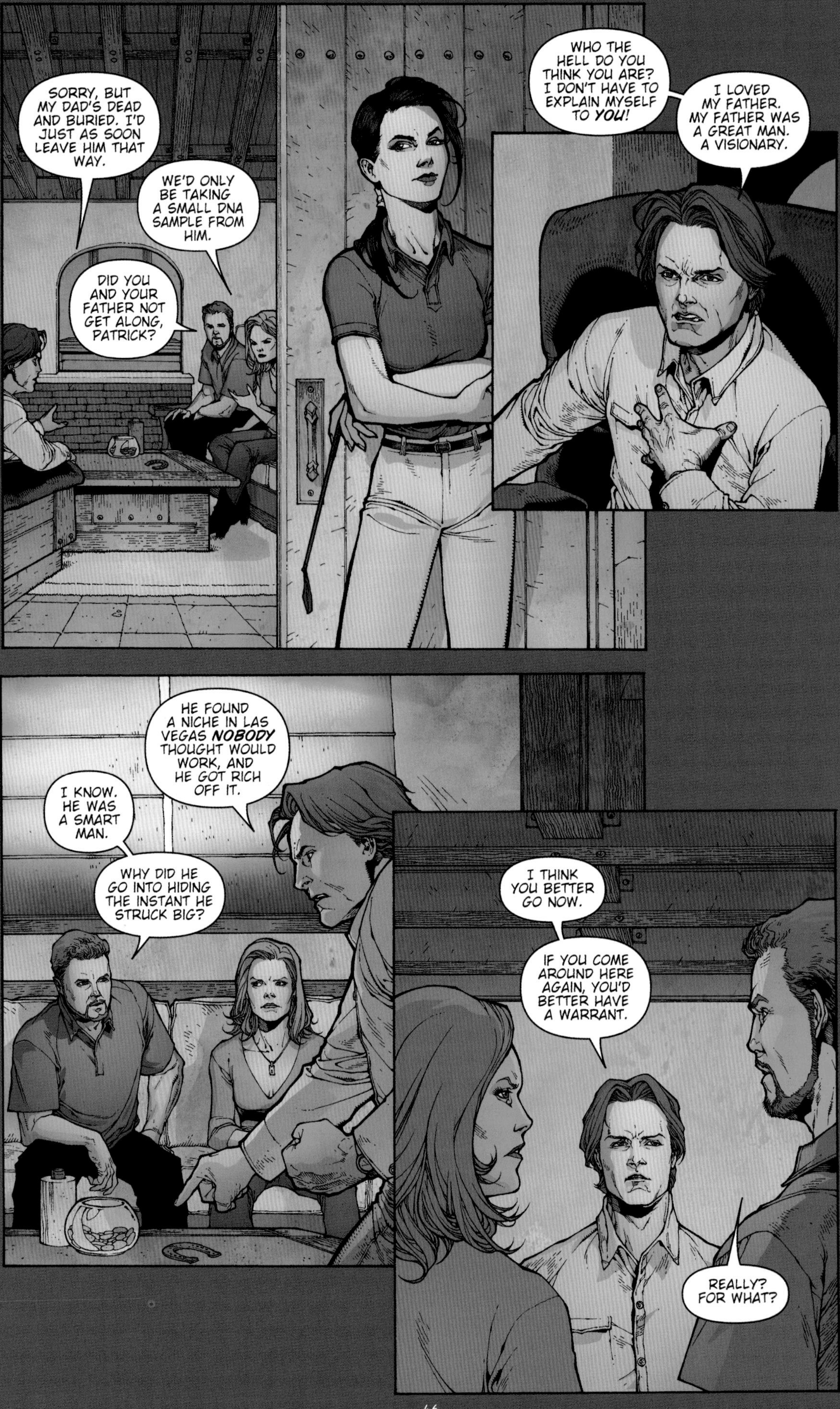
SORRY, BUT MY DAD'S DEAD AND BURIED. I'D JUST AS SOON LEAVE HIM THAT WAY.
WE'D ONLY BE TAKING A SMALL DNA SAMPLE FROM HIM.
DID YOU AND YOUR FATHER NOT GET ALONG, PATRICK?
WHO THE HELL DO YOU THINK YOU ARE? I DON'T HAVE TO EXPLAIN MYSELF TO *YOU*!
I LOVED MY FATHER. MY FATHER WAS A GREAT MAN. A VISIONARY.
HE FOUND A NICHE IN LAS VEGAS *NOBODY* THOUGHT WOULD WORK, AND HE GOT RICH OFF IT.
I KNOW. HE WAS A SMART MAN.
WHY DID HE GO INTO HIDING THE INSTANT HE STRUCK BIG?
I THINK YOU BETTER GO NOW.
IF YOU COME AROUND HERE AGAIN, YOU'D BETTER HAVE A WARRANT.
REALLY? FOR WHAT?

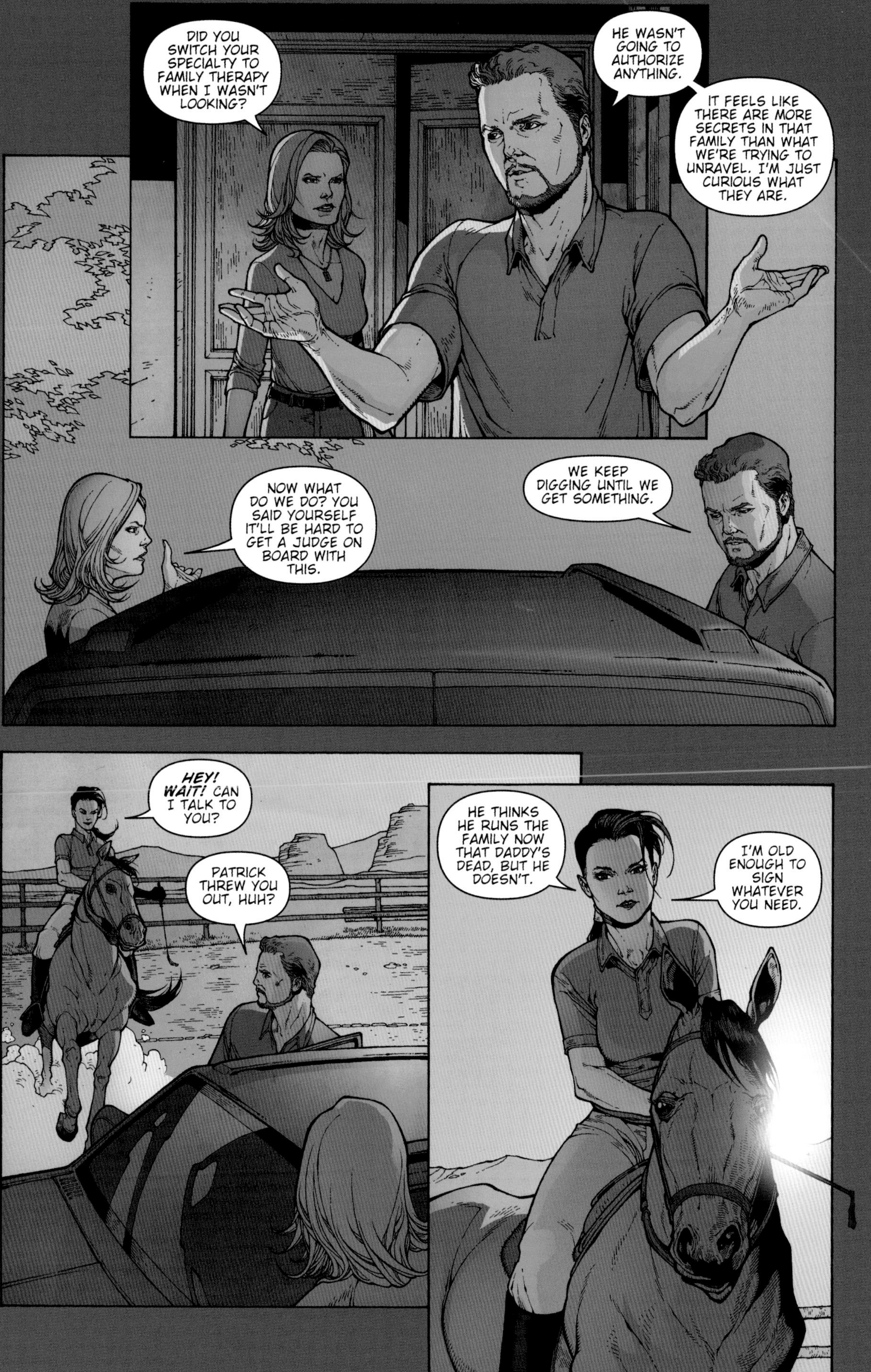
DID YOU SWITCH YOUR SPECIALTY TO FAMILY THERAPY WHEN I WASN'T LOOKING?
HE WASN'T GOING TO AUTHORIZE ANYTHING.
IT FEELS LIKE THERE ARE MORE SECRETS IN THAT FAMILY THAN WHAT WE'RE TRYING TO UNRAVEL. I'M JUST CURIOUS WHAT THEY ARE.
NOW WHAT DO WE DO? YOU SAID YOURSELF IT'LL BE HARD TO GET A JUDGE ON BOARD WITH THIS.
WE KEEP DIGGING UNTIL WE GET SOMETHING.
HEY! WAIT! CAN I TALK TO YOU?
PATRICK THREW YOU OUT, HUH?
HE THINKS HE RUNS THE FAMILY NOW THAT DADDY'S DEAD, BUT HE DOESN'T.
I'M OLD ENOUGH TO SIGN WHATEVER YOU NEED.

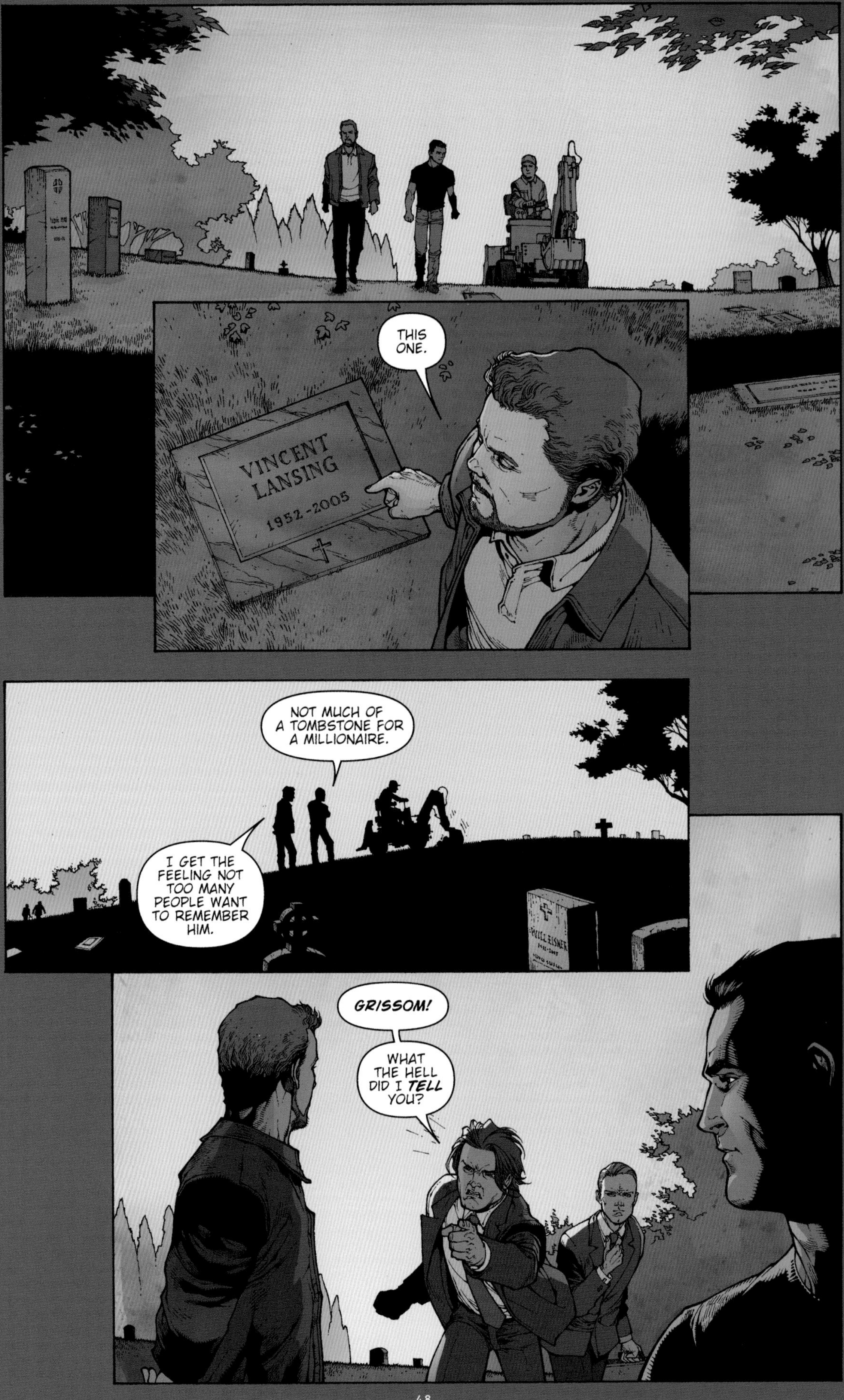
VINCENT LANSING
1952-2005
THIS ONE.
NOT MUCH OF A TOMBSTONE FOR A MILLIONAIRE.
I GET THE FEELING NOT TOO MANY PEOPLE WANT TO REMEMBER HIM.
GRISSOM!
WHAT THE HELL DID I *TELL* YOU?

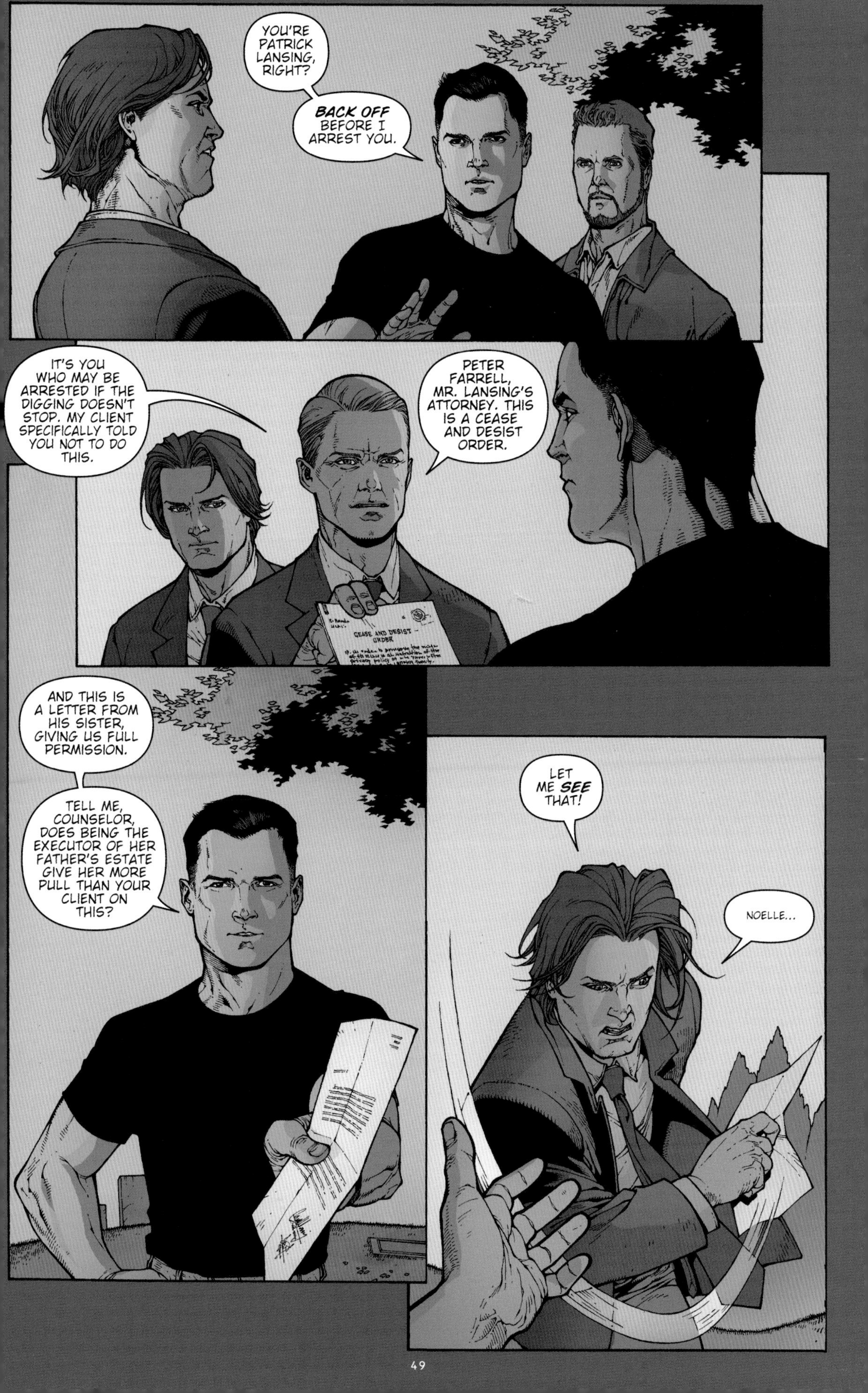
YOU'RE PATRICK LANSING, RIGHT?
BACK OFF BEFORE I ARREST YOU.
IT'S YOU WHO MAY BE ARRESTED IF THE DIGGING DOESN'T STOP. MY CLIENT SPECIFICALLY TOLD YOU NOT TO DO THIS.
PETER FARRELL, MR. LANSING'S ATTORNEY. THIS IS A CEASE AND DESIST ORDER.
CEASE AND DESIST - ORDER
AND THIS IS A LETTER FROM HIS SISTER, GIVING US FULL PERMISSION.
TELL ME, COUNSELOR, DOES BEING THE EXECUTOR OF HER FATHER'S ESTATE GIVE HER MORE PULL THAN YOUR CLIENT ON THIS?
LET ME **SEE** THAT!
NOELLE...

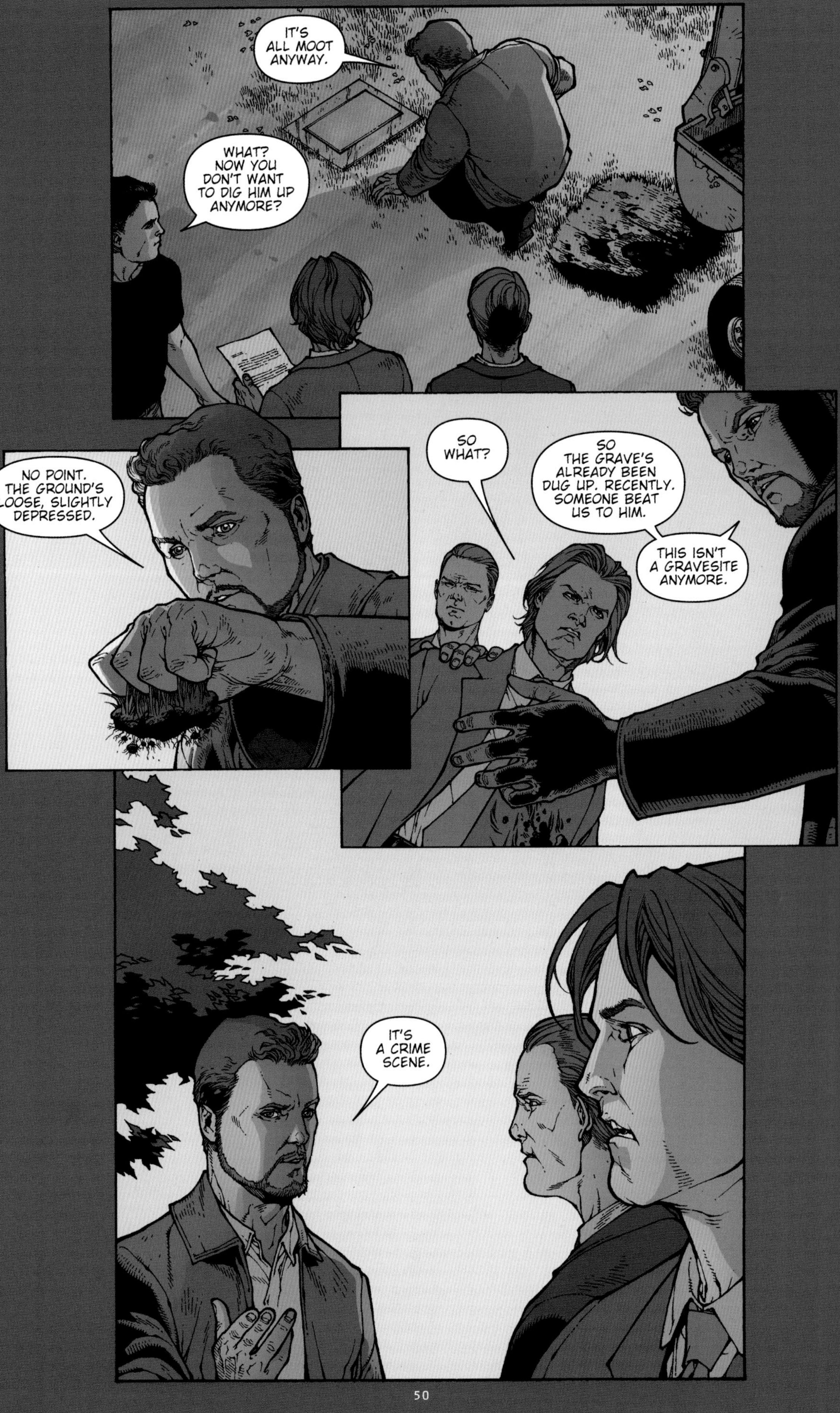
IT'S ALL MOOT ANYWAY.
WHAT? NOW YOU DON'T WANT TO DIG HIM UP ANYMORE?
NO POINT. THE GROUND'S LOOSE, SLIGHTLY DEPRESSED.
SO WHAT?
SO THE GRAVE'S ALREADY BEEN DUG UP. RECENTLY. SOMEONE BEAT US TO HIM.
THIS ISN'T A GRAVESITE ANYMORE.
IT'S A CRIME SCENE.

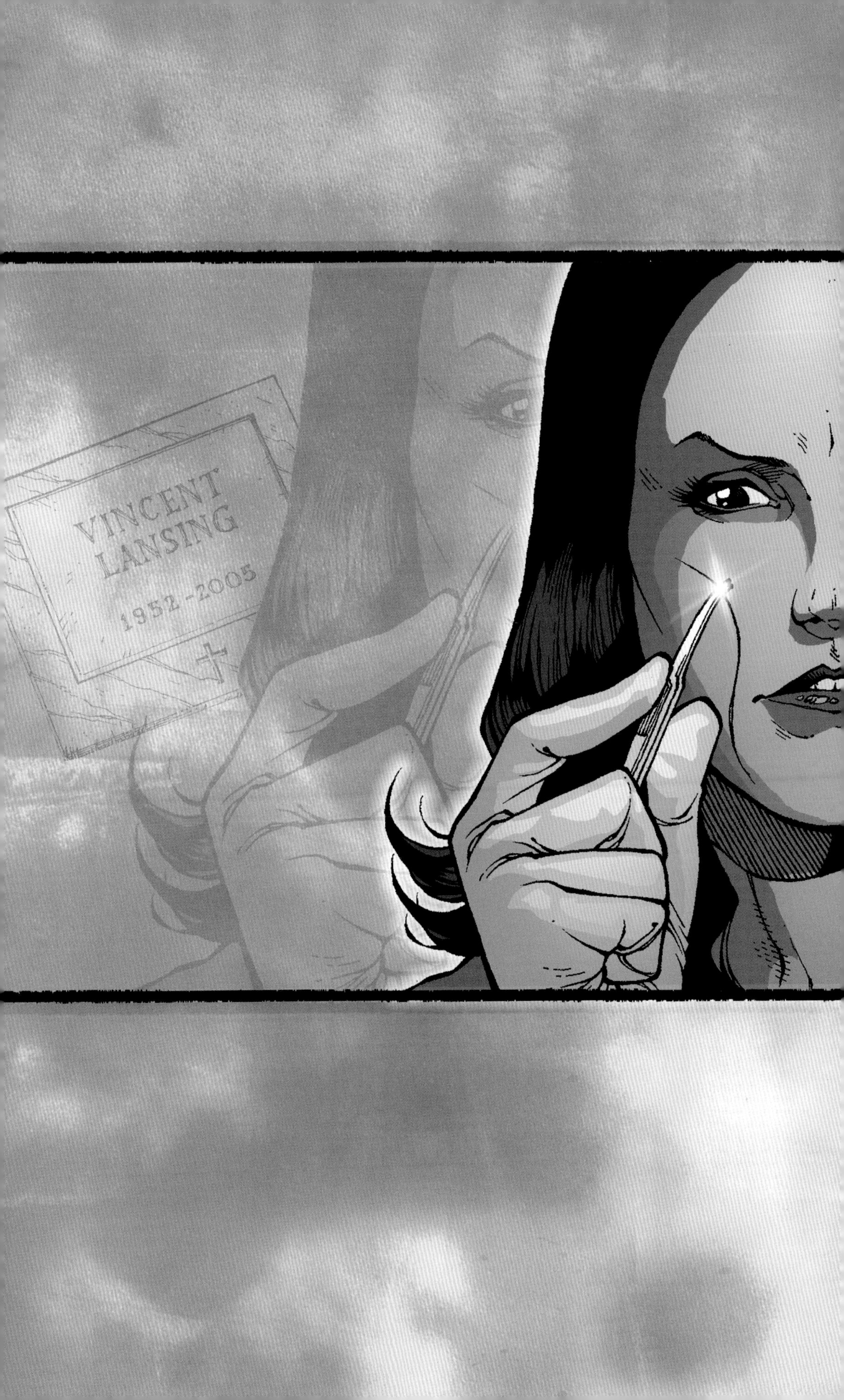
VINCENT LANSING
1952-2005

chapter three

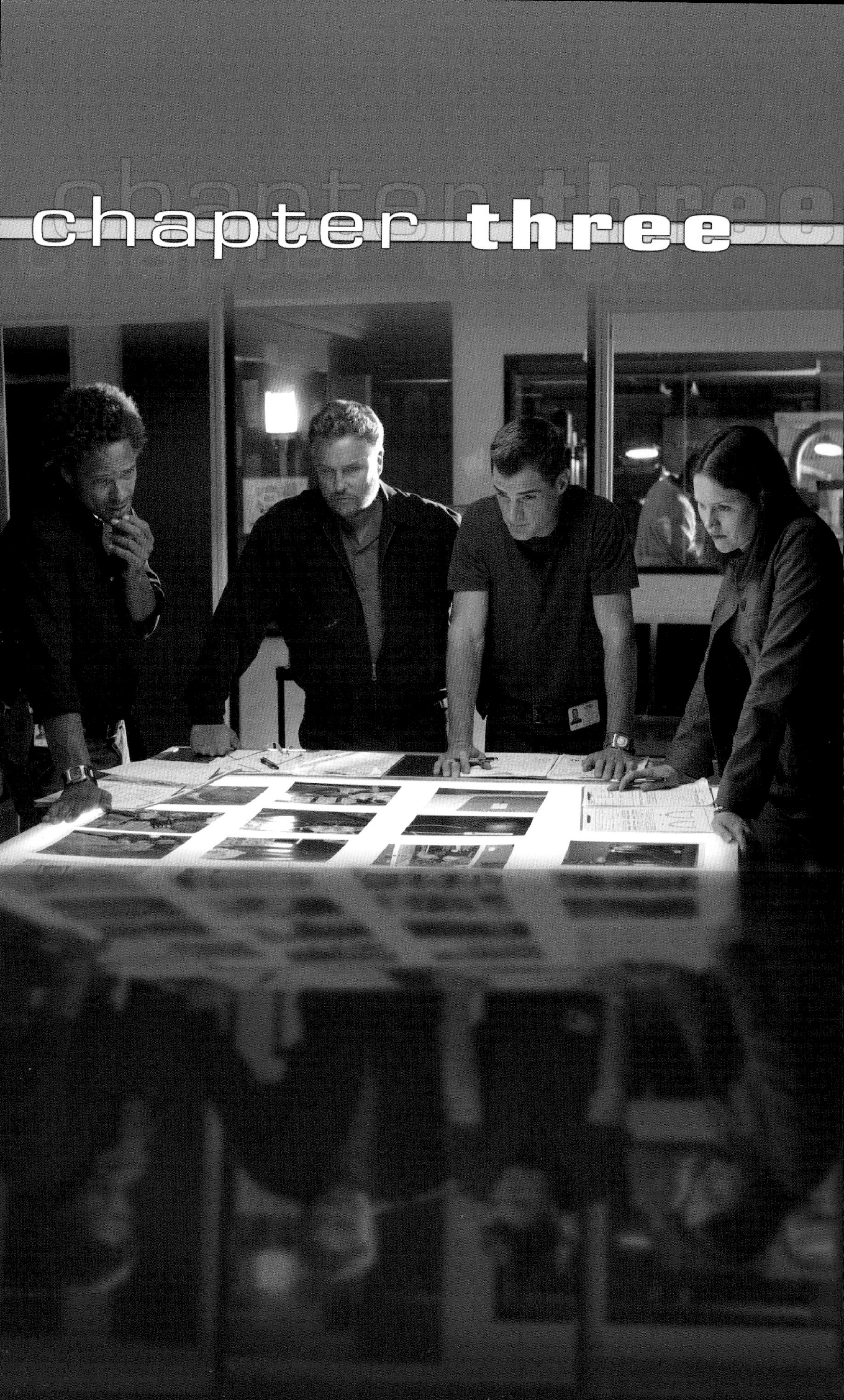

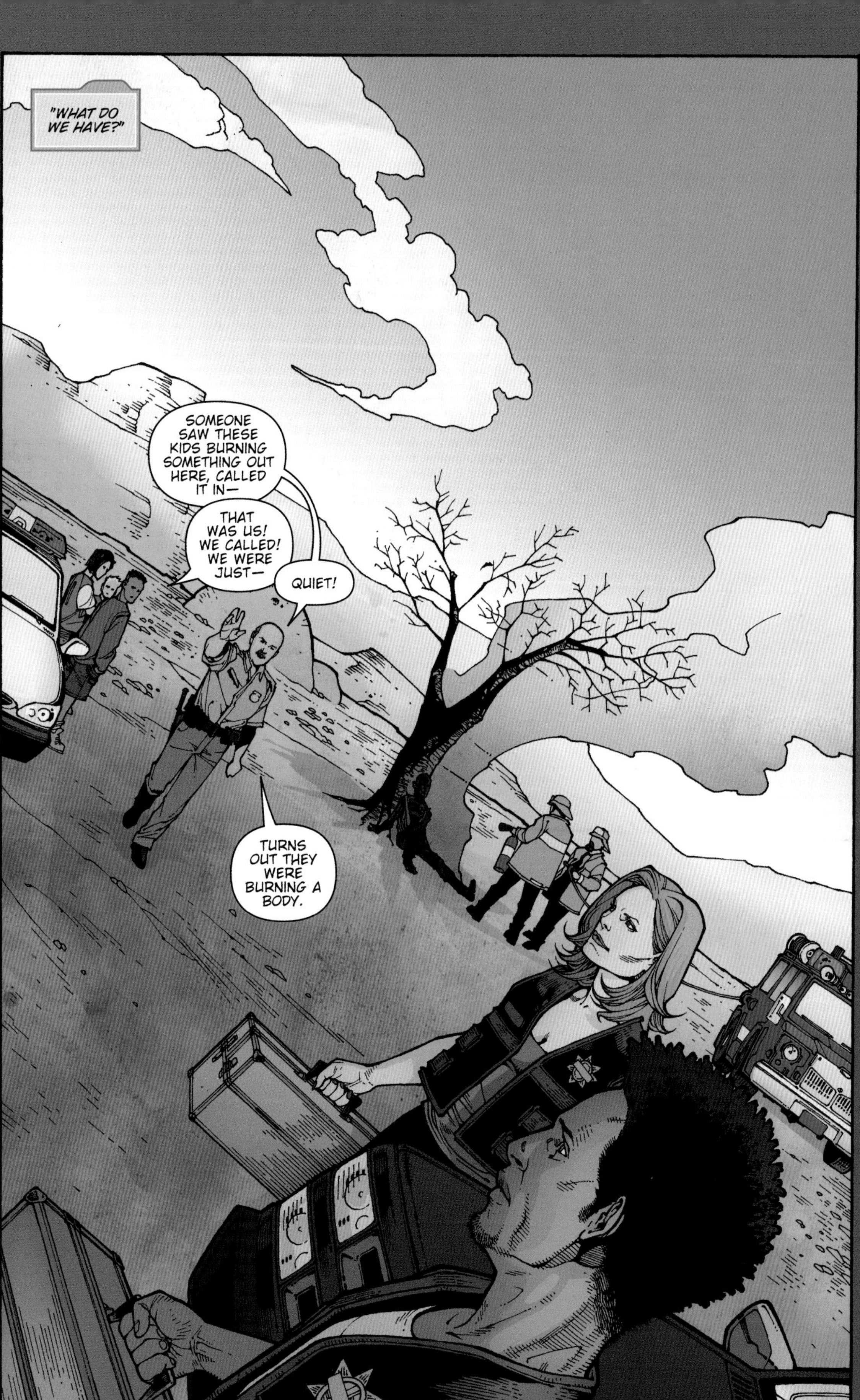
"WHAT DO WE HAVE?"
SOMEONE SAW THESE KIDS BURNING SOMETHING OUT HERE, CALLED IT IN—
THAT WAS US! WE CALLED! WE WERE JUST—
QUIET!
TURNS OUT THEY WERE BURNING A BODY.

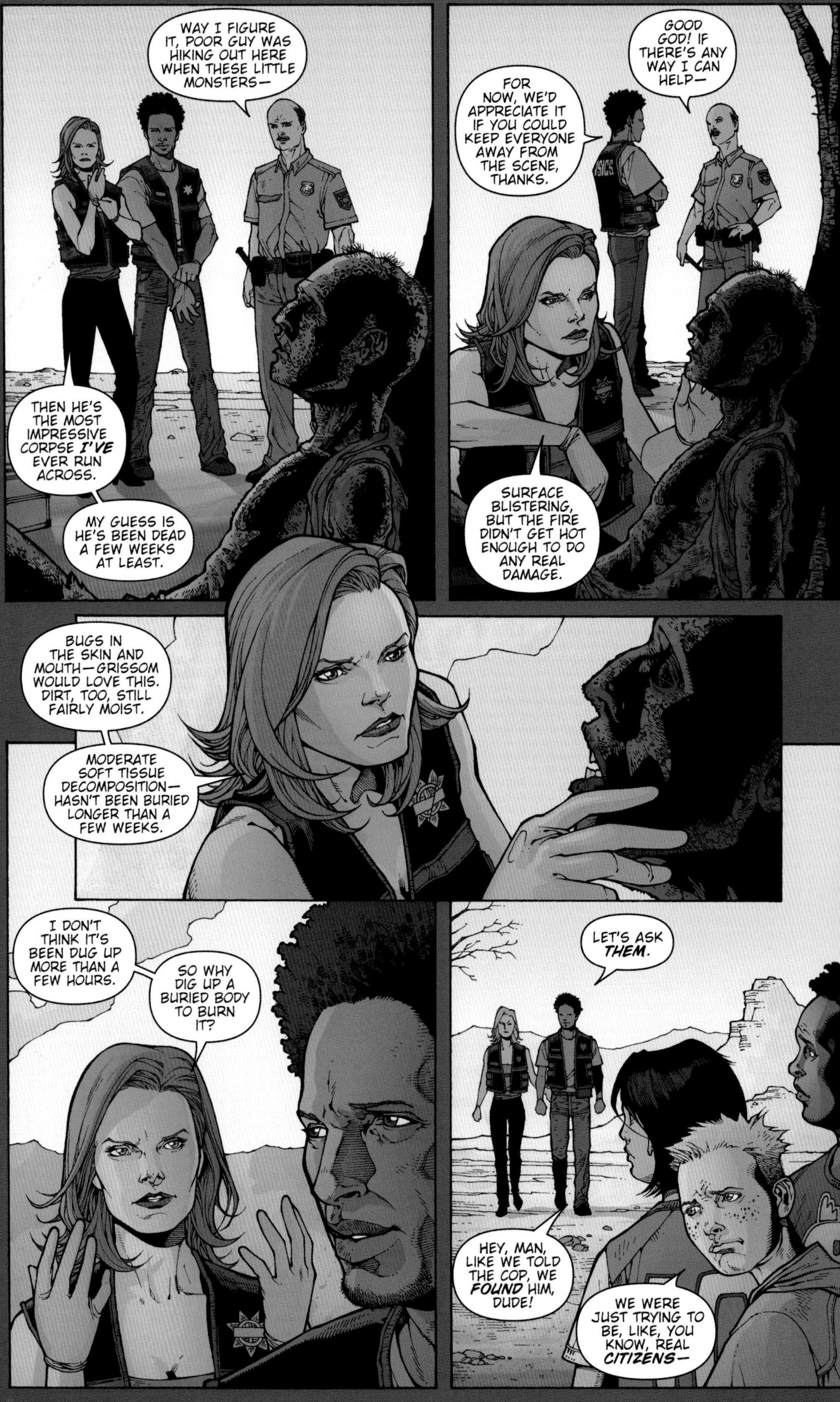
WAY I FIGURE IT, POOR GUY WAS HIKING OUT HERE WHEN THESE LITTLE MONSTERS—
THEN HE'S THE MOST IMPRESSIVE CORPSE I'VE EVER RUN ACROSS.
MY GUESS IS HE'S BEEN DEAD A FEW WEEKS AT LEAST.
GOOD GOD! IF THERE'S ANY WAY I CAN HELP—
FOR NOW, WE'D APPRECIATE IT IF YOU COULD KEEP EVERYONE AWAY FROM THE SCENE, THANKS.
SURFACE BLISTERING, BUT THE FIRE DIDN'T GET HOT ENOUGH TO DO ANY REAL DAMAGE.
BUGS IN THE SKIN AND MOUTH—GRISSOM WOULD LOVE THIS. DIRT, TOO, STILL FAIRLY MOIST.
MODERATE SOFT TISSUE DECOMPOSITION—HASN'T BEEN BURIED LONGER THAN A FEW WEEKS.
I DON'T THINK IT'S BEEN DUG UP MORE THAN A FEW HOURS.
SO WHY DIG UP A BURIED BODY TO BURN IT?
LET'S ASK THEM.
HEY, MAN, LIKE WE TOLD THE COP, WE FOUND HIM, DUDE!
WE WERE JUST TRYING TO BE, LIKE, YOU KNOW, REAL CITIZENS—

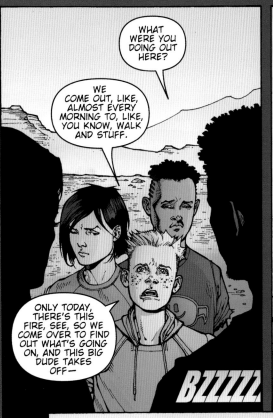

WHAT WERE YOU DOING OUT HERE?

WE COME OUT, LIKE, ALMOST EVERY MORNING TO, LIKE, YOU KNOW, WALK AND STUFF.

ONLY TODAY, THERE'S THIS FIRE, SEE, SO WE COME OVER TO FIND OUT WHAT'S GOING ON, AND THIS BIG DUDE TAKES OFF—

BZZZZZ

CAN YOU TELL ME WHAT THIS "DUDE" LOOKED LIKE?

AW, MAN, IT WAS STILL DARK...

YEAH?

OH, HI. WE GOT A CALL, SOME SORT OF DO-IT-YOURSELF CREMATION OUT HERE IN THE CANYON.

FIGURE A COUPLE HOURS.

WHAT?

REALLY?

I DON'T THINK THEY HAD ANYTHING TO DO WITH IT.

ME, NEITHER. THAT WAS GRISSOM. HE WANTS US BACK ASAP.

SEEMS SOMEONE DUG UP VINCENT LANSING'S GRAVE LAST NIGHT.

CLIP

BROWN

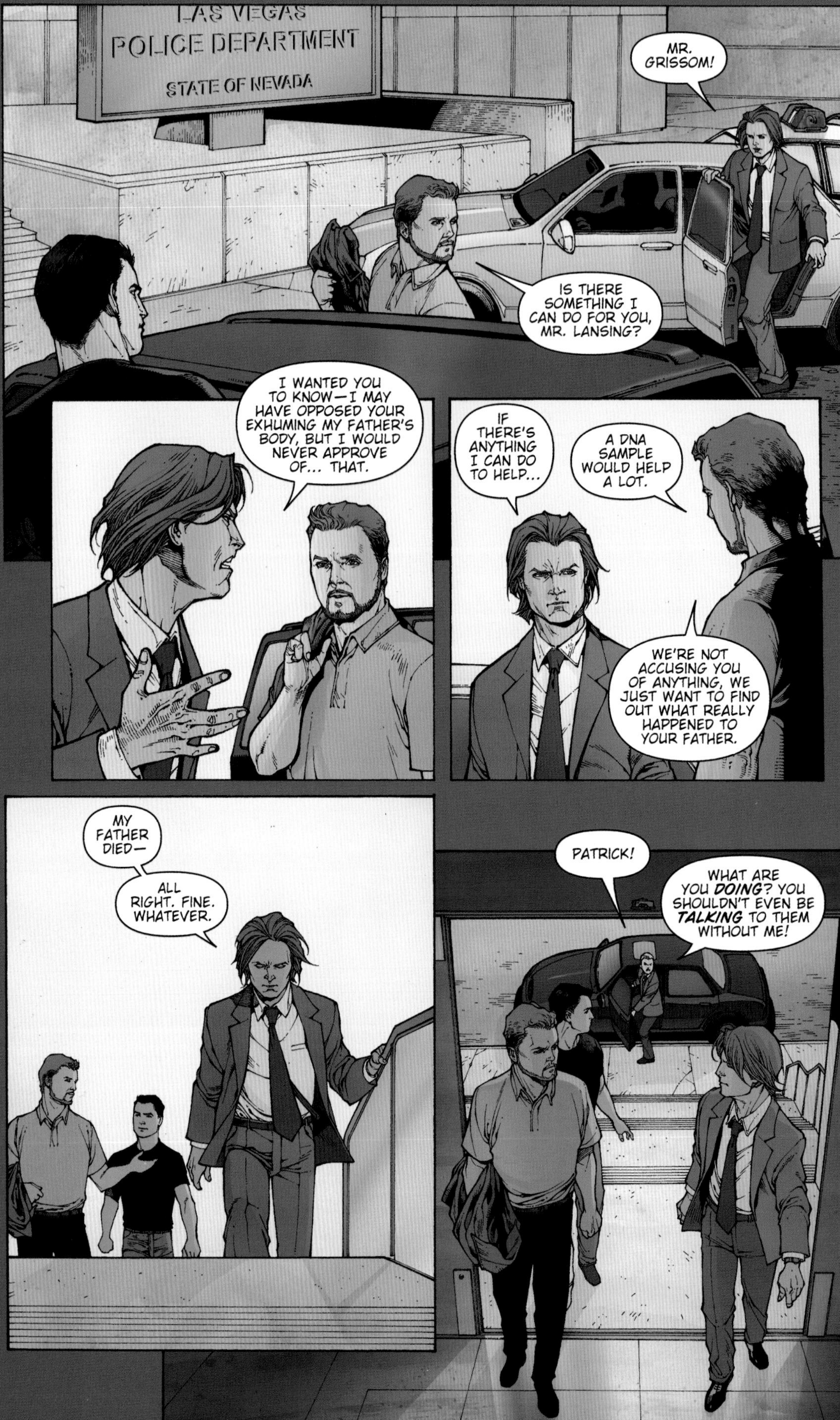
LAS VEGAS
POLICE DEPARTMENT
STATE OF NEVADA
MR. GRISSOM!
IS THERE SOMETHING I CAN DO FOR YOU, MR. LANSING?
I WANTED YOU TO KNOW—I MAY HAVE OPPOSED YOUR EXHUMING MY FATHER'S BODY, BUT I WOULD NEVER APPROVE OF... THAT.
IF THERE'S ANYTHING I CAN DO TO HELP...
A DNA SAMPLE WOULD HELP A LOT.
WE'RE NOT ACCUSING YOU OF ANYTHING, WE JUST WANT TO FIND OUT WHAT REALLY HAPPENED TO YOUR FATHER.
MY FATHER DIED—
ALL RIGHT. FINE. WHATEVER.
PATRICK!
WHAT ARE YOU **DOING**? YOU SHOULDN'T EVEN BE ***TALKING*** TO THEM WITHOUT ME!

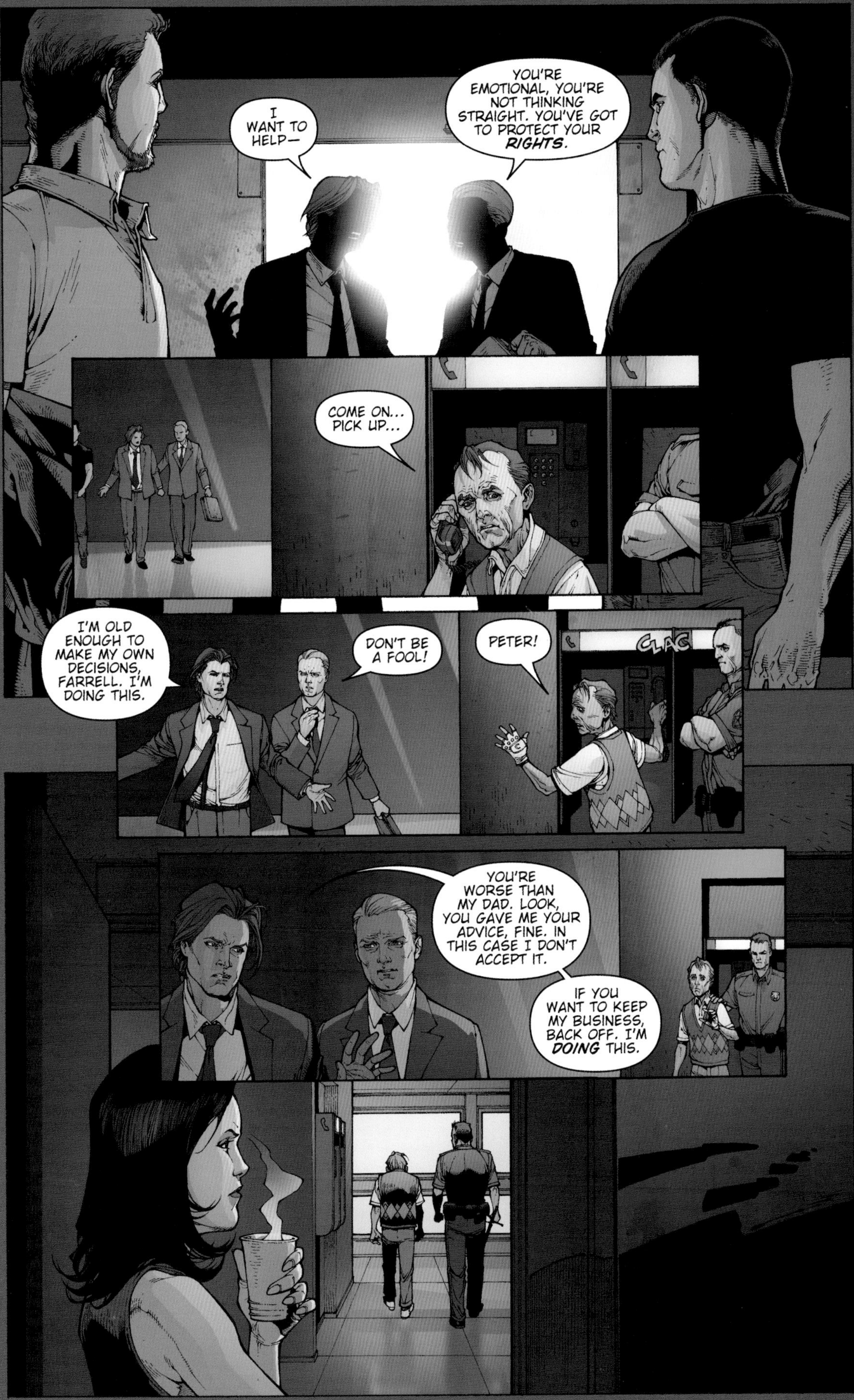
I WANT TO HELP—
YOU'RE EMOTIONAL, YOU'RE NOT THINKING STRAIGHT. YOU'VE GOT TO PROTECT YOUR ***RIGHTS***.
COME ON... PICK UP...
I'M OLD ENOUGH TO MAKE MY OWN DECISIONS, FARRELL. I'M DOING THIS.
DON'T BE A FOOL!
PETER!
CLAC
YOU'RE WORSE THAN MY DAD. LOOK, YOU GAVE ME YOUR ADVICE, FINE. IN THIS CASE I DON'T ACCEPT IT.
IF YOU WANT TO KEEP MY BUSINESS, BACK OFF. I'M ***DOING*** THIS.

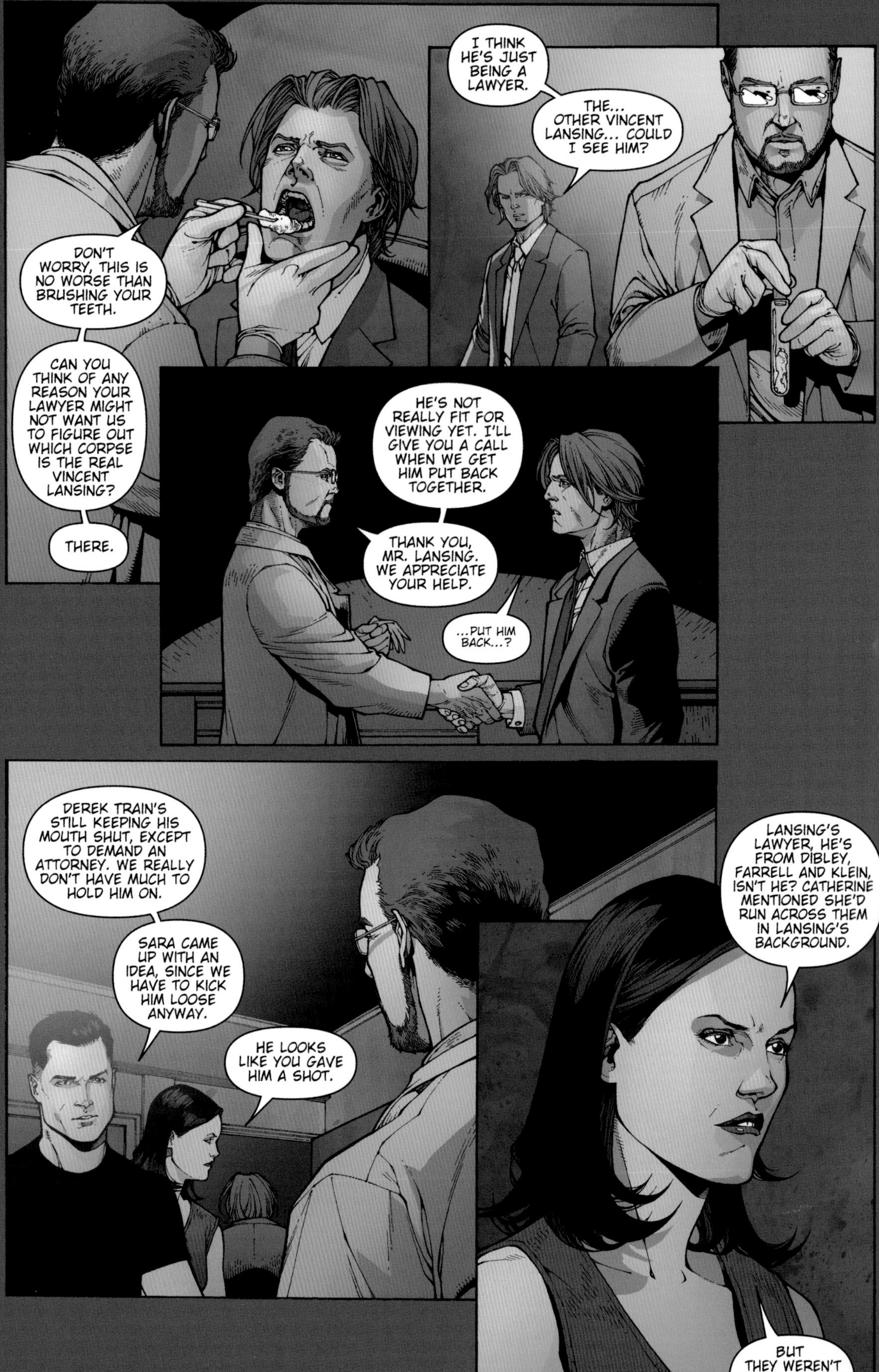
DON'T WORRY, THIS IS NO WORSE THAN BRUSHING YOUR TEETH.
CAN YOU THINK OF ANY REASON YOUR LAWYER MIGHT NOT WANT US TO FIGURE OUT WHICH CORPSE IS THE REAL VINCENT LANSING?
THERE.
I THINK HE'S JUST BEING A LAWYER.
THE... OTHER VINCENT LANSING... COULD I SEE HIM?
HE'S NOT REALLY FIT FOR VIEWING YET. I'LL GIVE YOU A CALL WHEN WE GET HIM PUT BACK TOGETHER.
THANK YOU, MR. LANSING. WE APPRECIATE YOUR HELP.
...PUT HIM BACK...?
DEREK TRAIN'S STILL KEEPING HIS MOUTH SHUT, EXCEPT TO DEMAND AN ATTORNEY. WE REALLY DON'T HAVE MUCH TO HOLD HIM ON.
SARA CAME UP WITH AN IDEA, SINCE WE HAVE TO KICK HIM LOOSE ANYWAY.
HE LOOKS LIKE YOU GAVE HIM A SHOT.
LANSING'S LAWYER, HE'S FROM DIBLEY, FARRELL AND KLEIN, ISN'T HE? CATHERINE MENTIONED SHE'D RUN ACROSS THEM IN LANSING'S BACKGROUND.
BUT THEY WEREN'T REPRESENTING LANSING THEN...

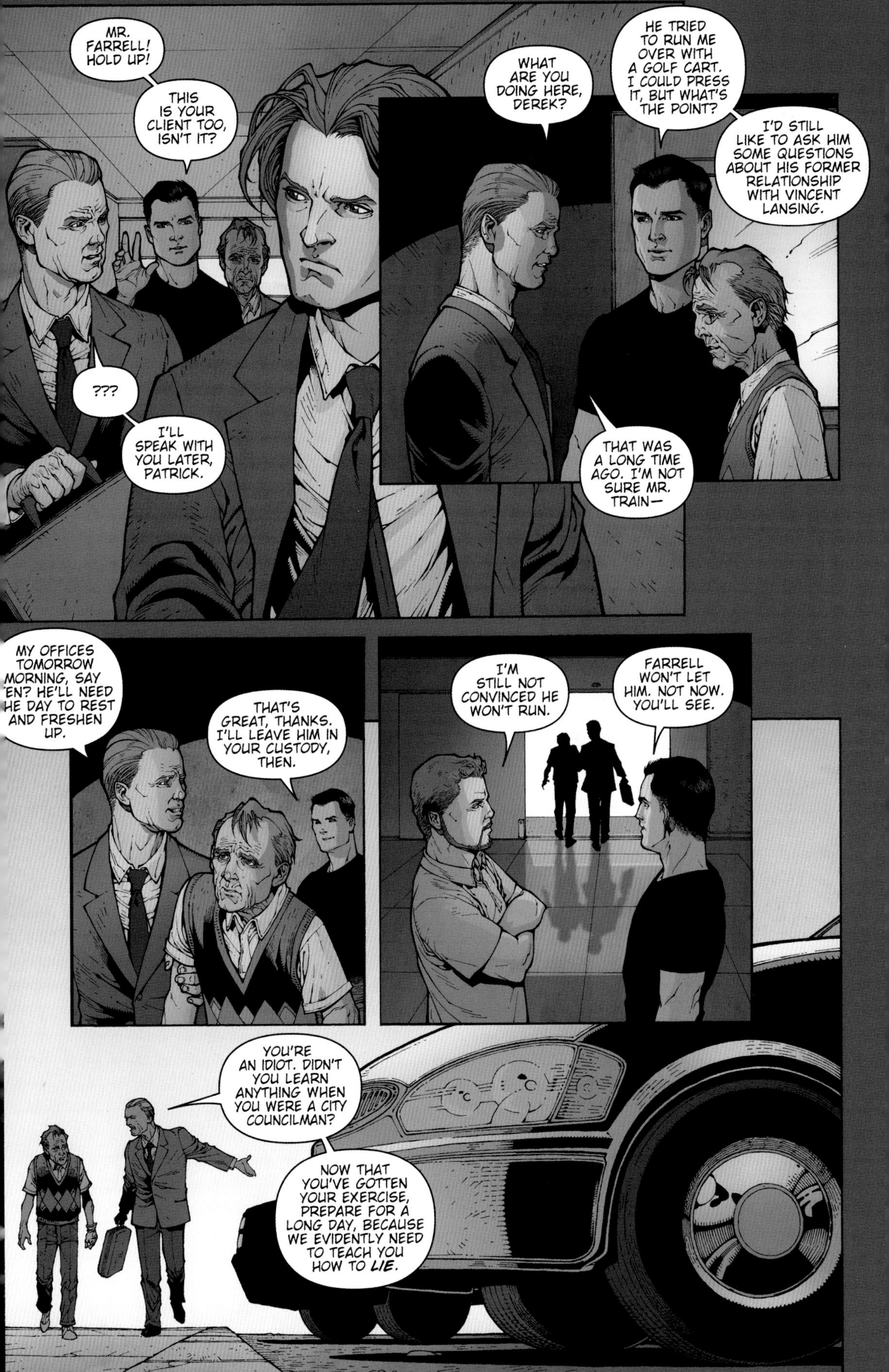
MR. FARRELL! HOLD UP!
THIS IS YOUR CLIENT TOO, ISN'T IT?
???
I'LL SPEAK WITH YOU LATER, PATRICK.
WHAT ARE YOU DOING HERE, DEREK?
HE TRIED TO RUN ME OVER WITH A GOLF CART. I COULD PRESS IT, BUT WHAT'S THE POINT?
I'D STILL LIKE TO ASK HIM SOME QUESTIONS ABOUT HIS FORMER RELATIONSHIP WITH VINCENT LANSING.
THAT WAS A LONG TIME AGO. I'M NOT SURE MR. TRAIN—
MY OFFICES TOMORROW MORNING, SAY 'EN? HE'LL NEED HE DAY TO REST AND FRESHEN UP.
THAT'S GREAT, THANKS. I'LL LEAVE HIM IN YOUR CUSTODY, THEN.
I'M STILL NOT CONVINCED HE WON'T RUN.
FARRELL WON'T LET HIM. NOT NOW. YOU'LL SEE.
YOU'RE AN IDIOT. DIDN'T YOU LEARN ANYTHING WHEN YOU WERE A CITY COUNCILMAN?
NOW THAT YOU'VE GOTTEN YOUR EXERCISE, PREPARE FOR A LONG DAY, BECAUSE WE EVIDENTLY NEED TO TEACH YOU HOW TO *LIE*.

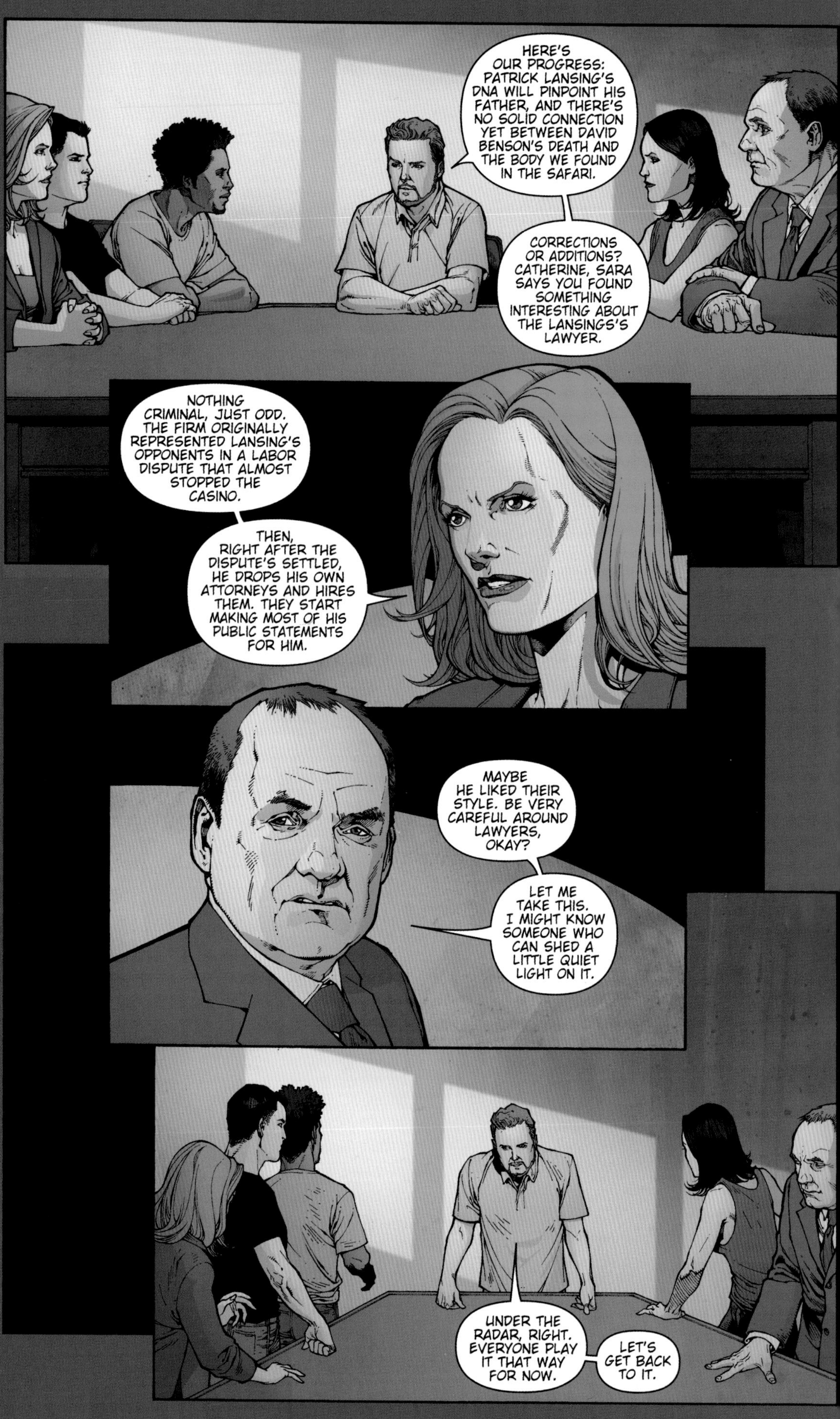
HERE'S OUR PROGRESS: PATRICK LANSING'S DNA WILL PINPOINT HIS FATHER, AND THERE'S NO SOLID CONNECTION YET BETWEEN DAVID BENSON'S DEATH AND THE BODY WE FOUND IN THE SAFARI.
CORRECTIONS OR ADDITIONS? CATHERINE, SARA SAYS YOU FOUND SOMETHING INTERESTING ABOUT THE LANSINGS'S LAWYER.
NOTHING CRIMINAL, JUST ODD. THE FIRM ORIGINALLY REPRESENTED LANSING'S OPPONENTS IN A LABOR DISPUTE THAT ALMOST STOPPED THE CASINO.
THEN, RIGHT AFTER THE DISPUTE'S SETTLED, HE DROPS HIS OWN ATTORNEYS AND HIRES THEM. THEY START MAKING MOST OF HIS PUBLIC STATEMENTS FOR HIM.
MAYBE HE LIKED THEIR STYLE. BE VERY CAREFUL AROUND LAWYERS, OKAY?
LET ME TAKE THIS. I MIGHT KNOW SOMEONE WHO CAN SHED A LITTLE QUIET LIGHT ON IT.
UNDER THE RADAR, RIGHT. EVERYONE PLAY IT THAT WAY FOR NOW.
LET'S GET BACK TO IT.

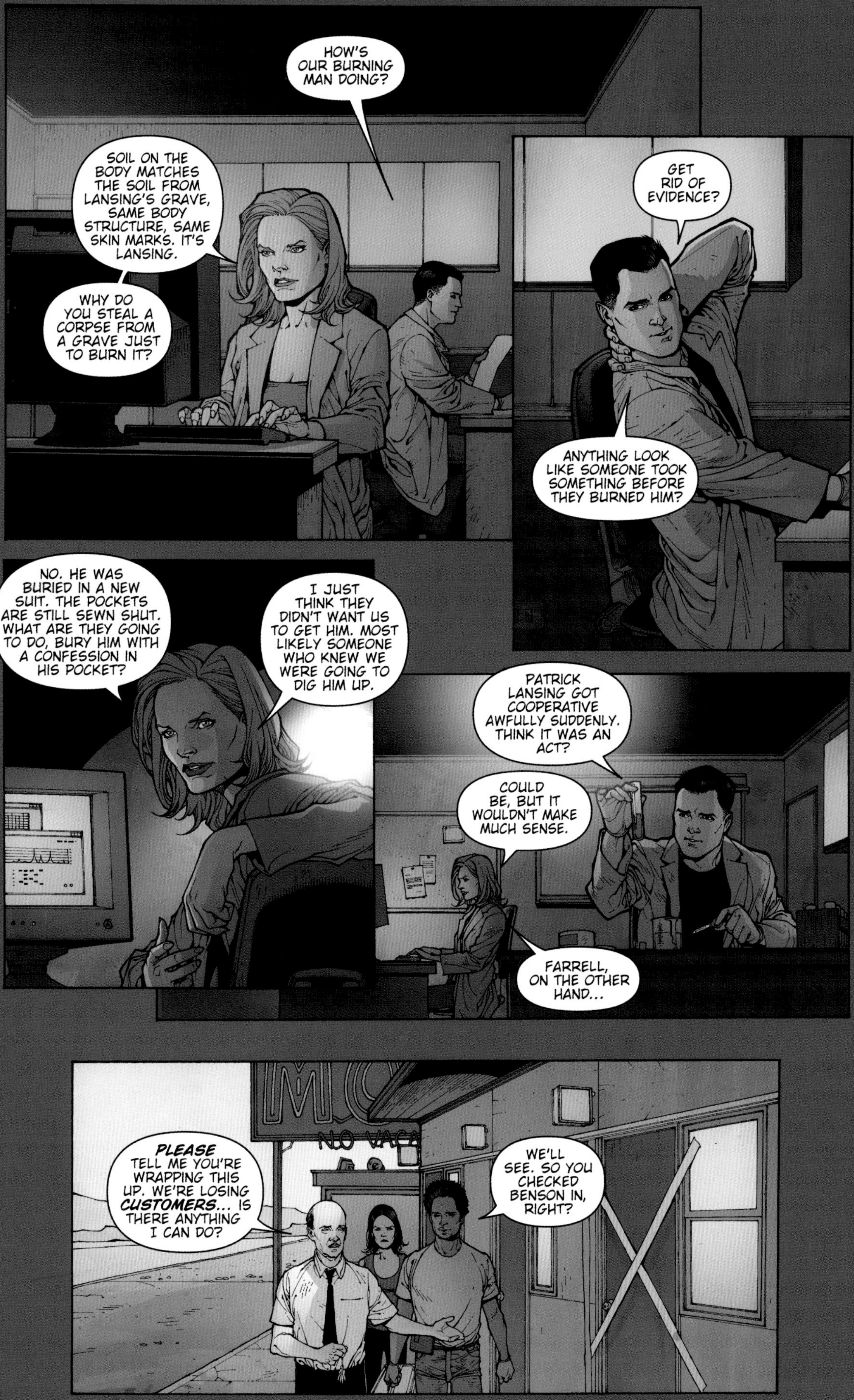
HOW'S OUR BURNING MAN DOING?
SOIL ON THE BODY MATCHES THE SOIL FROM LANSING'S GRAVE, SAME BODY STRUCTURE, SAME SKIN MARKS. IT'S LANSING.
WHY DO YOU STEAL A CORPSE FROM A GRAVE JUST TO BURN IT?
GET RID OF EVIDENCE?
ANYTHING LOOK LIKE SOMEONE TOOK SOMETHING BEFORE THEY BURNED HIM?
NO. HE WAS BURIED IN A NEW SUIT. THE POCKETS ARE STILL SEWN SHUT. WHAT ARE THEY GOING TO DO, BURY HIM WITH A CONFESSION IN HIS POCKET?
I JUST THINK THEY DIDN'T WANT US TO GET HIM. MOST LIKELY SOMEONE WHO KNEW WE WERE GOING TO DIG HIM UP.
PATRICK LANSING GOT COOPERATIVE AWFULLY SUDDENLY. THINK IT WAS AN ACT?
COULD BE, BUT IT WOULDN'T MAKE MUCH SENSE.
FARRELL, ON THE OTHER HAND...
PLEASE TELL ME YOU'RE WRAPPING THIS UP. WE'RE LOSING CUSTOMERS... IS THERE ANYTHING I CAN DO?
WE'LL SEE. SO YOU CHECKED BENSON IN, RIGHT?

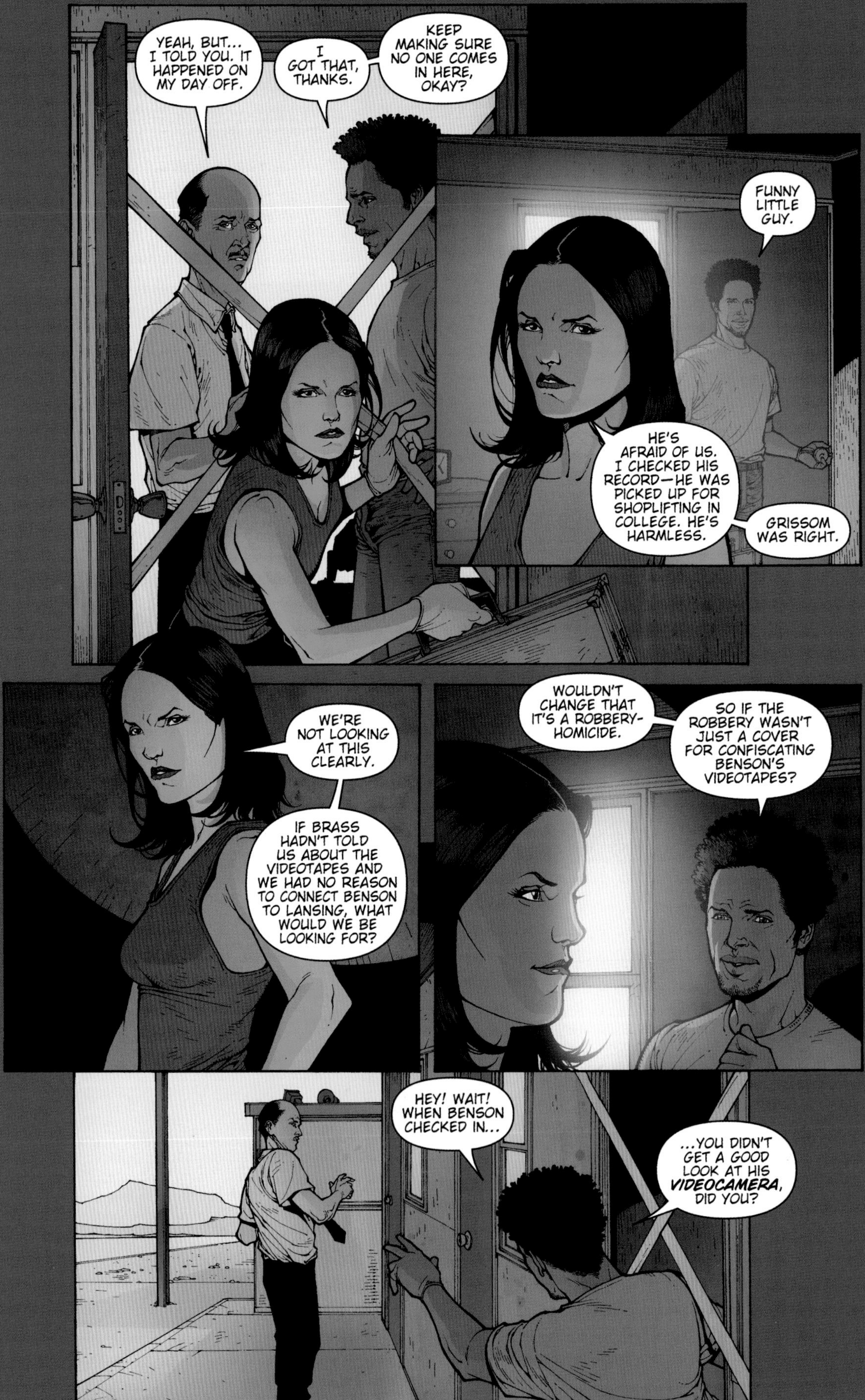

YEAH, BUT... I TOLD YOU. IT HAPPENED ON MY DAY OFF.
I GOT THAT, THANKS.
KEEP MAKING SURE NO ONE COMES IN HERE, OKAY?
FUNNY LITTLE GUY.
HE'S AFRAID OF US. I CHECKED HIS RECORD—HE WAS PICKED UP FOR SHOPLIFTING IN COLLEGE. HE'S HARMLESS.
GRISSOM WAS RIGHT.
WE'RE NOT LOOKING AT THIS CLEARLY.
IF BRASS HADN'T TOLD US ABOUT THE VIDEOTAPES AND WE HAD NO REASON TO CONNECT BENSON TO LANSING, WHAT WOULD WE BE LOOKING FOR?
WOULDN'T CHANGE THAT IT'S A ROBBERY-HOMICIDE.
SO IF THE ROBBERY WASN'T JUST A COVER FOR CONFISCATING BENSON'S VIDEOTAPES?
HEY! WAIT! WHEN BENSON CHECKED IN...
...YOU DIDN'T GET A GOOD LOOK AT HIS ***VIDEOCAMERA***, DID YOU?

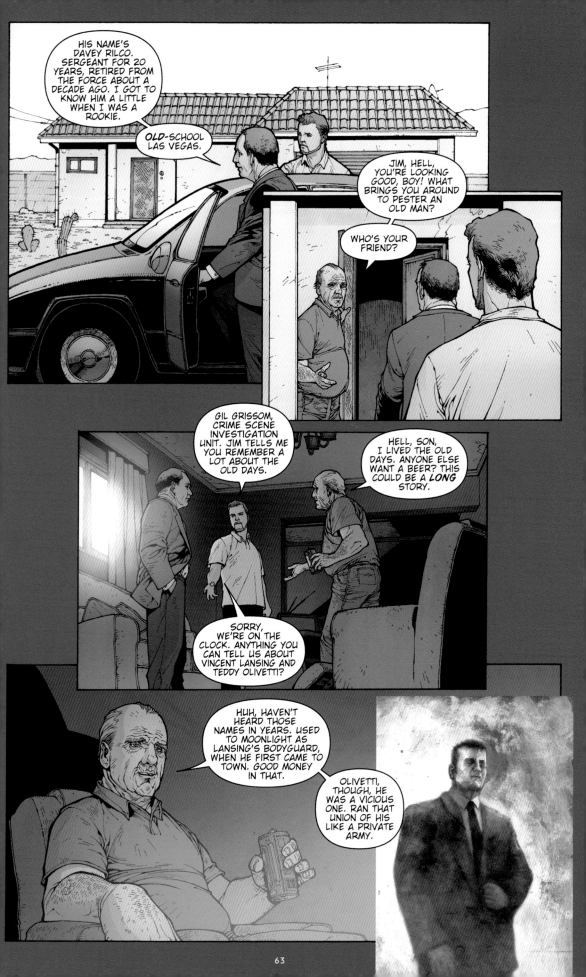

HIS NAME'S DAVEY RILCO. SERGEANT FOR 20 YEARS, RETIRED FROM THE FORCE ABOUT A DECADE AGO. I GOT TO KNOW HIM A LITTLE WHEN I WAS A ROOKIE.

OLD-SCHOOL LAS VEGAS.

JIM, HELL, YOU'RE LOOKING GOOD, BOY! WHAT BRINGS YOU AROUND TO PESTER AN OLD MAN?

WHO'S YOUR FRIEND?

GIL GRISSOM, CRIME SCENE INVESTIGATION UNIT. JIM TELLS ME YOU REMEMBER A LOT ABOUT THE OLD DAYS.

HELL, SON, I LIVED THE OLD DAYS. ANYONE ELSE WANT A BEER? THIS COULD BE A *LONG* STORY.

SORRY, WE'RE ON THE CLOCK. ANYTHING YOU CAN TELL US ABOUT VINCENT LANSING AND TEDDY OLIVETTI?

HUH, HAVEN'T HEARD THOSE NAMES IN YEARS. USED TO MOONLIGHT AS LANSING'S BODYGUARD, WHEN HE FIRST CAME TO TOWN. GOOD MONEY IN THAT.

OLIVETTI, THOUGH, HE WAS A VICIOUS ONE. RAN THAT UNION OF HIS LIKE A PRIVATE ARMY.

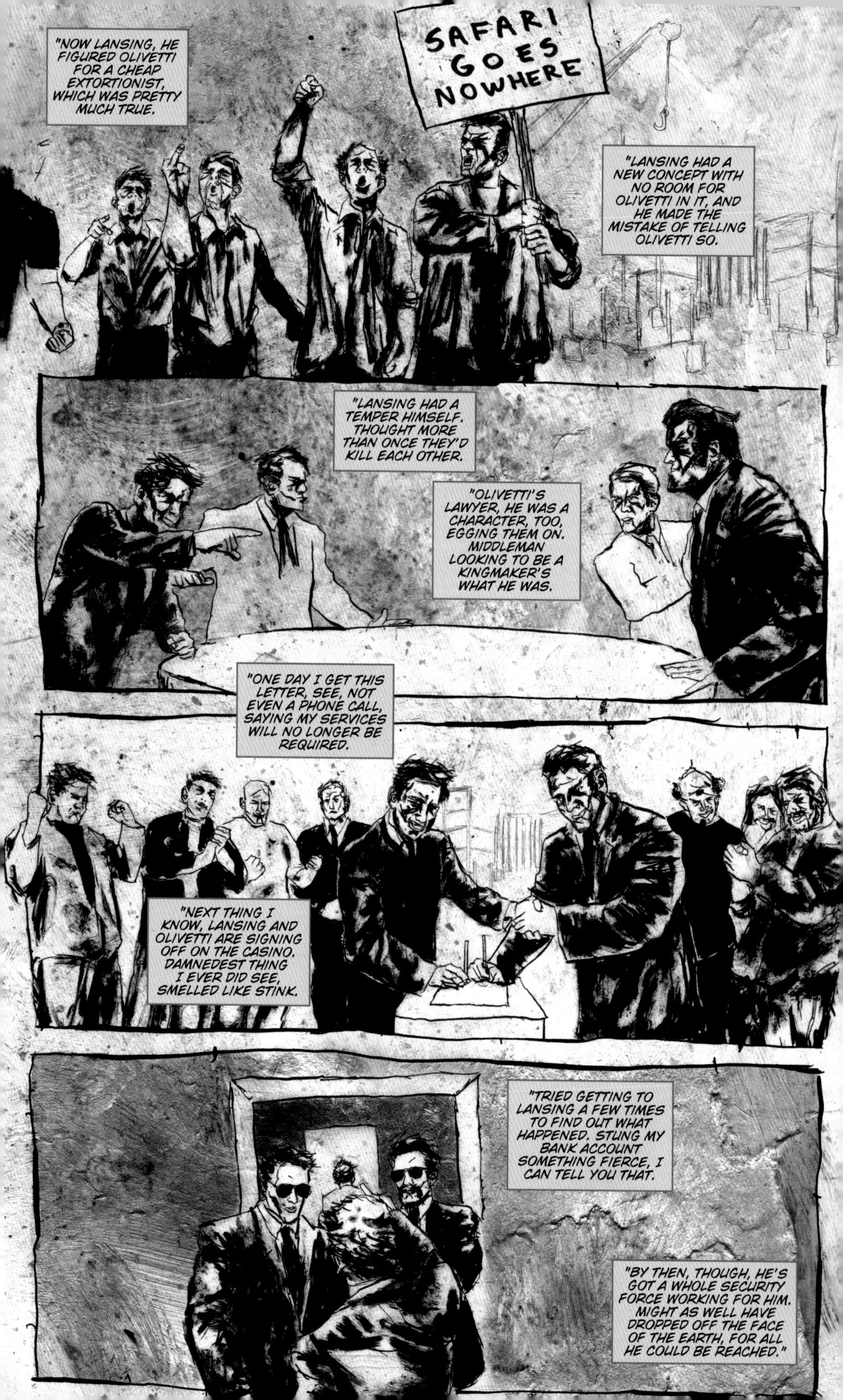
"NOW LANSING, HE FIGURED OLIVETTI FOR A CHEAP EXTORTIONIST, WHICH WAS PRETTY MUCH TRUE.
SAFARI GOES NOWHERE
"LANSING HAD A NEW CONCEPT WITH NO ROOM FOR OLIVETTI IN IT, AND HE MADE THE MISTAKE OF TELLING OLIVETTI SO.
"LANSING HAD A TEMPER HIMSELF. THOUGHT MORE THAN ONCE THEY'D KILL EACH OTHER.
"OLIVETTI'S LAWYER, HE WAS A CHARACTER, TOO, EGGING THEM ON. MIDDLEMAN LOOKING TO BE A KINGMAKER'S WHAT HE WAS.
"ONE DAY I GET THIS LETTER, SEE, NOT EVEN A PHONE CALL, SAYING MY SERVICES WILL NO LONGER BE REQUIRED.
"NEXT THING I KNOW, LANSING AND OLIVETTI ARE SIGNING OFF ON THE CASINO. DAMNEDEST THING I EVER DID SEE, SMELLED LIKE STINK.
"TRIED GETTING TO LANSING A FEW TIMES TO FIND OUT WHAT HAPPENED. STUNG MY BANK ACCOUNT SOMETHING FIERCE, I CAN TELL YOU THAT.
"BY THEN, THOUGH, HE'S GOT A WHOLE SECURITY FORCE WORKING FOR HIM. MIGHT AS WELL HAVE DROPPED OFF THE FACE OF THE EARTH, FOR ALL HE COULD BE REACHED."

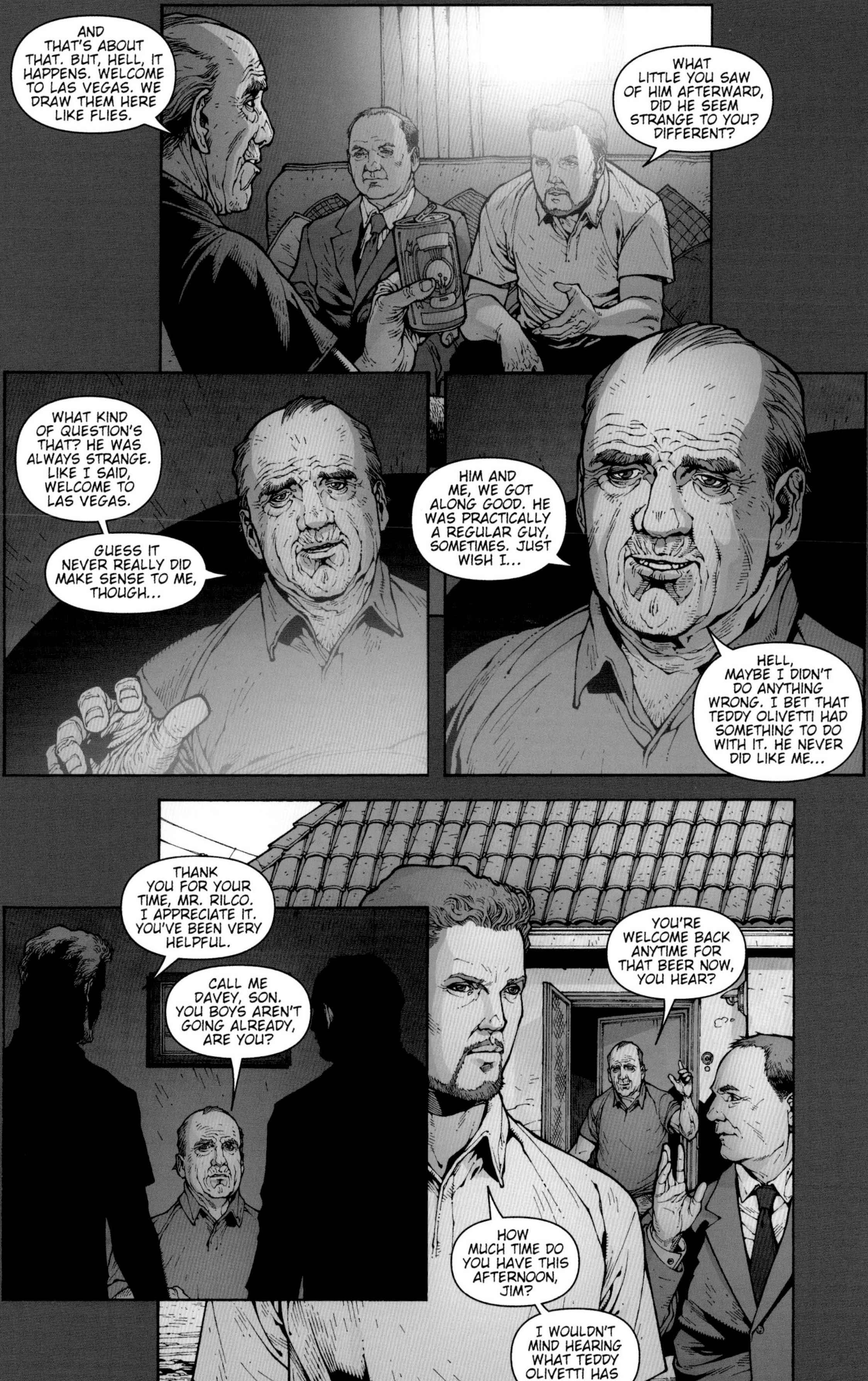
AND THAT'S ABOUT THAT. BUT, HELL, IT HAPPENS. WELCOME TO LAS VEGAS. WE DRAW THEM HERE LIKE FLIES.
WHAT LITTLE YOU SAW OF HIM AFTERWARD, DID HE SEEM STRANGE TO YOU? DIFFERENT?
WHAT KIND OF QUESTION'S THAT? HE WAS ALWAYS STRANGE. LIKE I SAID, WELCOME TO LAS VEGAS.
GUESS IT NEVER REALLY DID MAKE SENSE TO ME, THOUGH...
HIM AND ME, WE GOT ALONG GOOD. HE WAS PRACTICALLY A REGULAR GUY, SOMETIMES. JUST WISH I...
HELL, MAYBE I DIDN'T DO ANYTHING WRONG. I BET THAT TEDDY OLIVETTI HAD SOMETHING TO DO WITH IT. HE NEVER DID LIKE ME...
THANK YOU FOR YOUR TIME, MR. RILCO. I APPRECIATE IT. YOU'VE BEEN VERY HELPFUL.
CALL ME DAVEY, SON. YOU BOYS AREN'T GOING ALREADY, ARE YOU?
YOU'RE WELCOME BACK ANYTIME FOR THAT BEER NOW, YOU HEAR?
HOW MUCH TIME DO YOU HAVE THIS AFTERNOON, JIM?
I WOULDN'T MIND HEARING WHAT TEDDY OLIVETTI HAS TO SAY.

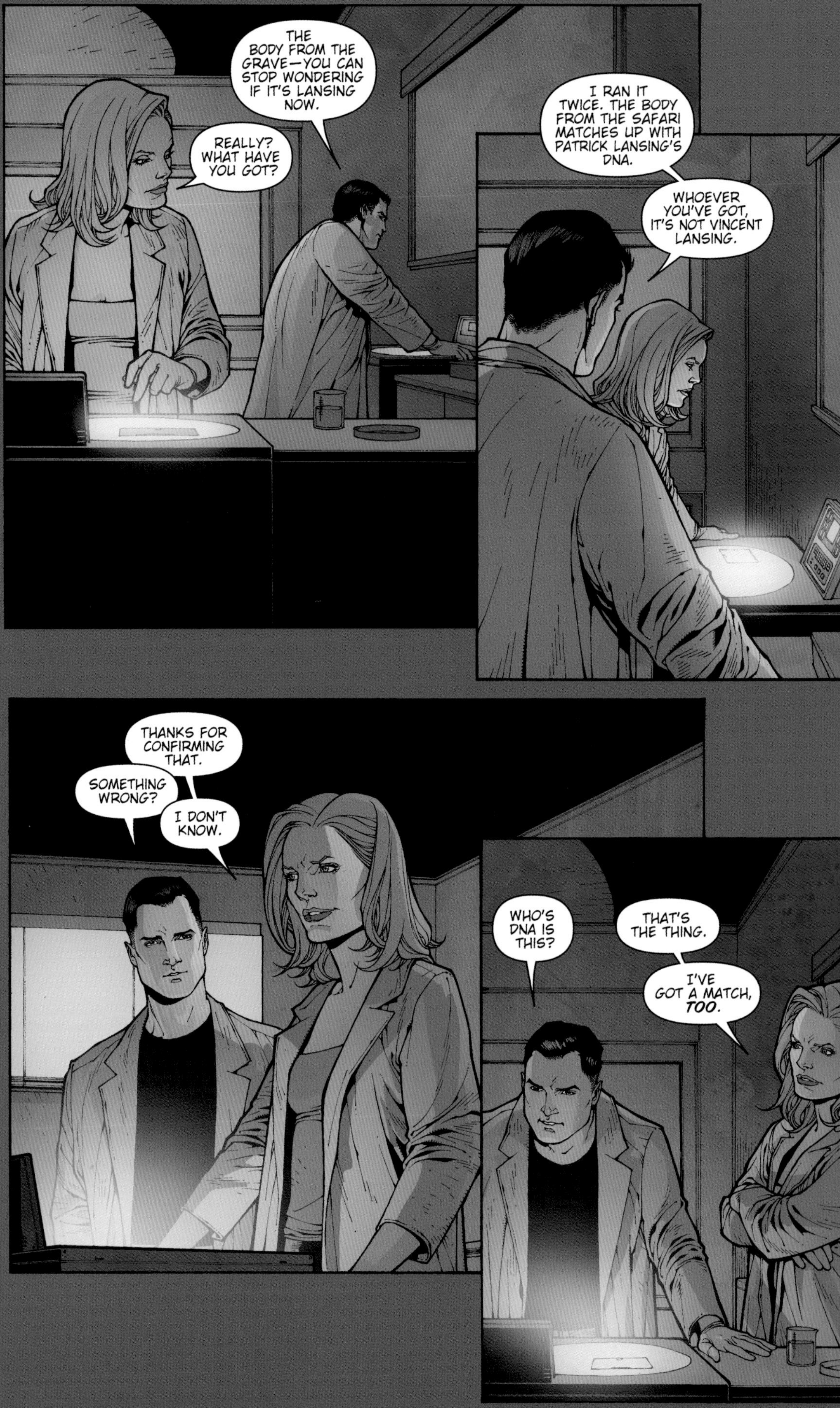
THE BODY FROM THE GRAVE—YOU CAN STOP WONDERING IF IT'S LANSING NOW.
REALLY? WHAT HAVE YOU GOT?
I RAN IT TWICE. THE BODY FROM THE SAFARI MATCHES UP WITH PATRICK LANSING'S DNA.
WHOEVER YOU'VE GOT, IT'S NOT VINCENT LANSING.
THANKS FOR CONFIRMING THAT.
SOMETHING WRONG?
I DON'T KNOW.
WHO'S DNA IS THIS?
THAT'S THE THING.
I'VE GOT A MATCH, ***TOO.***

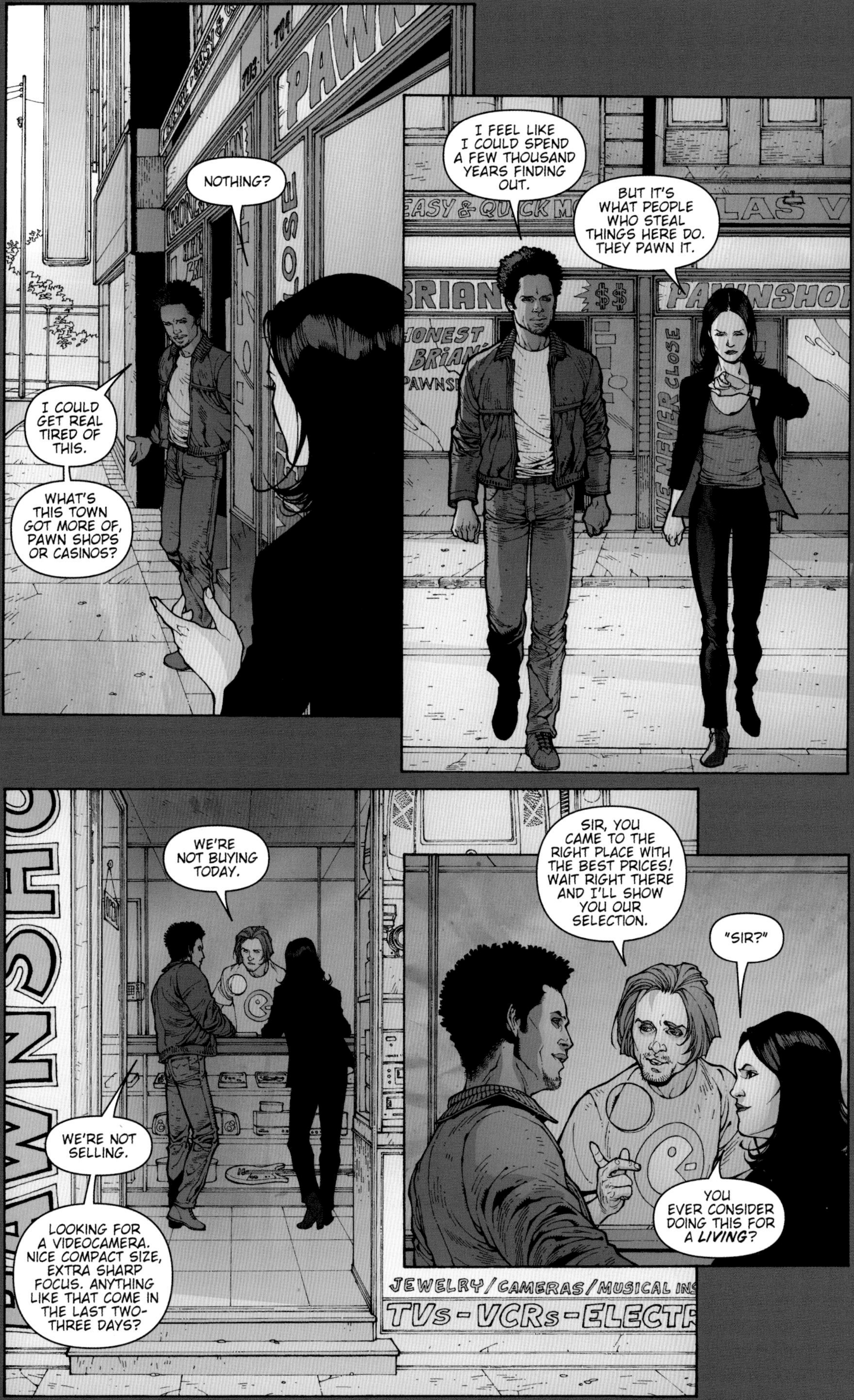
PAWN
NOTHING?
I COULD GET REAL TIRED OF THIS.
WHAT'S THIS TOWN GOT MORE OF, PAWN SHOPS OR CASINOS?
I FEEL LIKE I COULD SPEND A FEW THOUSAND YEARS FINDING OUT.
BUT IT'S WHAT PEOPLE WHO STEAL THINGS HERE DO. THEY PAWN IT.
WE NEVER CLOSE
WE'RE NOT BUYING TODAY.
WE'RE NOT SELLING.
LOOKING FOR A VIDEOCAMERA. NICE COMPACT SIZE, EXTRA SHARP FOCUS. ANYTHING LIKE THAT COME IN THE LAST TWO-THREE DAYS?
SIR, YOU CAME TO THE RIGHT PLACE WITH THE BEST PRICES! WAIT RIGHT THERE AND I'LL SHOW YOU OUR SELECTION.
"SIR?"
YOU EVER CONSIDER DOING THIS FOR A *LIVING*?
JEWELRY/CAMERAS/MUSICAL INS
TVs - VCRs - ELECTR

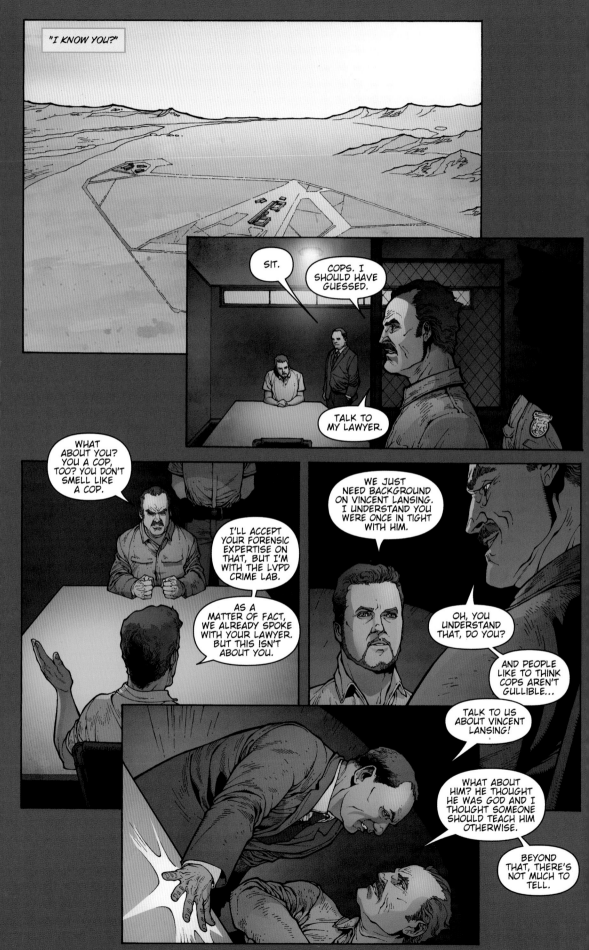

"I KNOW YOU?"

SIT.

COPS. I SHOULD HAVE GUESSED.

TALK TO MY LAWYER.

WHAT ABOUT YOU? YOU A COP, TOO? YOU DON'T SMELL LIKE A COP.

I'LL ACCEPT YOUR FORENSIC EXPERTISE ON THAT, BUT I'M WITH THE LVPD CRIME LAB.

AS A MATTER OF FACT, WE ALREADY SPOKE WITH YOUR LAWYER. BUT THIS ISN'T ABOUT YOU.

WE JUST NEED BACKGROUND ON VINCENT LANSING. I UNDERSTAND YOU WERE ONCE IN TIGHT WITH HIM.

OH, YOU UNDERSTAND THAT, DO YOU?

AND PEOPLE LIKE TO THINK COPS AREN'T GULLIBLE...

TALK TO US ABOUT VINCENT LANSING!

WHAT ABOUT HIM? HE THOUGHT HE WAS GOD AND I THOUGHT SOMEONE SHOULD TEACH HIM OTHERWISE.

BEYOND THAT, THERE'S NOT MUCH TO TELL.

68

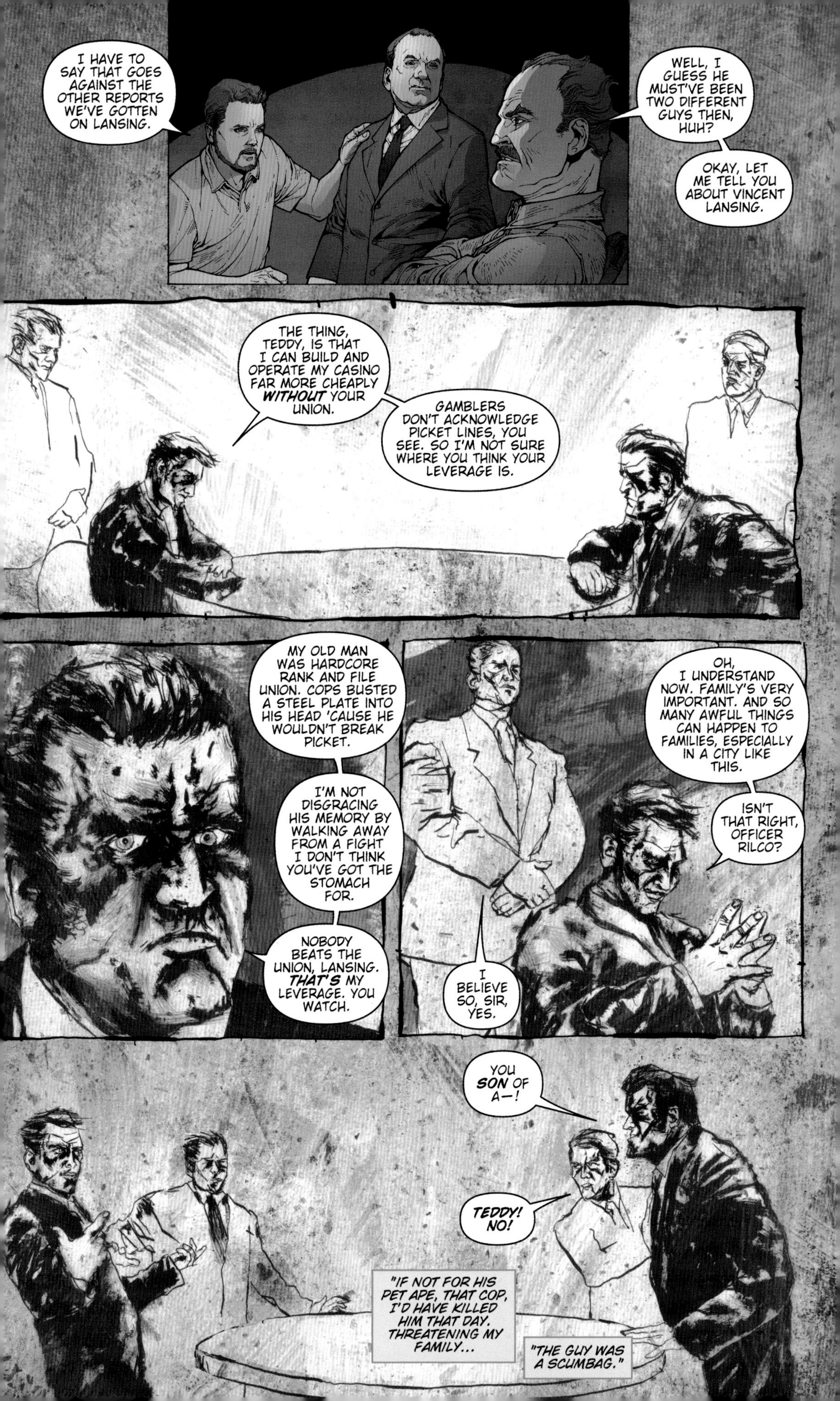
I HAVE TO SAY THAT GOES AGAINST THE OTHER REPORTS WE'VE GOTTEN ON LANSING.
WELL, I GUESS HE MUST'VE BEEN TWO DIFFERENT GUYS THEN, HUH?
OKAY, LET ME TELL YOU ABOUT VINCENT LANSING.
THE THING, TEDDY, IS THAT I CAN BUILD AND OPERATE MY CASINO FAR MORE CHEAPLY *WITHOUT* YOUR UNION.
GAMBLERS DON'T ACKNOWLEDGE PICKET LINES, YOU SEE. SO I'M NOT SURE WHERE YOU THINK YOUR LEVERAGE IS.
MY OLD MAN WAS HARDCORE RANK AND FILE UNION. COPS BUSTED A STEEL PLATE INTO HIS HEAD 'CAUSE HE WOULDN'T BREAK PICKET.
I'M NOT DISGRACING HIS MEMORY BY WALKING AWAY FROM A FIGHT I DON'T THINK YOU'VE GOT THE STOMACH FOR.
NOBODY BEATS THE UNION, LANSING. ***THAT'S*** MY LEVERAGE. YOU WATCH.
OH, I UNDERSTAND NOW. FAMILY'S VERY IMPORTANT. AND SO MANY AWFUL THINGS CAN HAPPEN TO FAMILIES, ESPECIALLY IN A CITY LIKE THIS.
ISN'T THAT RIGHT, OFFICER RILCO?
I BELIEVE SO, SIR, YES.
YOU ***SON*** OF A—!
TEDDY! NO!
"IF NOT FOR HIS PET APE, THAT COP, I'D HAVE KILLED HIM THAT DAY. THREATENING MY FAMILY...
"THE GUY WAS A SCUMBAG."

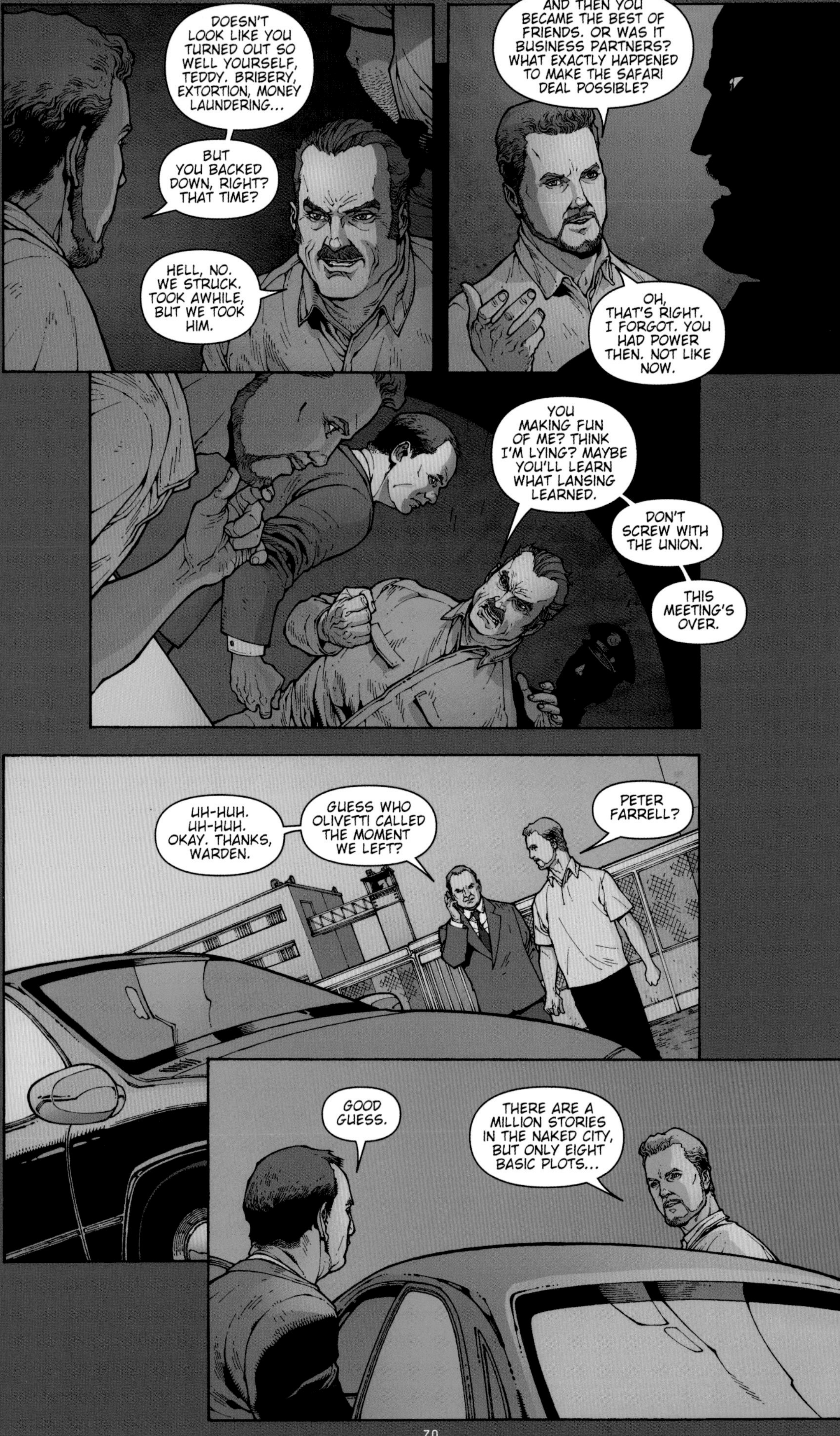
DOESN'T LOOK LIKE YOU TURNED OUT SO WELL YOURSELF, TEDDY. BRIBERY, EXTORTION, MONEY LAUNDERING...
BUT YOU BACKED DOWN, RIGHT? THAT TIME?
HELL, NO. WE STRUCK. TOOK AWHILE, BUT WE TOOK HIM.
AND THEN YOU BECAME THE BEST OF FRIENDS. OR WAS IT BUSINESS PARTNERS? WHAT EXACTLY HAPPENED TO MAKE THE SAFARI DEAL POSSIBLE?
OH, THAT'S RIGHT. I FORGOT. YOU HAD POWER THEN. NOT LIKE NOW.
YOU MAKING FUN OF ME? THINK I'M LYING? MAYBE YOU'LL LEARN WHAT LANSING LEARNED.
DON'T SCREW WITH THE UNION.
THIS MEETING'S OVER.
UH-HUH. UH-HUH. OKAY. THANKS, WARDEN.
GUESS WHO OLIVETTI CALLED THE MOMENT WE LEFT?
PETER FARRELL?
GOOD GUESS.
THERE ARE A MILLION STORIES IN THE NAKED CITY, BUT ONLY EIGHT BASIC PLOTS...

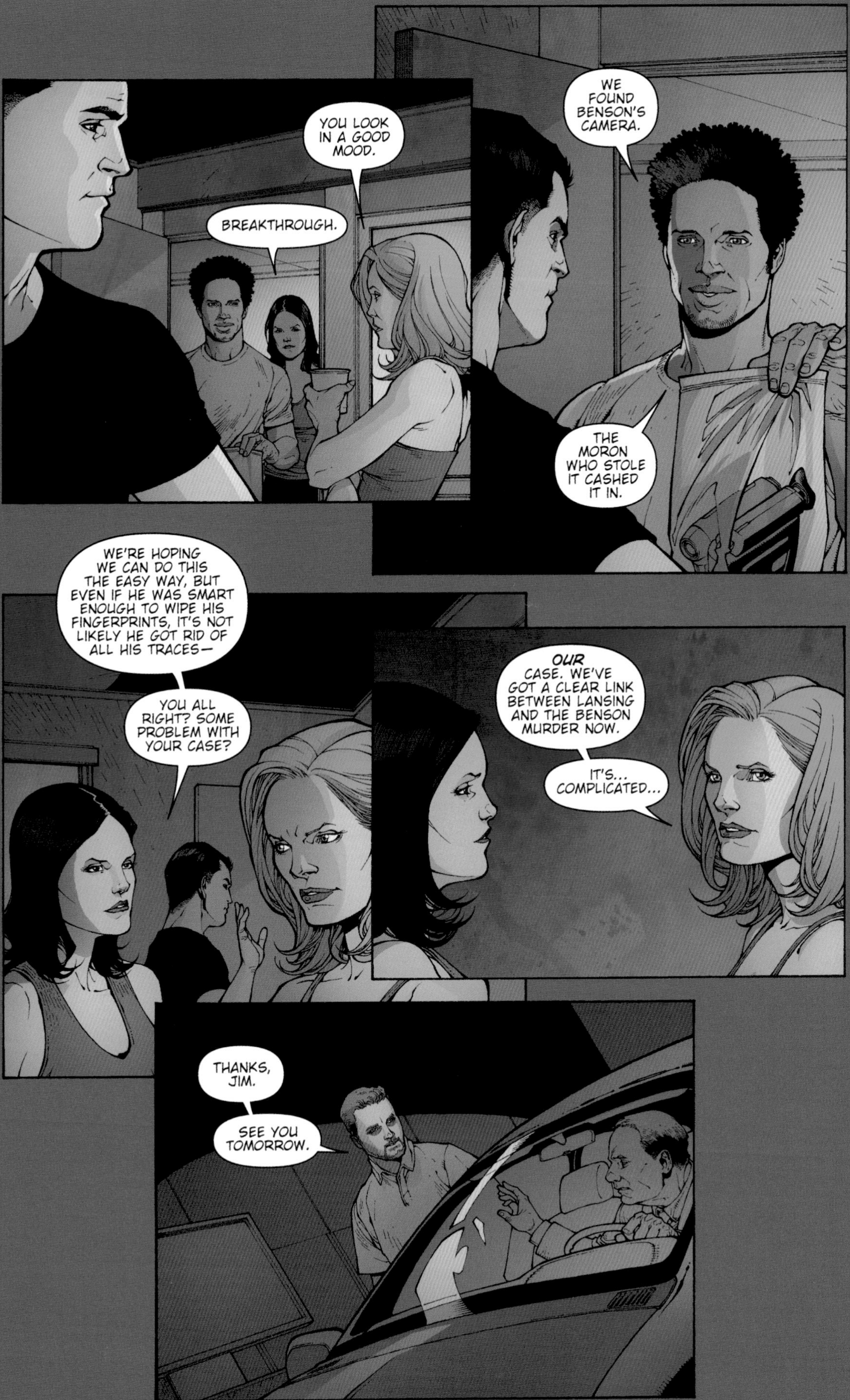
YOU LOOK IN A GOOD MOOD.
BREAKTHROUGH.
WE FOUND BENSON'S CAMERA.
THE MORON WHO STOLE IT CASHED IT IN.
WE'RE HOPING WE CAN DO THIS THE EASY WAY, BUT EVEN IF HE WAS SMART ENOUGH TO WIPE HIS FINGERPRINTS, IT'S NOT LIKELY HE GOT RID OF ALL HIS TRACES—
YOU ALL RIGHT? SOME PROBLEM WITH YOUR CASE?
OUR CASE. WE'VE GOT A CLEAR LINK BETWEEN LANSING AND THE BENSON MURDER NOW.
IT'S... COMPLICATED...
THANKS, JIM.
SEE YOU TOMORROW.

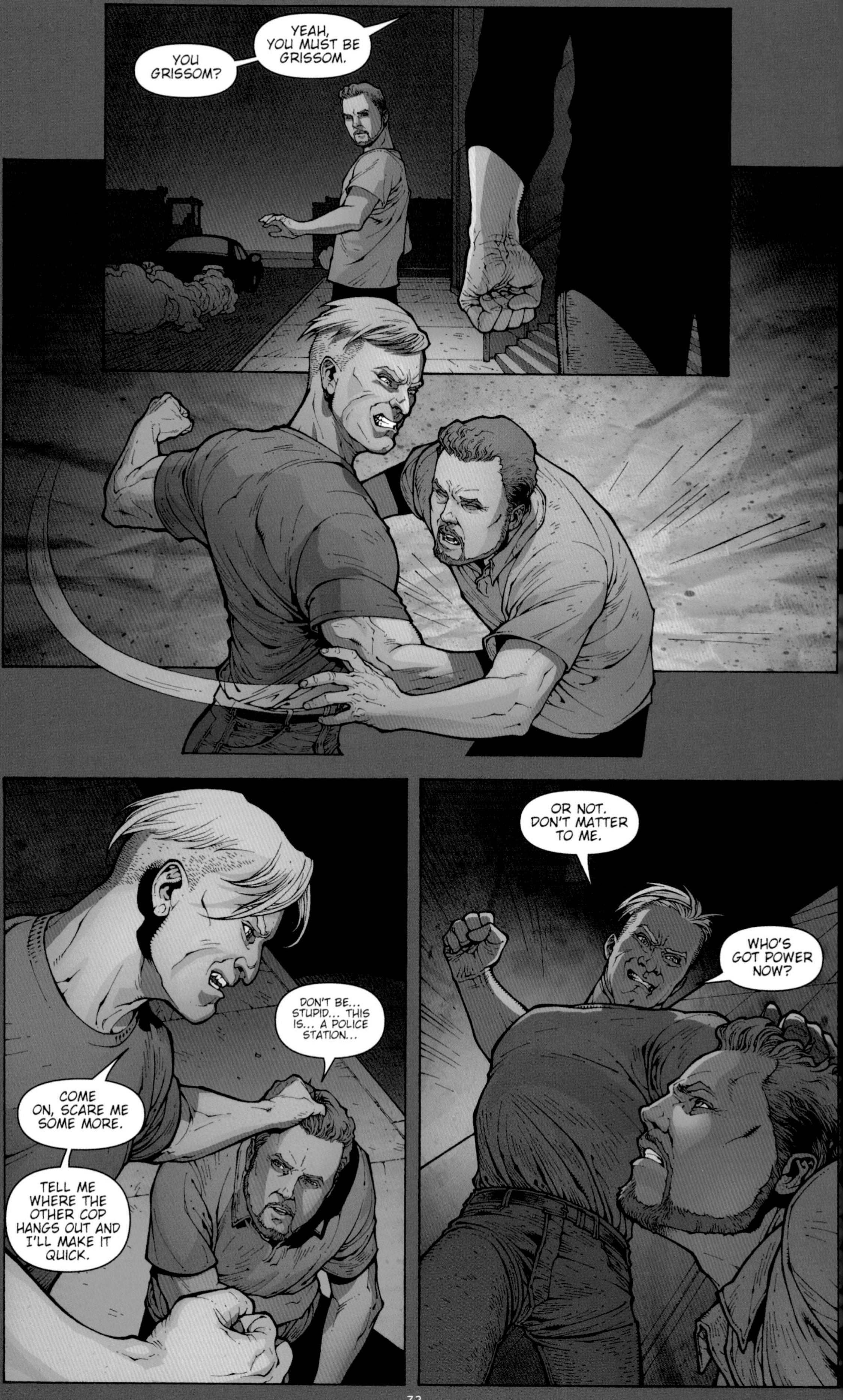
YOU GRISSOM?
YEAH, YOU MUST BE GRISSOM.
DON'T BE... STUPID... THIS IS... A POLICE STATION...
COME ON, SCARE ME SOME MORE.
TELL ME WHERE THE OTHER COP HANGS OUT AND I'LL MAKE IT QUICK.
OR NOT. DON'T MATTER TO ME.
WHO'S GOT POWER NOW?

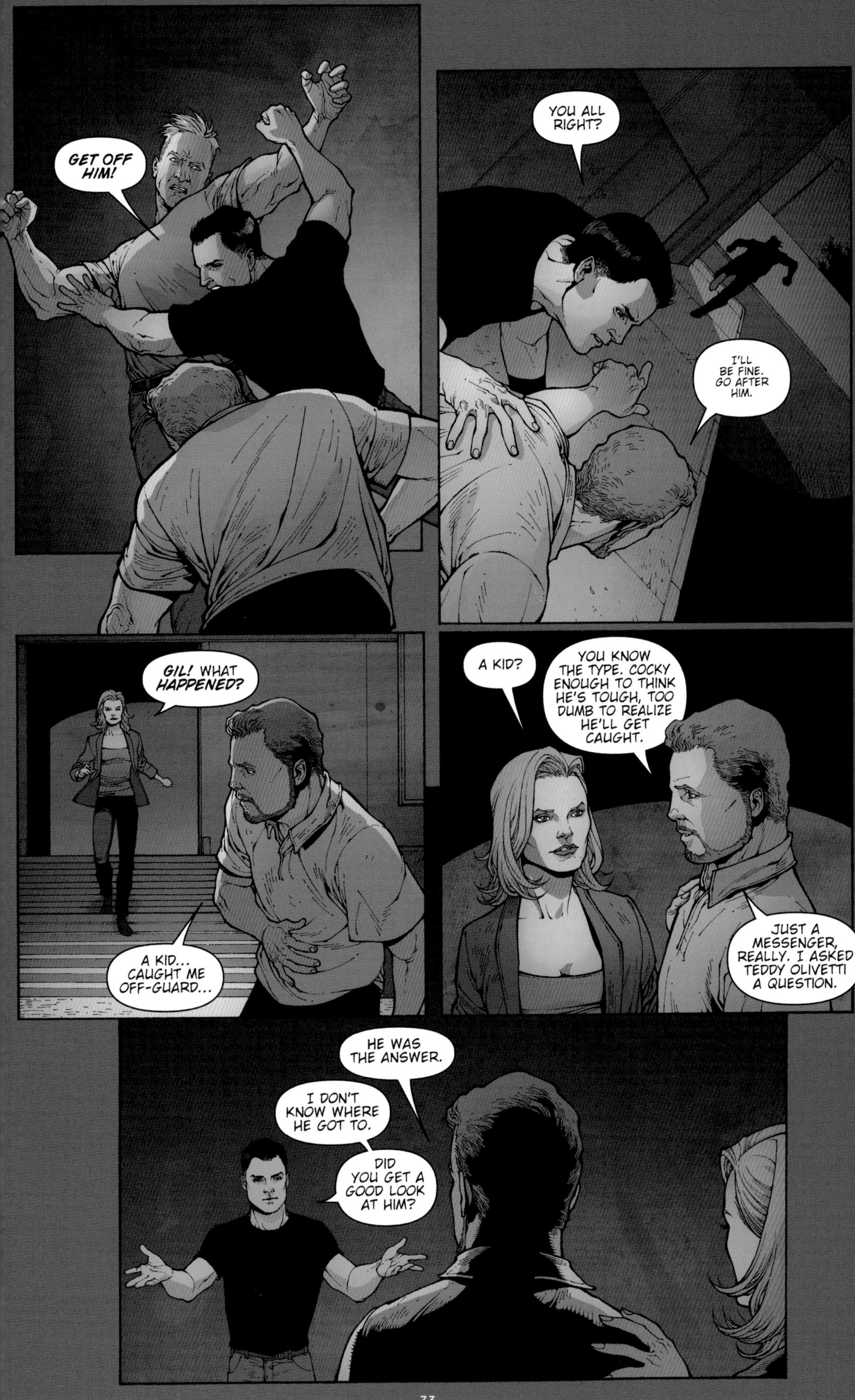
GET OFF HIM!
YOU ALL RIGHT?
I'LL BE FINE. GO AFTER HIM.
GIL! WHAT HAPPENED?
A KID... CAUGHT ME OFF-GUARD...
A KID?
YOU KNOW THE TYPE. COCKY ENOUGH TO THINK HE'S TOUGH, TOO DUMB TO REALIZE HE'LL GET CAUGHT.
JUST A MESSENGER, REALLY. I ASKED TEDDY OLIVETTI A QUESTION.
HE WAS THE ANSWER.
I DON'T KNOW WHERE HE GOT TO.
DID YOU GET A GOOD LOOK AT HIM?

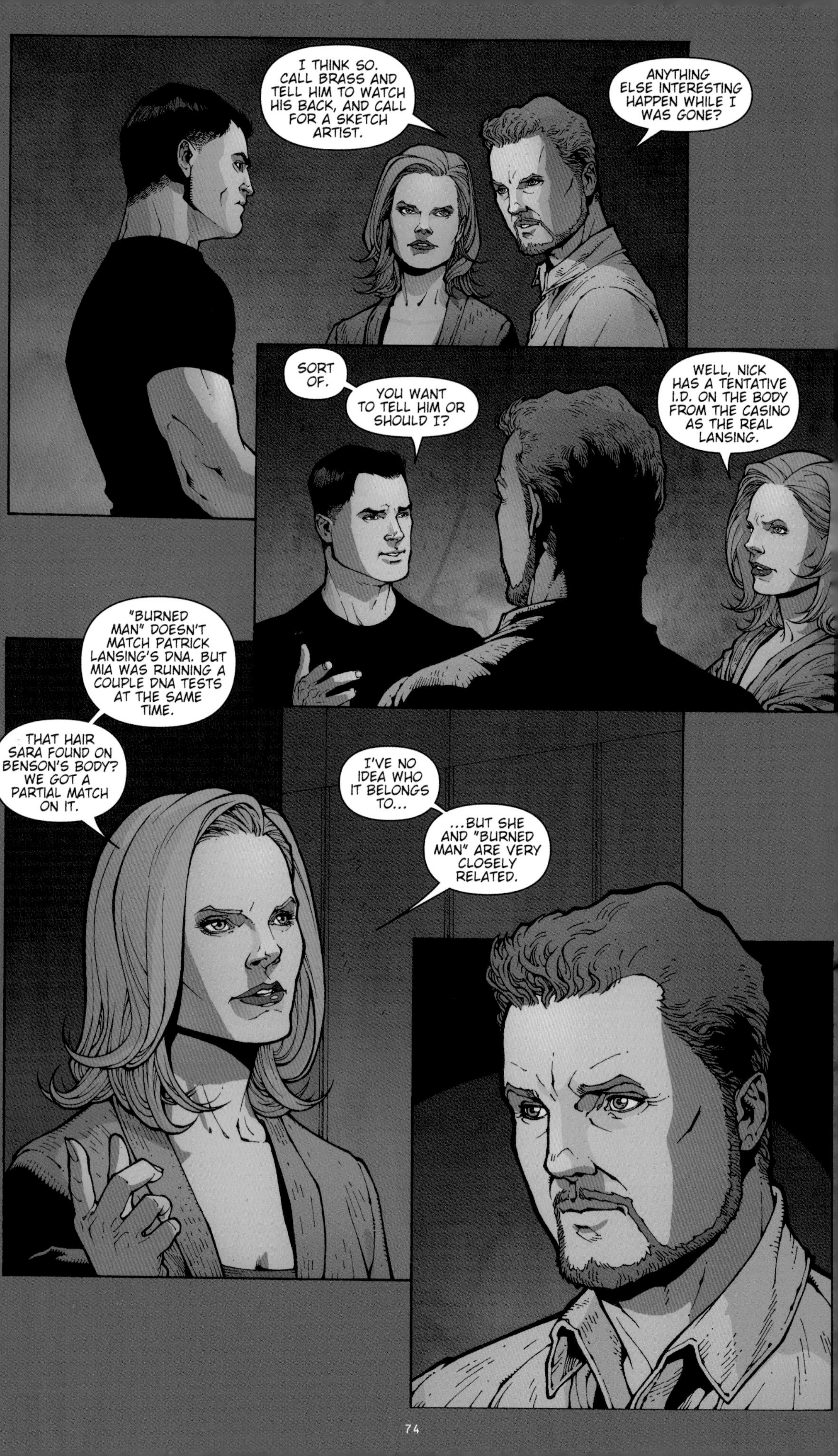
I THINK SO. CALL BRASS AND TELL HIM TO WATCH HIS BACK, AND CALL FOR A SKETCH ARTIST.
ANYTHING ELSE INTERESTING HAPPEN WHILE I WAS GONE?
SORT OF.
YOU WANT TO TELL HIM OR SHOULD I?
WELL, NICK HAS A TENTATIVE I.D. ON THE BODY FROM THE CASINO AS THE REAL LANSING.
"BURNED MAN" DOESN'T MATCH PATRICK LANSING'S DNA. BUT MIA WAS RUNNING A COUPLE DNA TESTS AT THE SAME TIME.
THAT HAIR SARA FOUND ON BENSON'S BODY? WE GOT A PARTIAL MATCH ON IT.
I'VE NO IDEA WHO IT BELONGS TO...
...BUT SHE AND "BURNED MAN" ARE VERY CLOSELY RELATED.

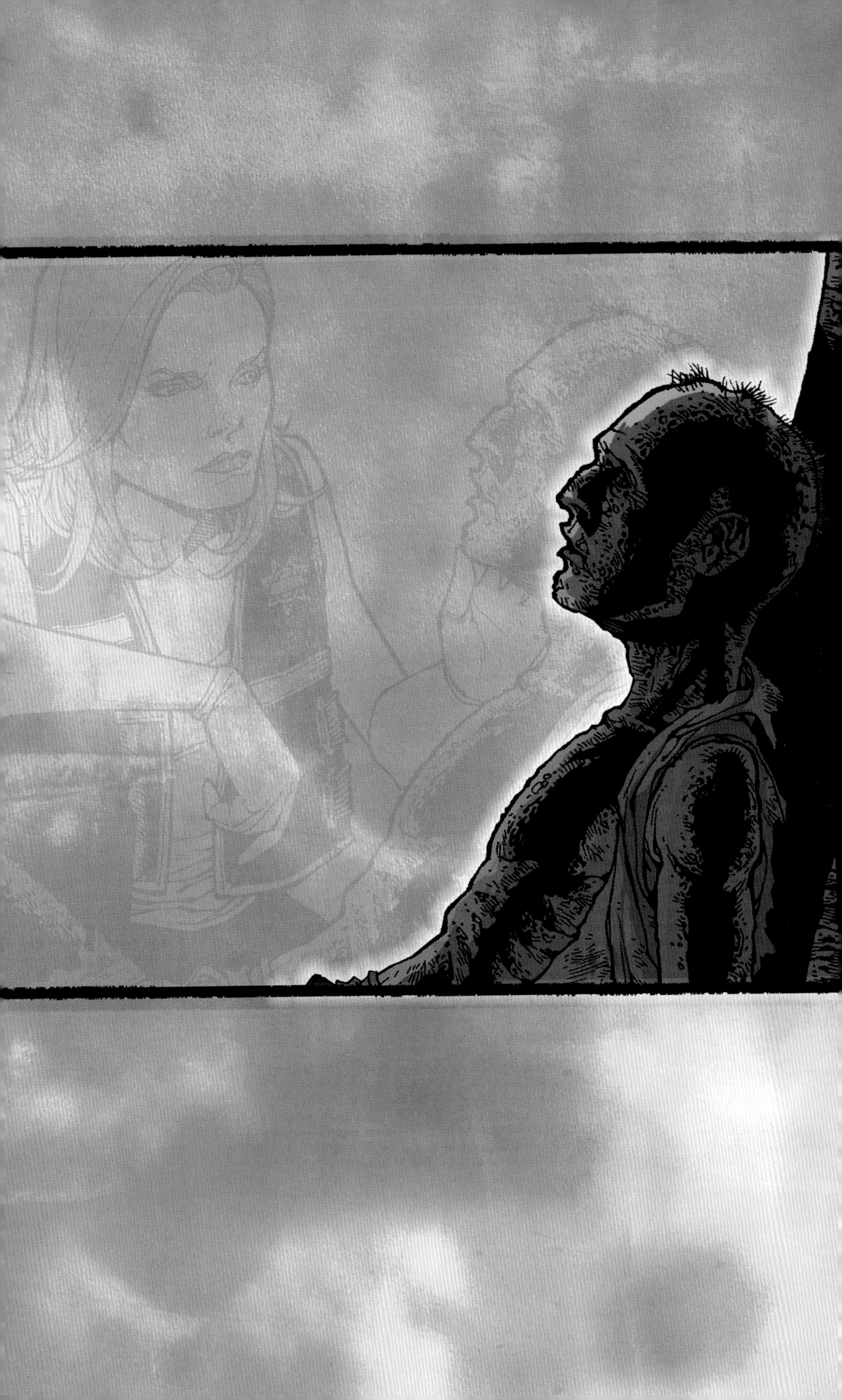

chapter four

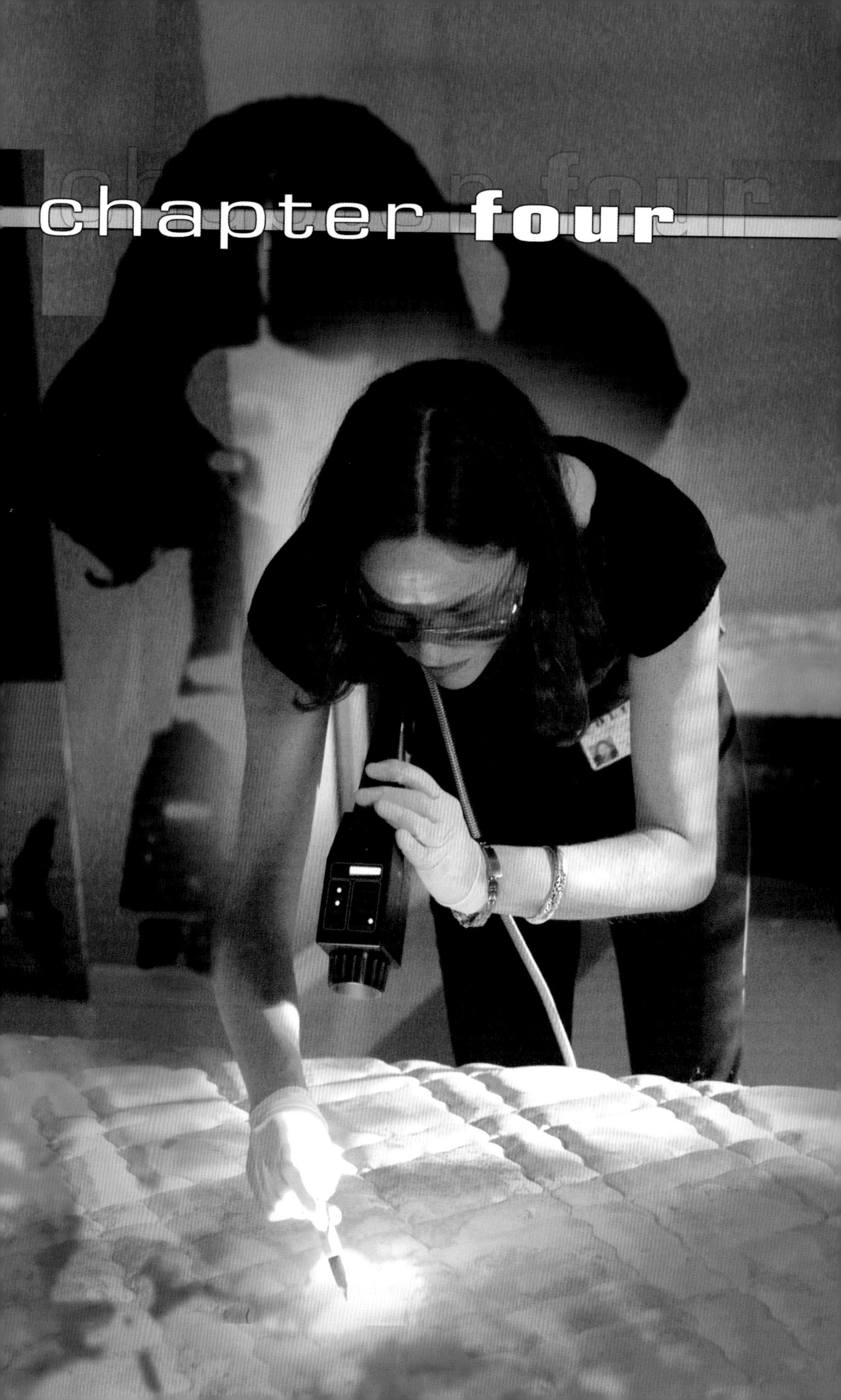

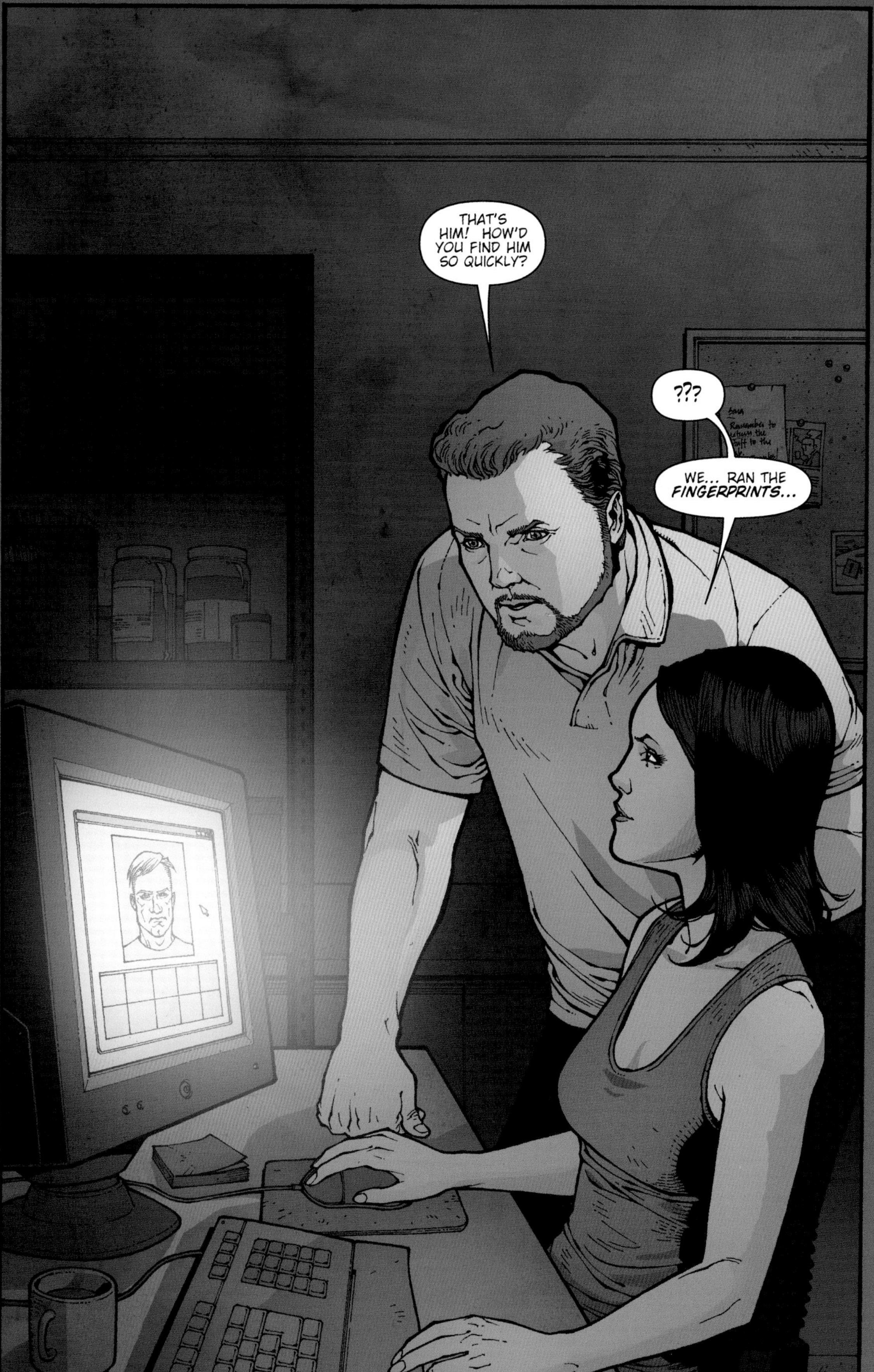
THAT'S HIM! HOW'D YOU FIND HIM SO QUICKLY?
???
WE... RAN THE *FINGERPRINTS...*

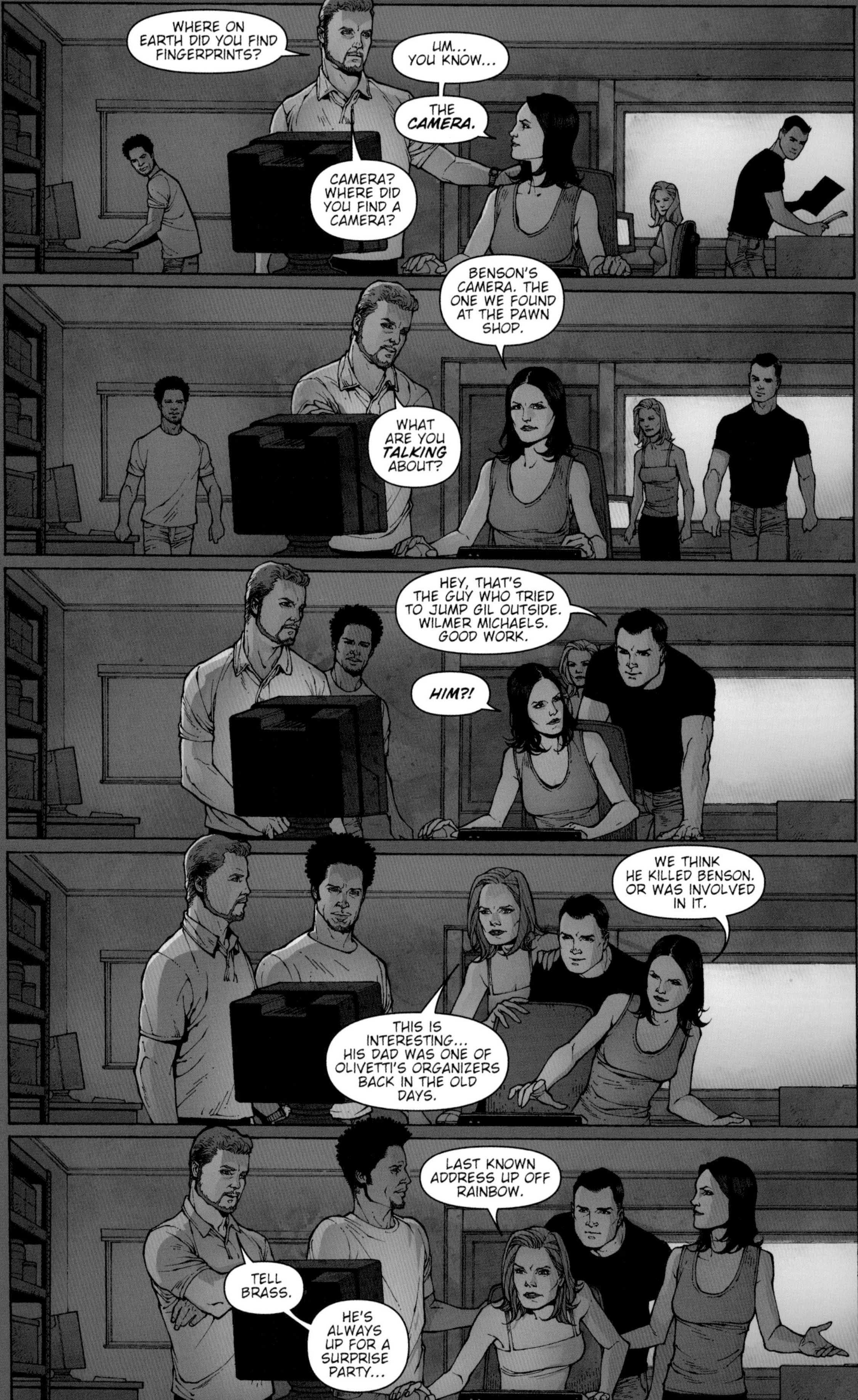
WHERE ON EARTH DID YOU FIND FINGERPRINTS?
UM... YOU KNOW...
THE *CAMERA.*
CAMERA? WHERE DID YOU FIND A CAMERA?
BENSON'S CAMERA. THE ONE WE FOUND AT THE PAWN SHOP.
WHAT ARE YOU *TALKING* ABOUT?
HEY, THAT'S THE GUY WHO TRIED TO JUMP GIL OUTSIDE. WILMER MICHAELS. GOOD WORK.
HIM?!
WE THINK HE KILLED BENSON. OR WAS INVOLVED IN IT.
THIS IS INTERESTING... HIS DAD WAS ONE OF OLIVETTI'S ORGANIZERS BACK IN THE OLD DAYS.
LAST KNOWN ADDRESS UP OFF RAINBOW.
TELL BRASS.
HE'S ALWAYS UP FOR A SURPRISE PARTY...

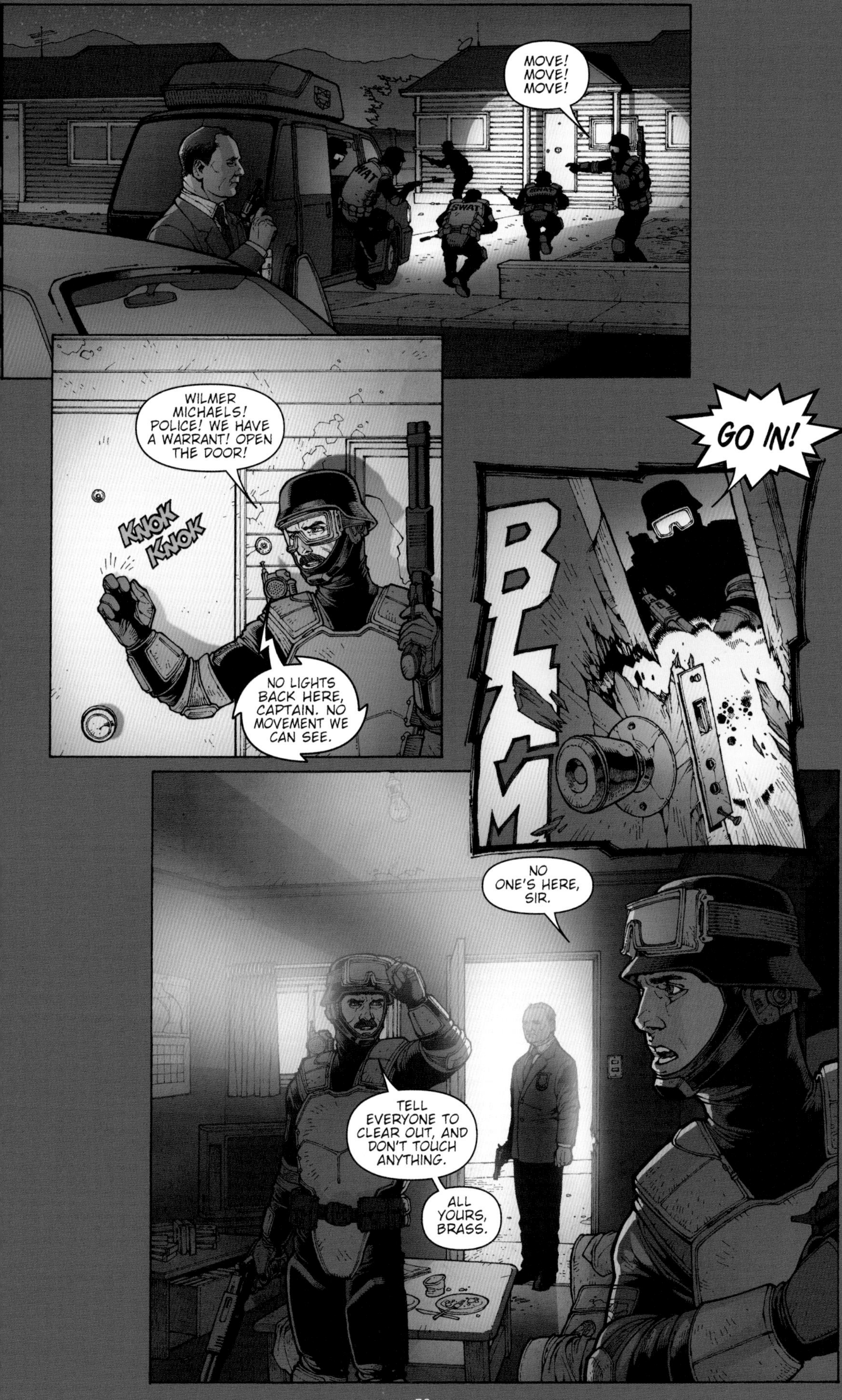
MOVE! MOVE! MOVE!
WILMER MICHAELS! POLICE! WE HAVE A WARRANT! OPEN THE DOOR!
KNOK KNOK
NO LIGHTS BACK HERE, CAPTAIN. NO MOVEMENT WE CAN SEE.
GO IN!
BLAM
NO ONE'S HERE, SIR.
TELL EVERYONE TO CLEAR OUT, AND DON'T TOUCH ANYTHING.
ALL YOURS, BRASS.

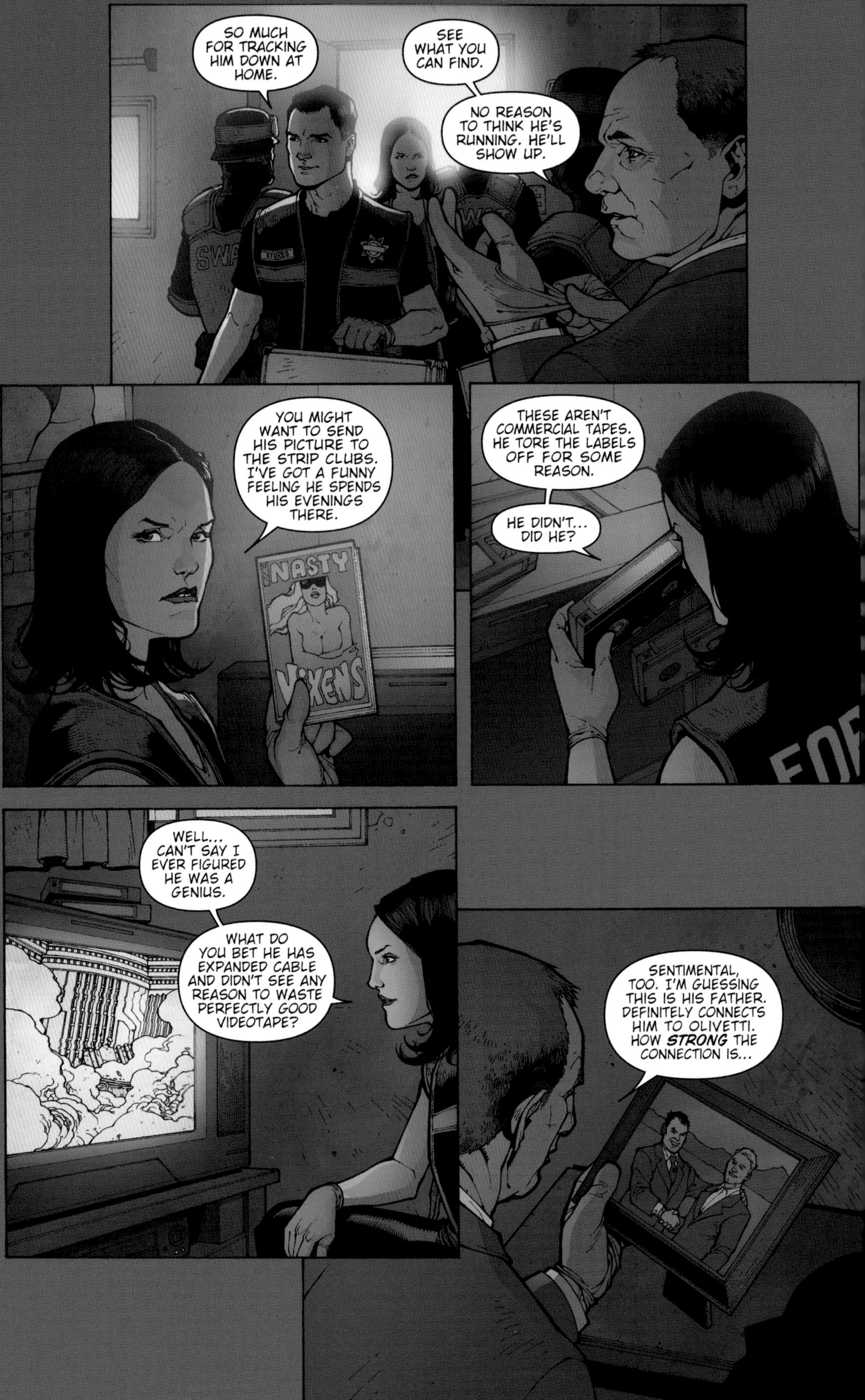
SO MUCH FOR TRACKING HIM DOWN AT HOME.
SEE WHAT YOU CAN FIND.
NO REASON TO THINK HE'S RUNNING. HE'LL SHOW UP.
SWA
STOKES
YOU MIGHT WANT TO SEND HIS PICTURE TO THE STRIP CLUBS. I'VE GOT A FUNNY FEELING HE SPENDS HIS EVENINGS THERE.
NASTY VIXENS
THESE AREN'T COMMERCIAL TAPES. HE TORE THE LABELS OFF FOR SOME REASON.
HE DIDN'T... DID HE?
WELL... CAN'T SAY I EVER FIGURED HE WAS A GENIUS.
WHAT DO YOU BET HE HAS EXPANDED CABLE AND DIDN'T SEE ANY REASON TO WASTE PERFECTLY GOOD VIDEOTAPE?
SENTIMENTAL, TOO. I'M GUESSING THIS IS HIS FATHER. DEFINITELY CONNECTS HIM TO OLIVETTI. HOW ***STRONG*** THE CONNECTION IS...

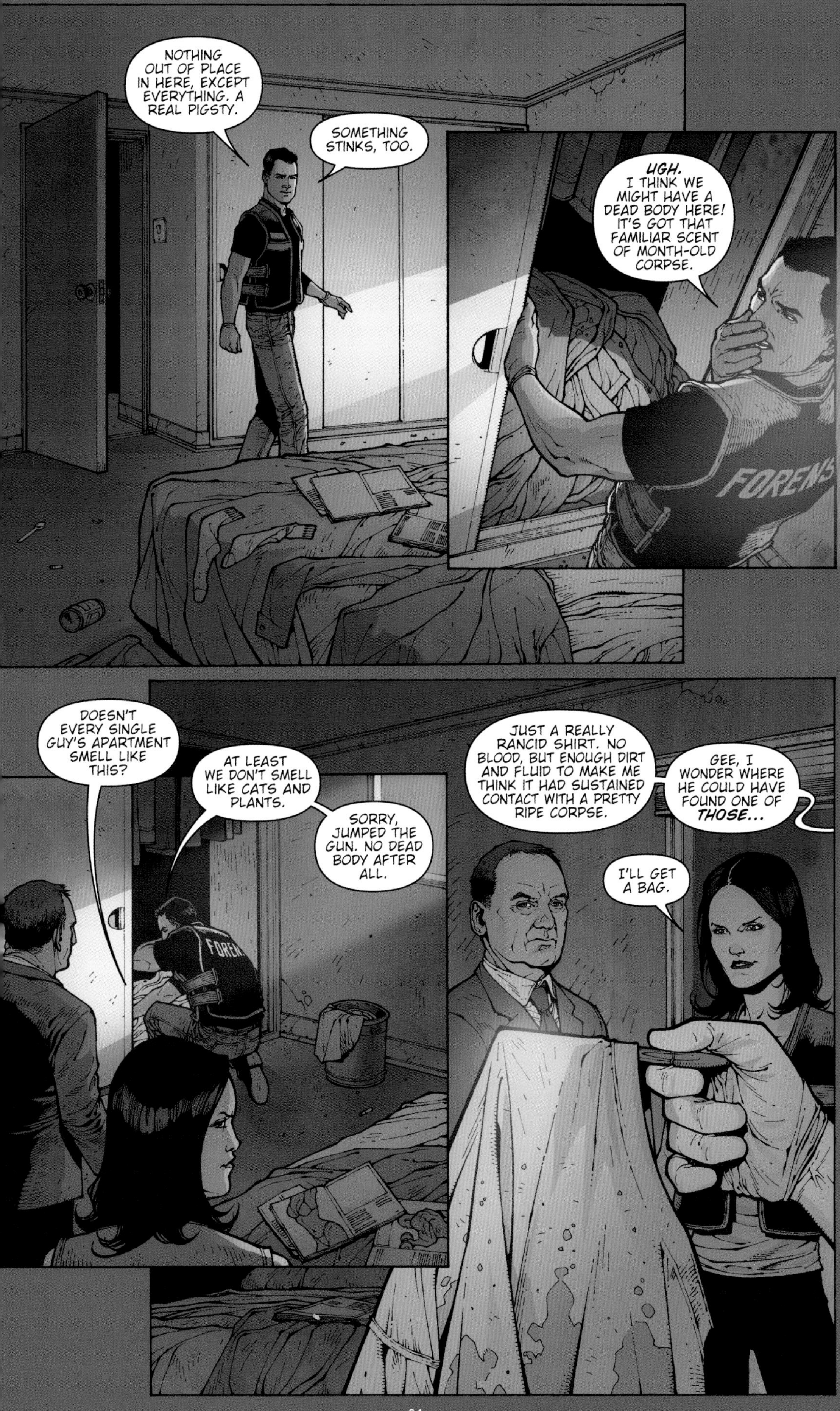
NOTHING OUT OF PLACE IN HERE, EXCEPT EVERYTHING. A REAL PIGSTY.
SOMETHING STINKS, TOO.
UGH. I THINK WE MIGHT HAVE A DEAD BODY HERE! IT'S GOT THAT FAMILIAR SCENT OF MONTH-OLD CORPSE.
FORENS
DOESN'T EVERY SINGLE GUY'S APARTMENT SMELL LIKE THIS?
AT LEAST WE DON'T SMELL LIKE CATS AND PLANTS.
SORRY, JUMPED THE GUN. NO DEAD BODY AFTER ALL.
FORENS
JUST A REALLY RANCID SHIRT. NO BLOOD, BUT ENOUGH DIRT AND FLUID TO MAKE ME THINK IT HAD SUSTAINED CONTACT WITH A PRETTY RIPE CORPSE.
GEE, I WONDER WHERE HE COULD HAVE FOUND ONE OF THOSE...
I'LL GET A BAG.

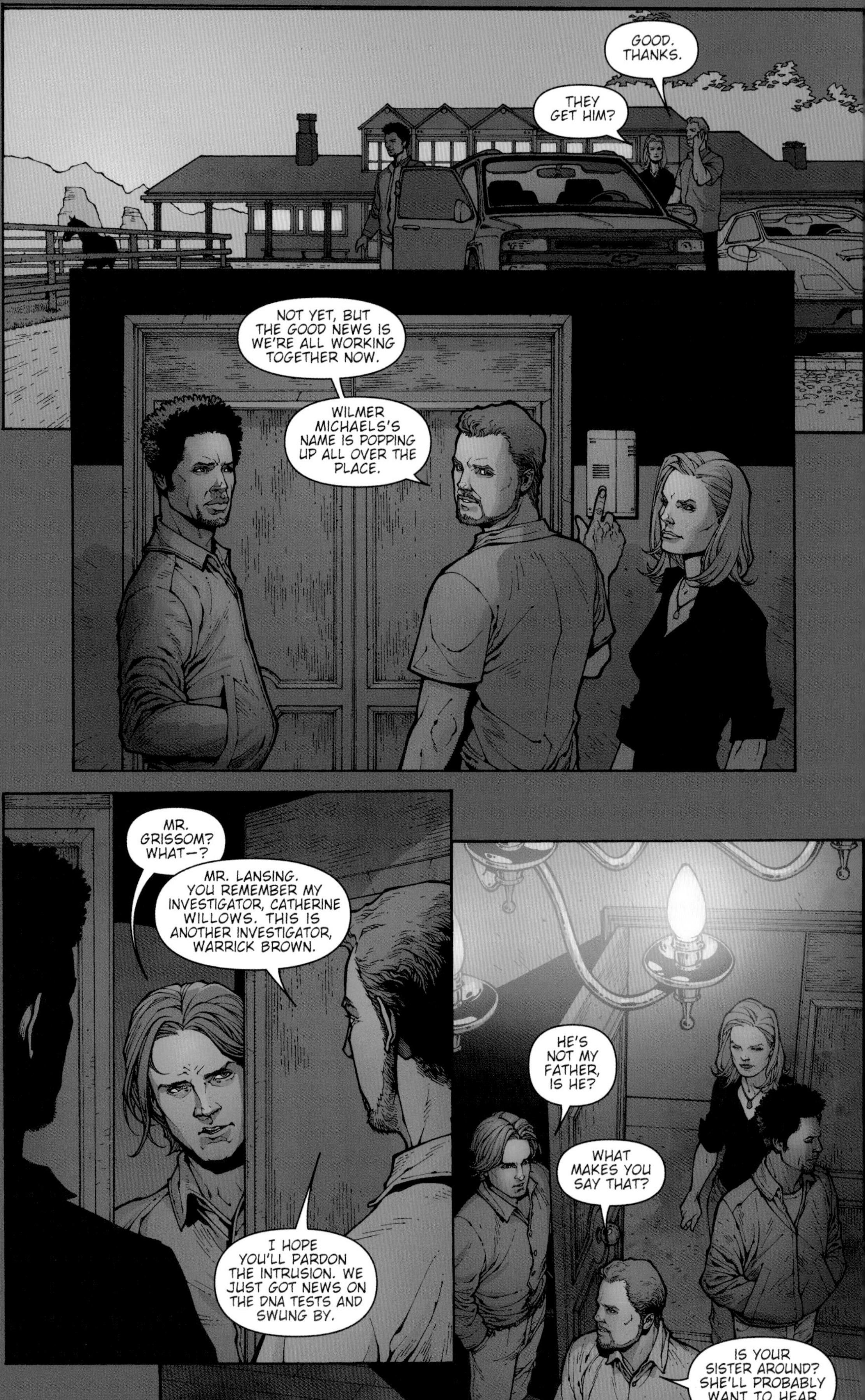

GOOD. THANKS.
THEY GET HIM?
NOT YET, BUT THE GOOD NEWS IS WE'RE ALL WORKING TOGETHER NOW.
WILMER MICHAELS'S NAME IS POPPING UP ALL OVER THE PLACE.
MR. GRISSOM? WHAT—?
MR. LANSING. YOU REMEMBER MY INVESTIGATOR, CATHERINE WILLOWS. THIS IS ANOTHER INVESTIGATOR, WARRICK BROWN.
I HOPE YOU'LL PARDON THE INTRUSION. WE JUST GOT NEWS ON THE DNA TESTS AND SWUNG BY.
HE'S NOT MY FATHER, IS HE?
WHAT MAKES YOU SAY THAT?
IS YOUR SISTER AROUND? SHE'LL PROBABLY WANT TO HEAR THIS TOO.

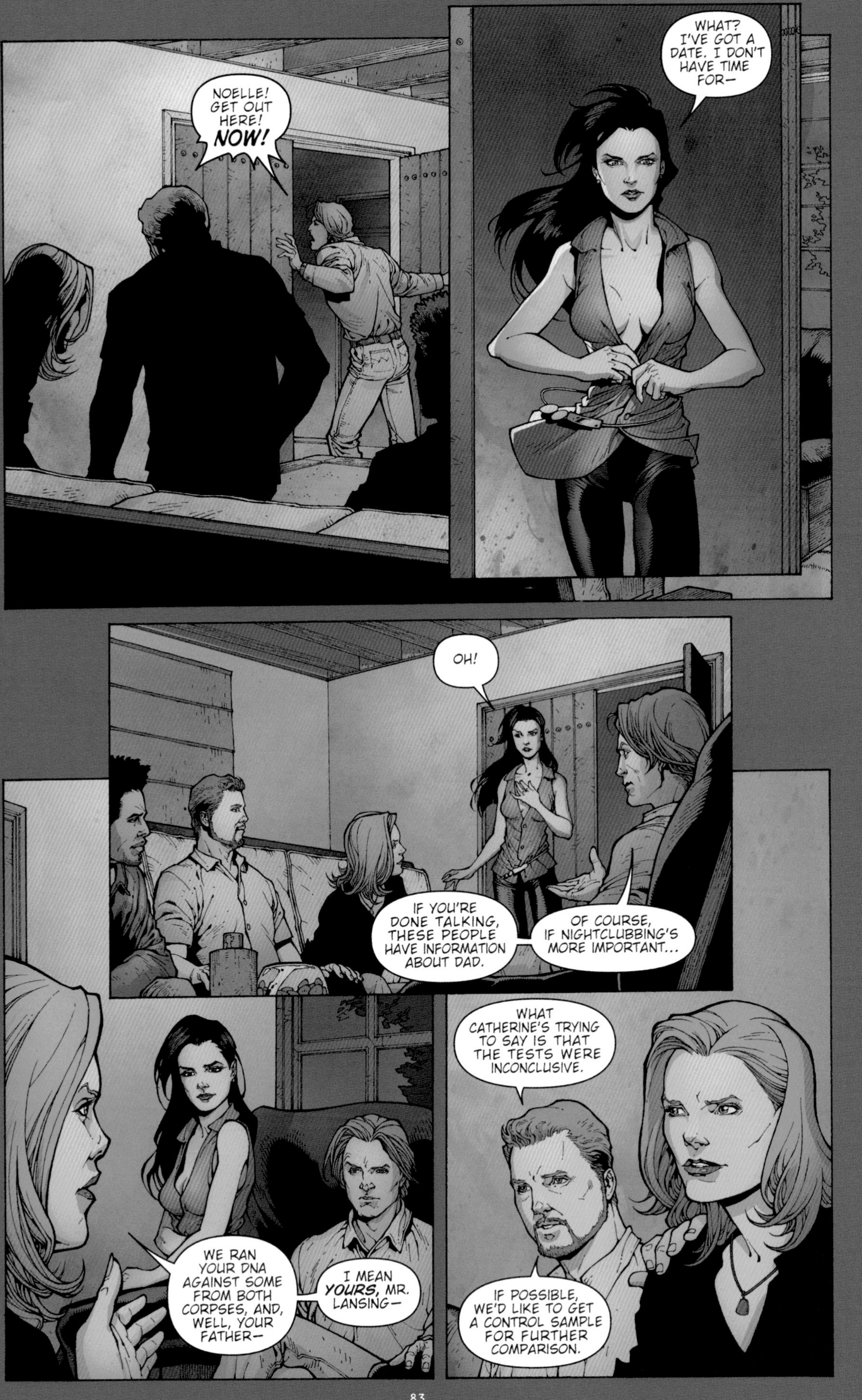

NOELLE! GET OUT HERE! **NOW!**
WHAT? I'VE GOT A DATE. I DON'T HAVE TIME FOR—
OH!
IF YOU'RE DONE TALKING, THESE PEOPLE HAVE INFORMATION ABOUT DAD.
OF COURSE, IF NIGHTCLUBBING'S MORE IMPORTANT...
WE RAN YOUR DNA AGAINST SOME FROM BOTH CORPSES, AND, WELL, YOUR FATHER—
I MEAN ***YOURS,*** MR. LANSING—
WHAT CATHERINE'S TRYING TO SAY IS THAT THE TESTS WERE INCONCLUSIVE.
IF POSSIBLE, WE'D LIKE TO GET A CONTROL SAMPLE FOR FURTHER COMPARISON.

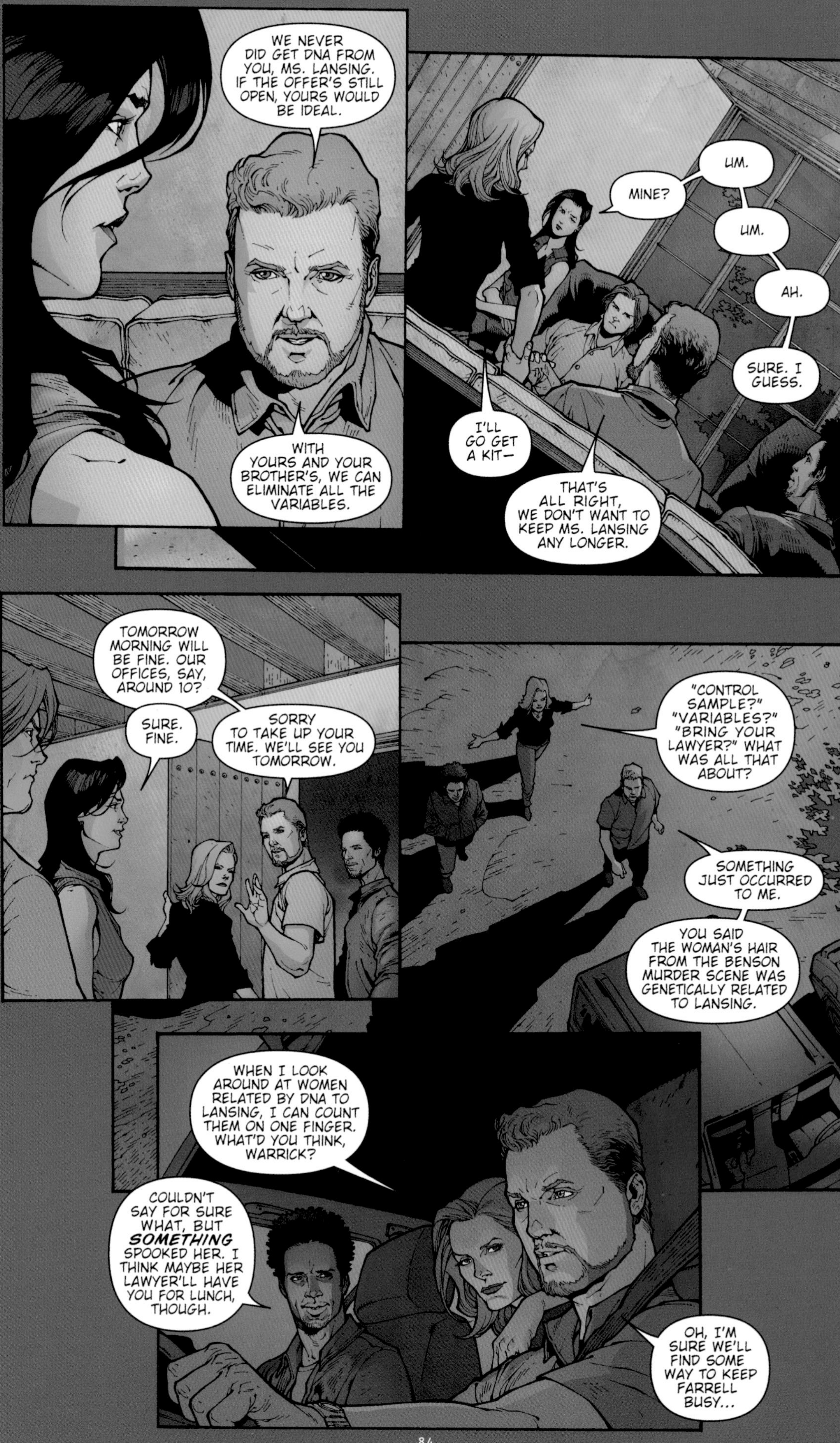
WE NEVER DID GET DNA FROM YOU, MS. LANSING. IF THE OFFER'S STILL OPEN, YOURS WOULD BE IDEAL.
WITH YOURS AND YOUR BROTHER'S, WE CAN ELIMINATE ALL THE VARIABLES.
UM.
MINE?
UM.
AH.
SURE. I GUESS.
I'LL GO GET A KIT—
THAT'S ALL RIGHT, WE DON'T WANT TO KEEP MS. LANSING ANY LONGER.
TOMORROW MORNING WILL BE FINE. OUR OFFICES, SAY, AROUND 10?
SURE. FINE.
SORRY TO TAKE UP YOUR TIME. WE'LL SEE YOU TOMORROW.
"CONTROL SAMPLE?" "VARIABLES?" "BRING YOUR LAWYER?" WHAT WAS ALL THAT ABOUT?
SOMETHING JUST OCCURRED TO ME.
YOU SAID THE WOMAN'S HAIR FROM THE BENSON MURDER SCENE WAS GENETICALLY RELATED TO LANSING.
WHEN I LOOK AROUND AT WOMEN RELATED BY DNA TO LANSING, I CAN COUNT THEM ON ONE FINGER. WHAT'D YOU THINK, WARRICK?
COULDN'T SAY FOR SURE WHAT, BUT ***SOMETHING*** SPOOKED HER. I THINK MAYBE HER LAWYER'LL HAVE YOU FOR LUNCH, THOUGH.
OH, I'M SURE WE'LL FIND SOME WAY TO KEEP FARRELL BUSY...

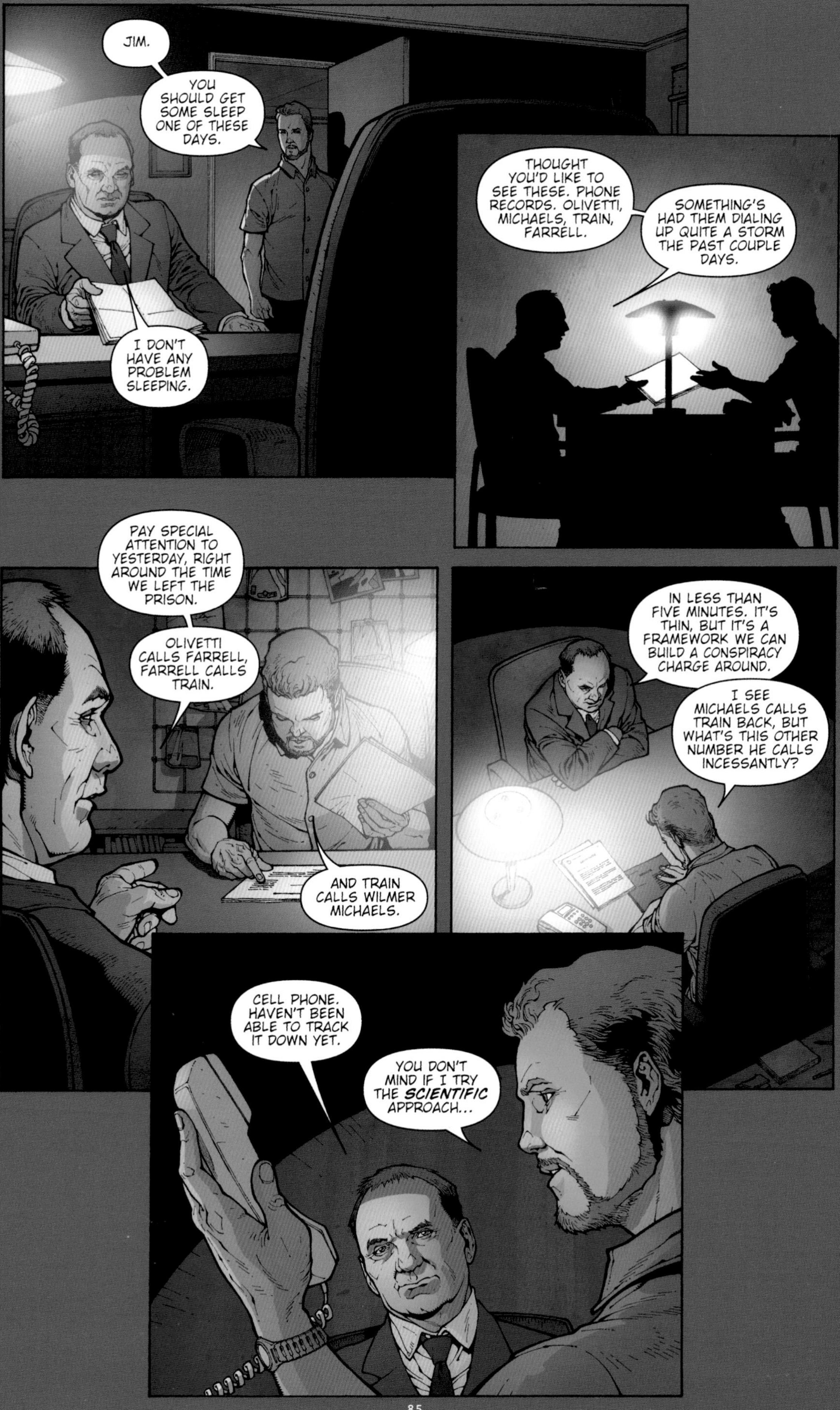
JIM.
YOU SHOULD GET SOME SLEEP ONE OF THESE DAYS.
I DON'T HAVE ANY PROBLEM SLEEPING.
THOUGHT YOU'D LIKE TO SEE THESE. PHONE RECORDS. OLIVETTI, MICHAELS, TRAIN, FARRELL.
SOMETHING'S HAD THEM DIALING UP QUITE A STORM THE PAST COUPLE DAYS.
PAY SPECIAL ATTENTION TO YESTERDAY, RIGHT AROUND THE TIME WE LEFT THE PRISON.
OLIVETTI CALLS FARRELL, FARRELL CALLS TRAIN.
AND TRAIN CALLS WILMER MICHAELS.
IN LESS THAN FIVE MINUTES. IT'S THIN, BUT IT'S A FRAMEWORK WE CAN BUILD A CONSPIRACY CHARGE AROUND.
I SEE MICHAELS CALLS TRAIN BACK, BUT WHAT'S THIS OTHER NUMBER HE CALLS INCESSANTLY?
CELL PHONE. HAVEN'T BEEN ABLE TO TRACK IT DOWN YET.
YOU DON'T MIND IF I TRY THE *SCIENTIFIC* APPROACH...

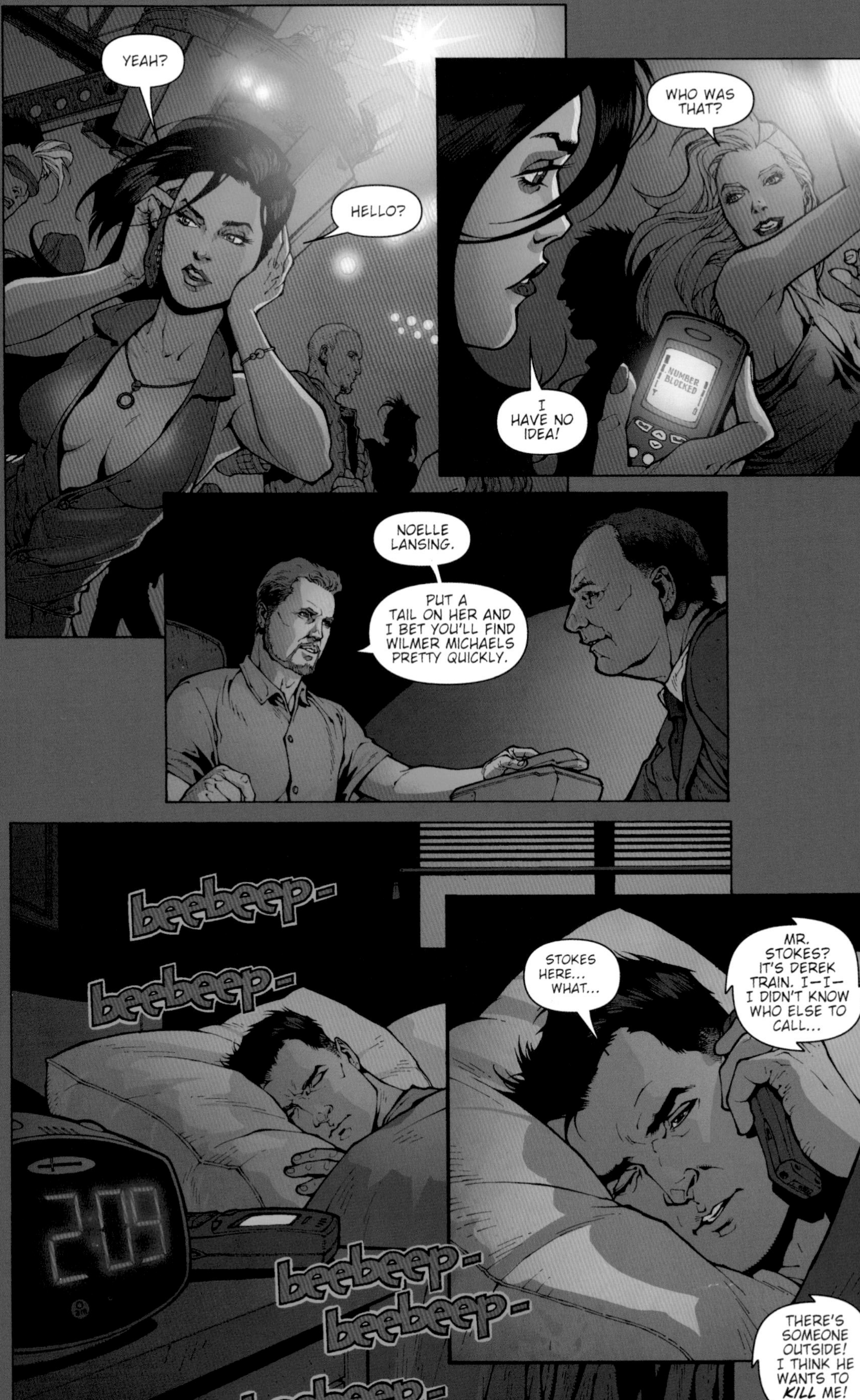
YEAH?
HELLO?
WHO WAS THAT?
NUMBER BLOCKED
I HAVE NO IDEA!
NOELLE LANSING.
PUT A TAIL ON HER AND I BET YOU'LL FIND WILMER MICHAELS PRETTY QUICKLY.
beebeep-
beebeep-
beebeep-
beebeep-
beebeep-
STOKES HERE... WHAT...
MR. STOKES? IT'S DEREK TRAIN. I—I— I DIDN'T KNOW WHO ELSE TO CALL...
THERE'S SOMEONE OUTSIDE! I THINK HE WANTS TO KILL ME!

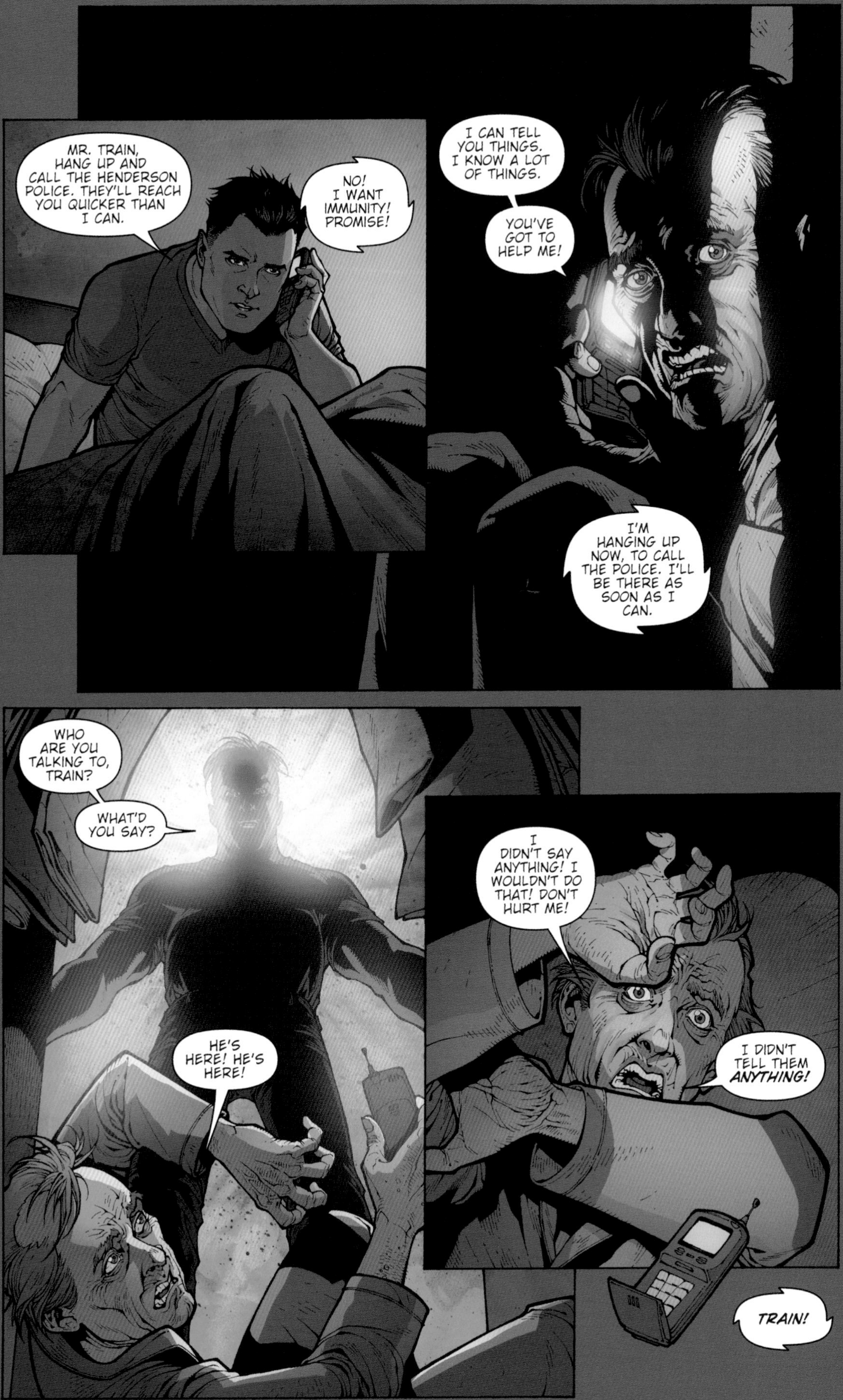
MR. TRAIN, HANG UP AND CALL THE HENDERSON POLICE. THEY'LL REACH YOU QUICKER THAN I CAN.
NO! I WANT IMMUNITY! PROMISE!
I CAN TELL YOU THINGS. I KNOW A LOT OF THINGS.
YOU'VE GOT TO HELP ME!
I'M HANGING UP NOW, TO CALL THE POLICE. I'LL BE THERE AS SOON AS I CAN.
WHO ARE YOU TALKING TO, TRAIN?
WHAT'D YOU SAY?
HE'S HERE! HE'S HERE!
I DIDN'T SAY ANYTHING! I WOULDN'T DO THAT! DON'T HURT ME!
I DIDN'T TELL THEM *ANYTHING!*
TRAIN!

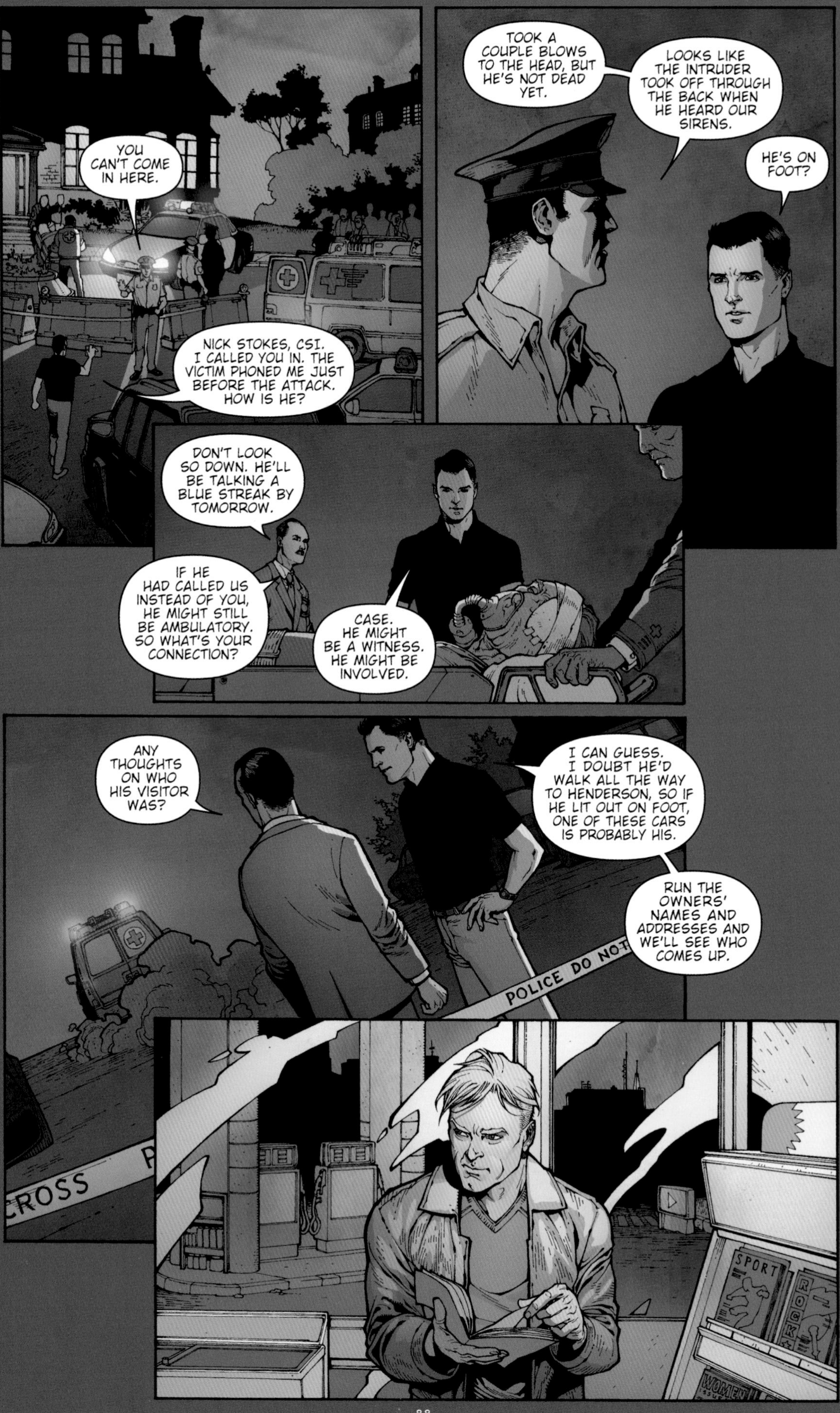
YOU CAN'T COME IN HERE.
NICK STOKES, CSI. I CALLED YOU IN. THE VICTIM PHONED ME JUST BEFORE THE ATTACK. HOW IS HE?
TOOK A COUPLE BLOWS TO THE HEAD, BUT HE'S NOT DEAD YET.
LOOKS LIKE THE INTRUDER TOOK OFF THROUGH THE BACK WHEN HE HEARD OUR SIRENS.
HE'S ON FOOT?
DON'T LOOK SO DOWN. HE'LL BE TALKING A BLUE STREAK BY TOMORROW.
IF HE HAD CALLED US INSTEAD OF YOU, HE MIGHT STILL BE AMBULATORY. SO WHAT'S YOUR CONNECTION?
CASE. HE MIGHT BE A WITNESS. HE MIGHT BE INVOLVED.
ANY THOUGHTS ON WHO HIS VISITOR WAS?
I CAN GUESS. I DOUBT HE'D WALK ALL THE WAY TO HENDERSON, SO IF HE LIT OUT ON FOOT, ONE OF THESE CARS IS PROBABLY HIS.
RUN THE OWNERS' NAMES AND ADDRESSES AND WE'LL SEE WHO COMES UP.
POLICE DO NOT
CROSS
SPORT

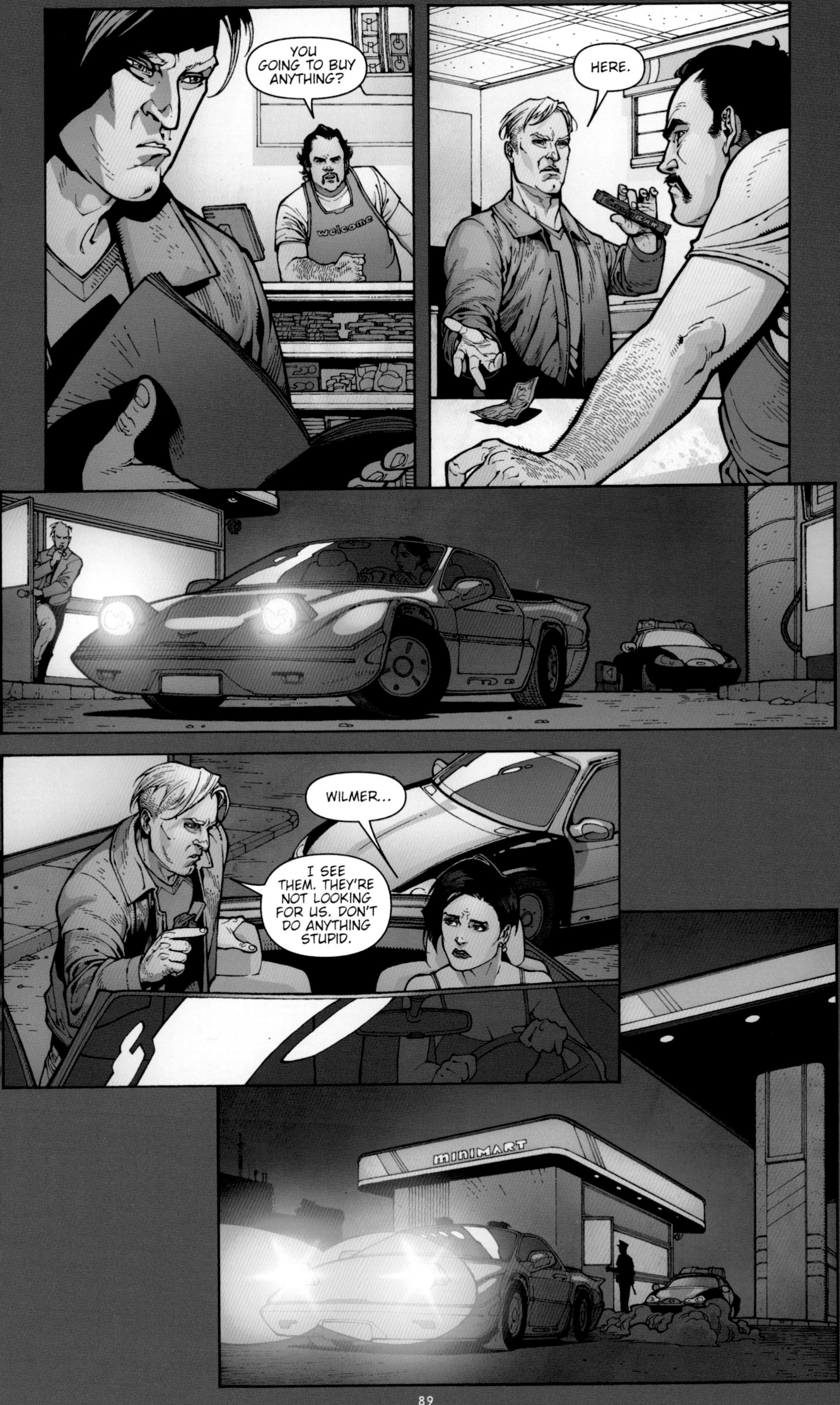
YOU GOING TO BUY ANYTHING?
welcome
HERE.
WILMER...
I SEE THEM. THEY'RE NOT LOOKING FOR US. DON'T DO ANYTHING STUPID.
MINIMART

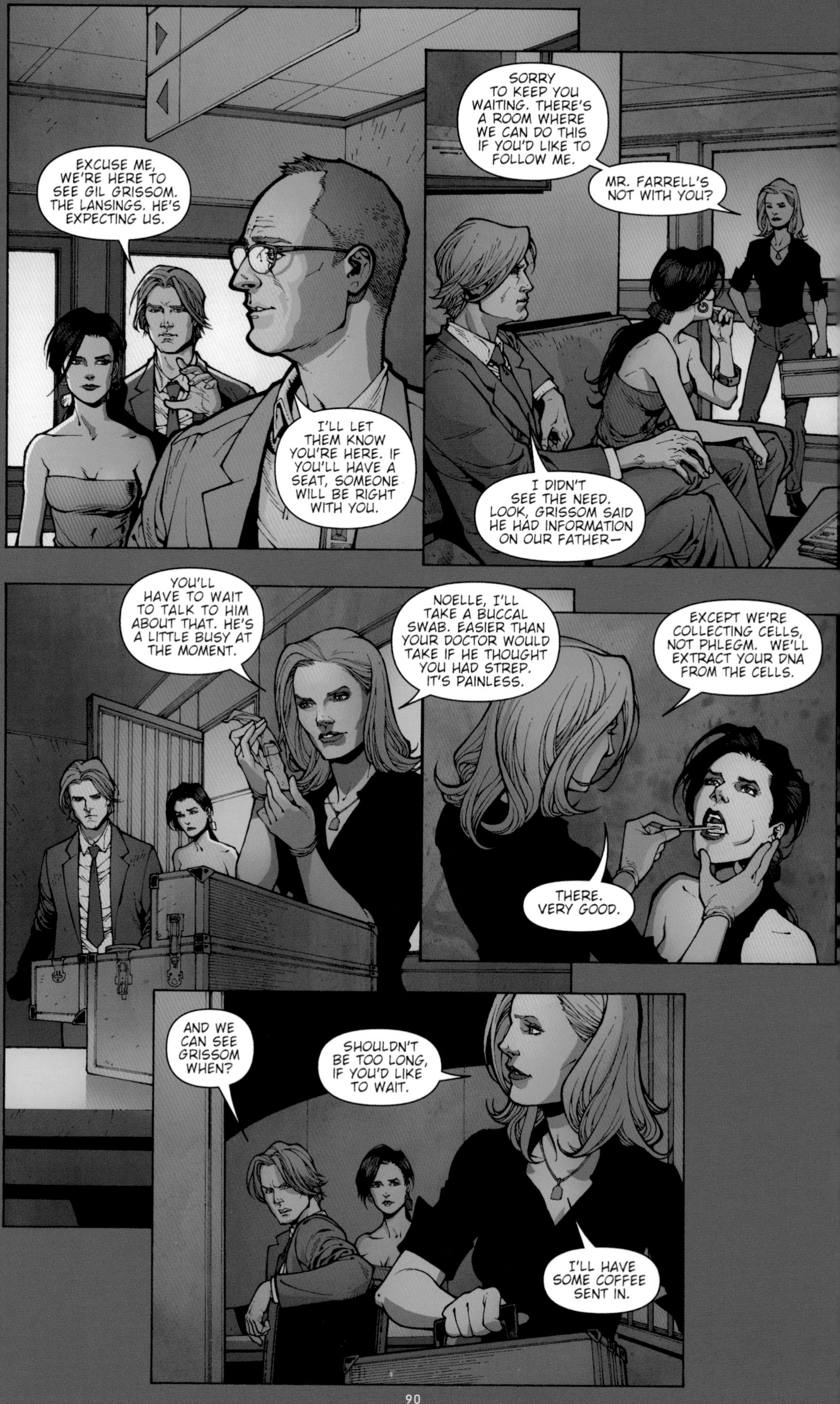
EXCUSE ME, WE'RE HERE TO SEE GIL GRISSOM. THE LANSINGS. HE'S EXPECTING US.
I'LL LET THEM KNOW YOU'RE HERE. IF YOU'LL HAVE A SEAT, SOMEONE WILL BE RIGHT WITH YOU.
SORRY TO KEEP YOU WAITING. THERE'S A ROOM WHERE WE CAN DO THIS IF YOU'D LIKE TO FOLLOW ME.
MR. FARRELL'S NOT WITH YOU?
I DIDN'T SEE THE NEED. LOOK, GRISSOM SAID HE HAD INFORMATION ON OUR FATHER—
YOU'LL HAVE TO WAIT TO TALK TO HIM ABOUT THAT. HE'S A LITTLE BUSY AT THE MOMENT.
NOELLE, I'LL TAKE A BUCCAL SWAB. EASIER THAN YOUR DOCTOR WOULD TAKE IF HE THOUGHT YOU HAD STREP. IT'S PAINLESS.
EXCEPT WE'RE COLLECTING CELLS, NOT PHLEGM. WE'LL EXTRACT YOUR DNA FROM THE CELLS.
THERE. VERY GOOD.
AND WE CAN SEE GRISSOM WHEN?
SHOULDN'T BE TOO LONG, IF YOU'D LIKE TO WAIT.
I'LL HAVE SOME COFFEE SENT IN.

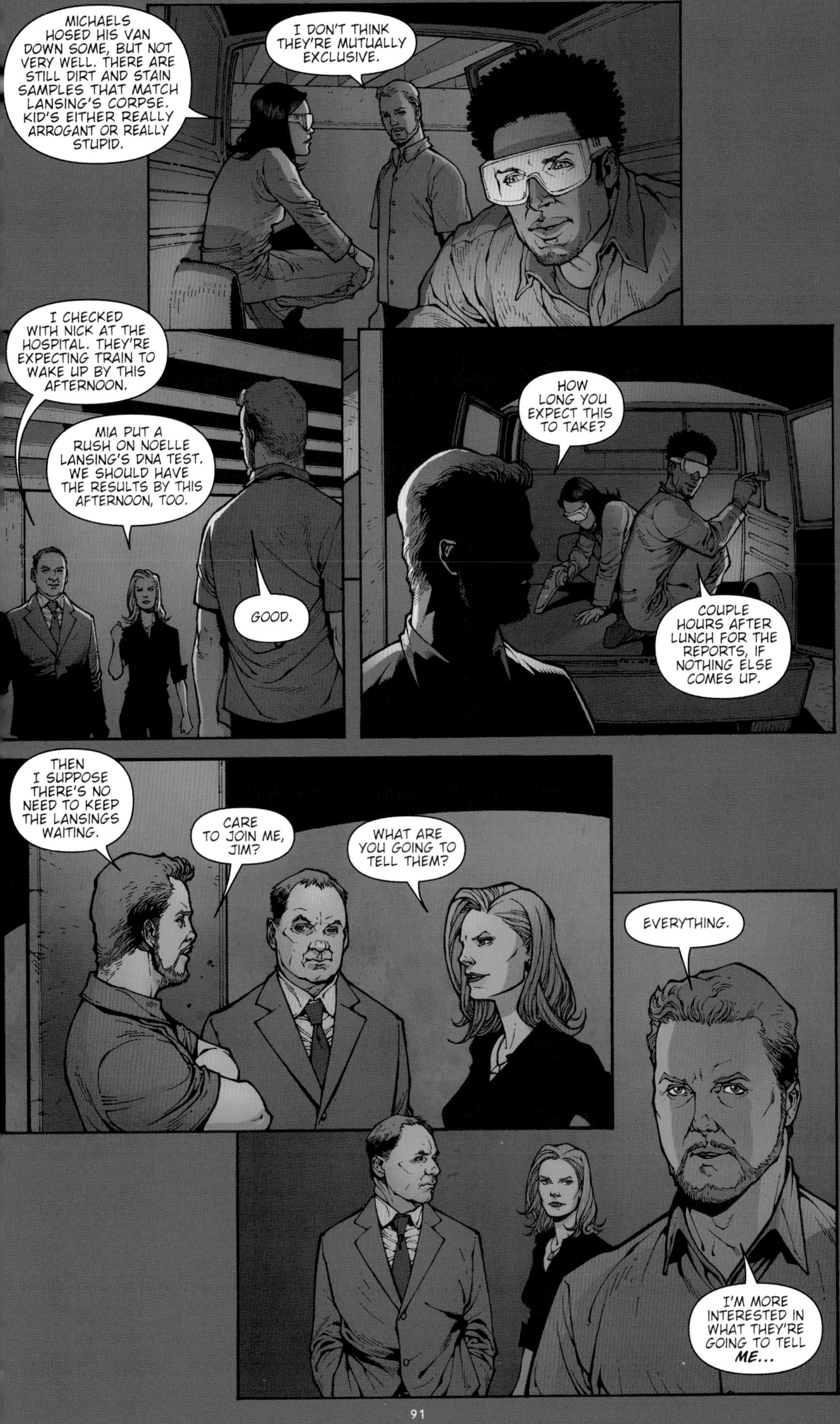

MICHAELS HOSED HIS VAN DOWN SOME, BUT NOT VERY WELL. THERE ARE STILL DIRT AND STAIN SAMPLES THAT MATCH LANSING'S CORPSE. KID'S EITHER REALLY ARROGANT OR REALLY STUPID.
I DON'T THINK THEY'RE MUTUALLY EXCLUSIVE.
I CHECKED WITH NICK AT THE HOSPITAL. THEY'RE EXPECTING TRAIN TO WAKE UP BY THIS AFTERNOON.
MIA PUT A RUSH ON NOELLE LANSING'S DNA TEST. WE SHOULD HAVE THE RESULTS BY THIS AFTERNOON, TOO.
GOOD.
HOW LONG YOU EXPECT THIS TO TAKE?
COUPLE HOURS AFTER LUNCH FOR THE REPORTS, IF NOTHING ELSE COMES UP.
THEN I SUPPOSE THERE'S NO NEED TO KEEP THE LANSINGS WAITING.
CARE TO JOIN ME, JIM?
WHAT ARE YOU GOING TO TELL THEM?
EVERYTHING.
I'M MORE INTERESTED IN WHAT THEY'RE GOING TO TELL **ME...**

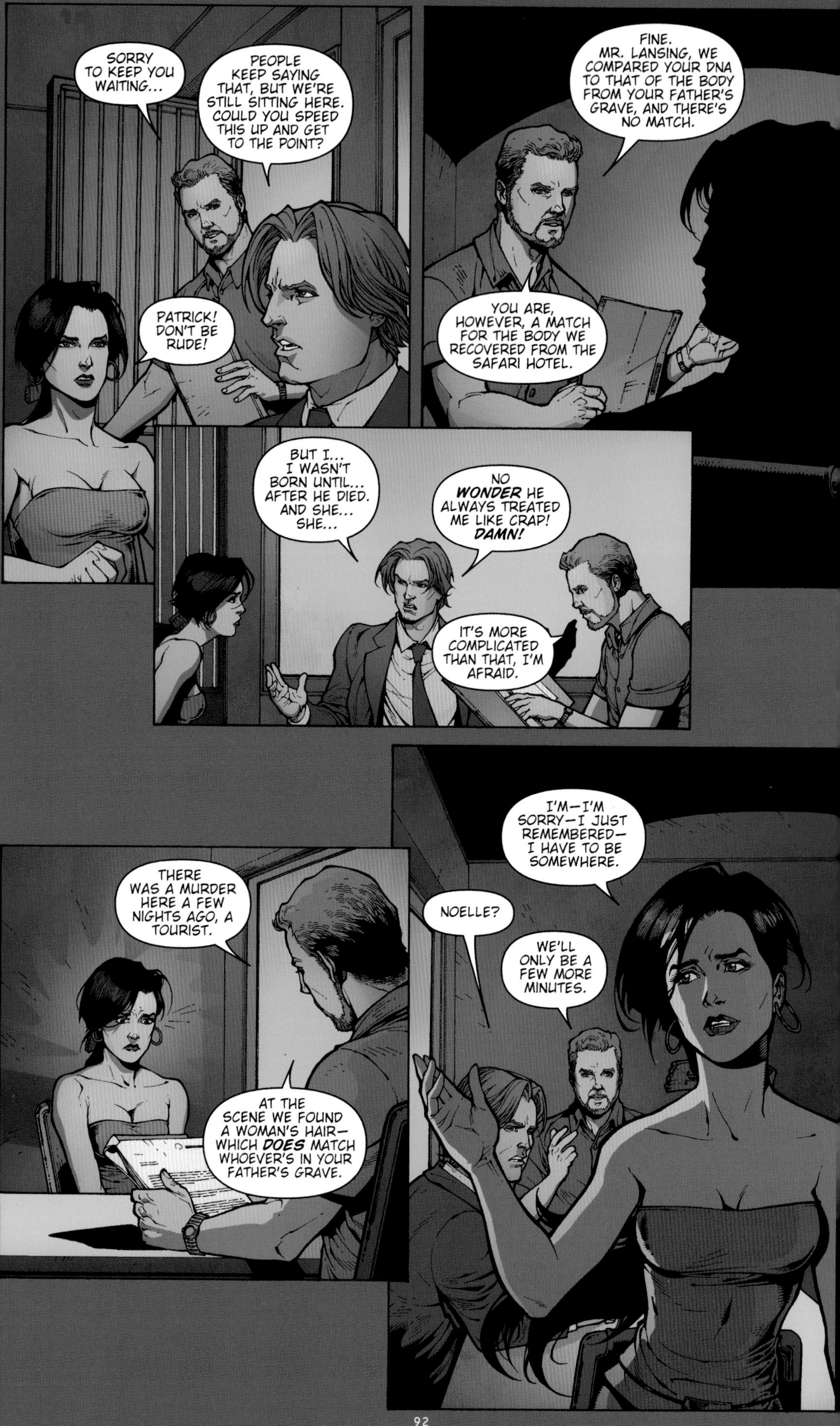
SORRY TO KEEP YOU WAITING...
PEOPLE KEEP SAYING THAT, BUT WE'RE STILL SITTING HERE. COULD YOU SPEED THIS UP AND GET TO THE POINT?
PATRICK! DON'T BE RUDE!
FINE. MR. LANSING, WE COMPARED YOUR DNA TO THAT OF THE BODY FROM YOUR FATHER'S GRAVE, AND THERE'S NO MATCH.
YOU ARE, HOWEVER, A MATCH FOR THE BODY WE RECOVERED FROM THE SAFARI HOTEL.
BUT I... I WASN'T BORN UNTIL... AFTER HE DIED. AND SHE... SHE...
NO *WONDER* HE ALWAYS TREATED ME LIKE CRAP! ***DAMN!***
IT'S MORE COMPLICATED THAN THAT, I'M AFRAID.
THERE WAS A MURDER HERE A FEW NIGHTS AGO, A TOURIST.
AT THE SCENE WE FOUND A WOMAN'S HAIR—WHICH *DOES* MATCH WHOEVER'S IN YOUR FATHER'S GRAVE.
I'M—I'M SORRY—I JUST REMEMBERED—I HAVE TO BE SOMEWHERE.
NOELLE?
WE'LL ONLY BE A FEW MORE MINUTES.

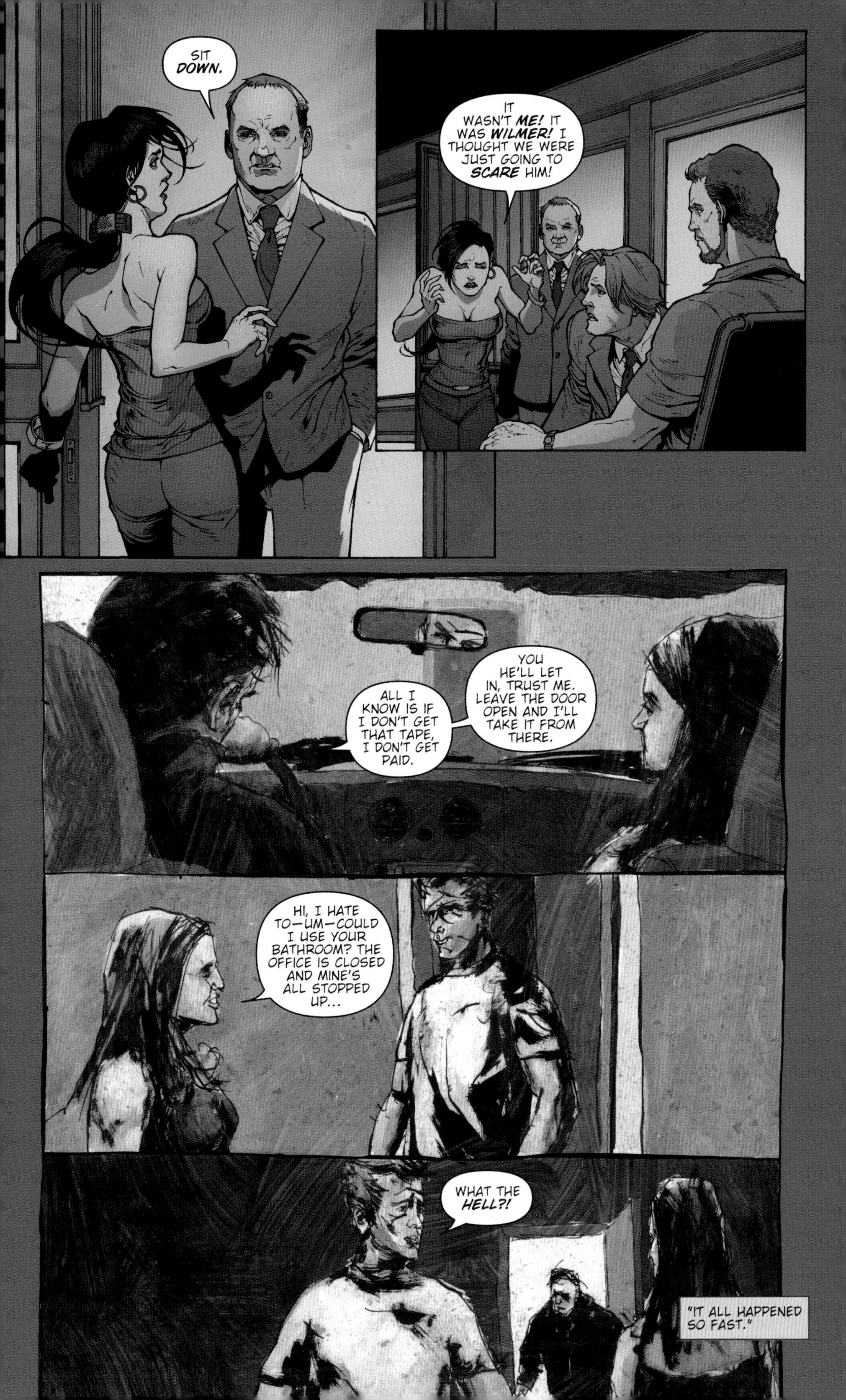
SIT DOWN.
IT WASN'T ME! IT WAS WILMER! I THOUGHT WE WERE JUST GOING TO SCARE HIM!
ALL I KNOW IS IF I DON'T GET THAT TAPE, I DON'T GET PAID.
YOU HE'LL LET IN, TRUST ME. LEAVE THE DOOR OPEN AND I'LL TAKE IT FROM THERE.
HI, I HATE TO—UM—COULD I USE YOUR BATHROOM? THE OFFICE IS CLOSED AND MINE'S ALL STOPPED UP...
WHAT THE HELL?!
"IT ALL HAPPENED SO FAST."

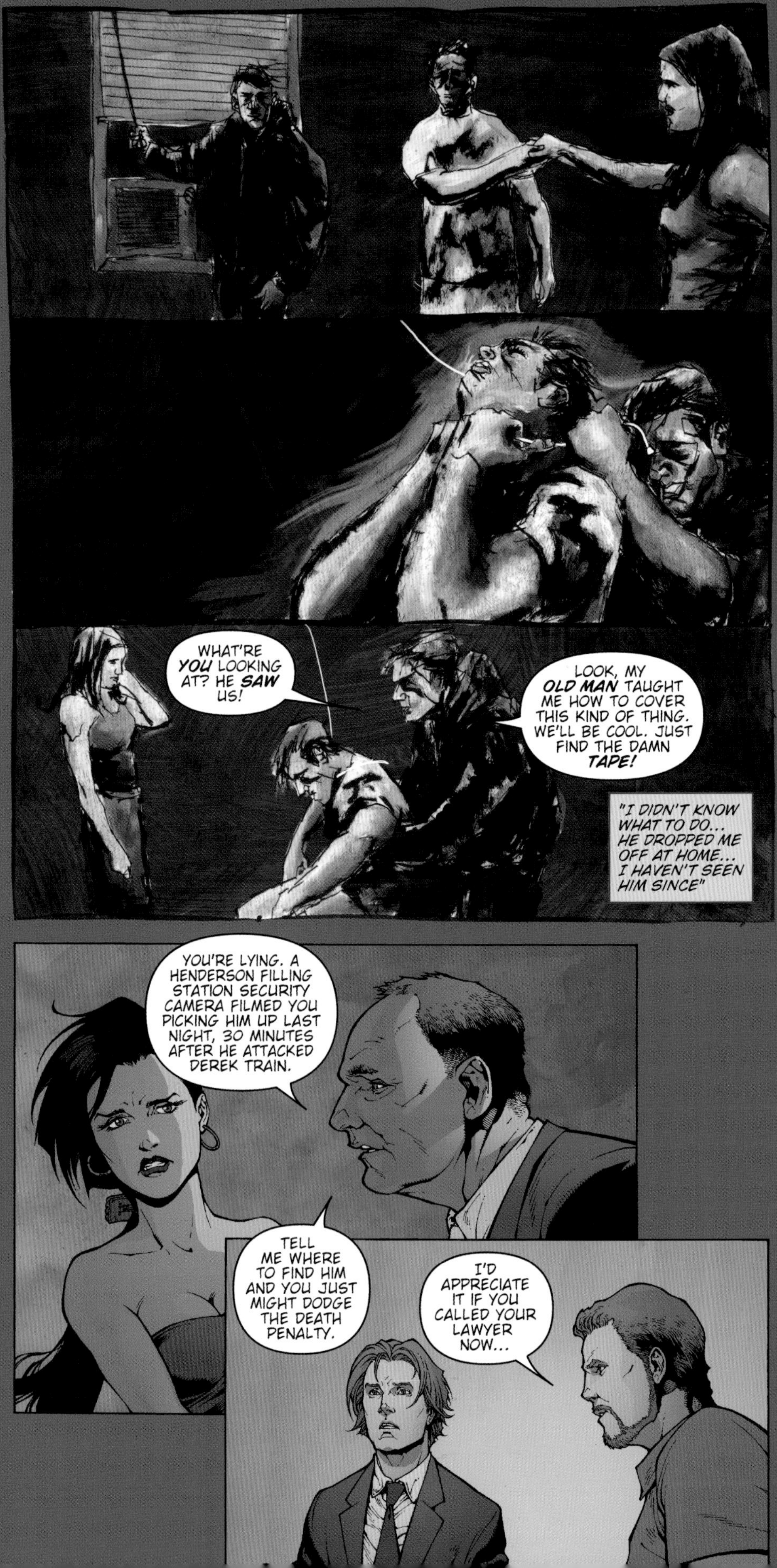

WHAT'RE YOU LOOKING AT? HE SAW US!
LOOK, MY OLD MAN TAUGHT ME HOW TO COVER THIS KIND OF THING. WE'LL BE COOL. JUST FIND THE DAMN TAPE!
"I DIDN'T KNOW WHAT TO DO... HE DROPPED ME OFF AT HOME... I HAVEN'T SEEN HIM SINCE"
YOU'RE LYING. A HENDERSON FILLING STATION SECURITY CAMERA FILMED YOU PICKING HIM UP LAST NIGHT, 30 MINUTES AFTER HE ATTACKED DEREK TRAIN.
TELL ME WHERE TO FIND HIM AND YOU JUST MIGHT DODGE THE DEATH PENALTY.
I'D APPRECIATE IT IF YOU CALLED YOUR LAWYER NOW...

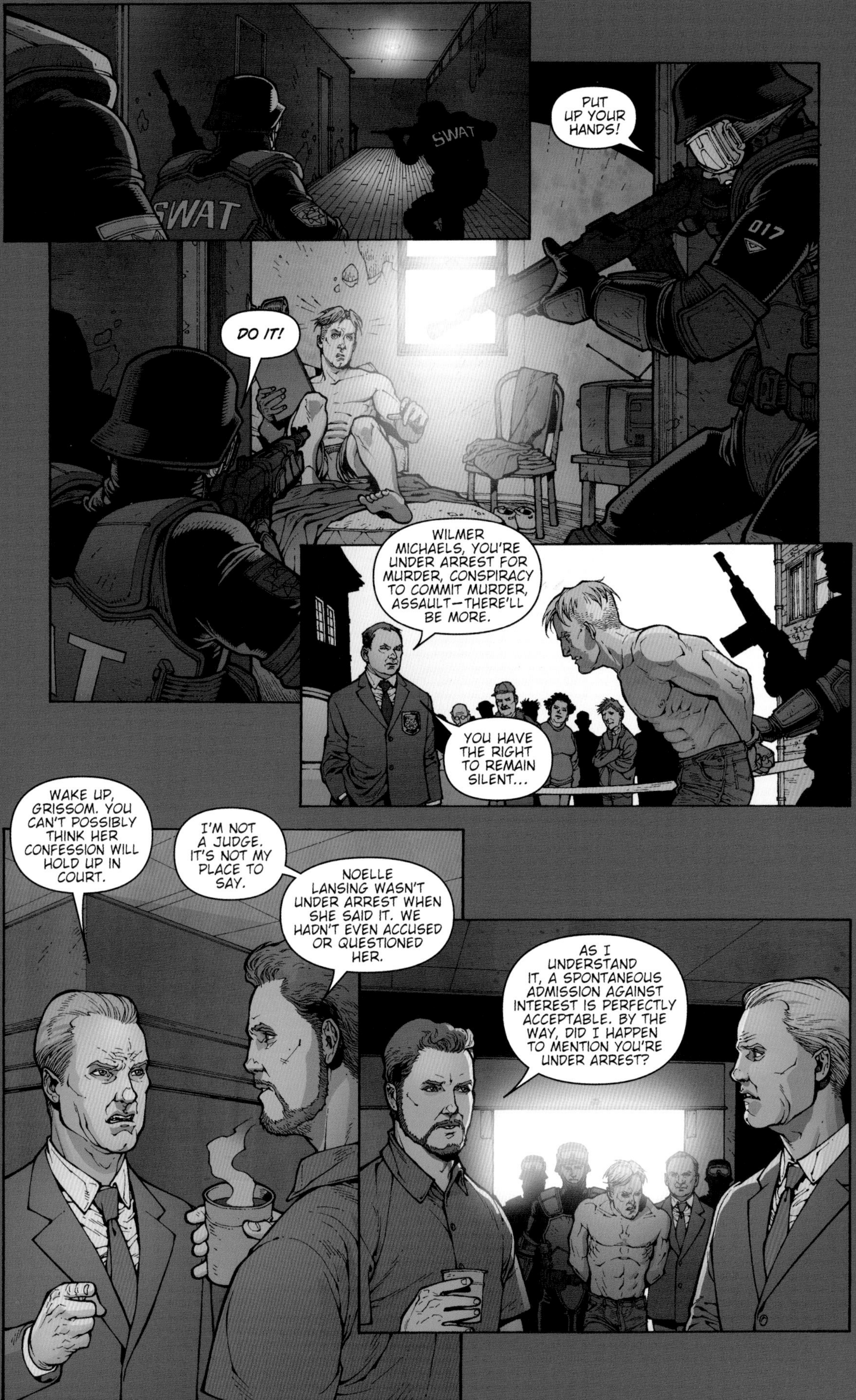
SWAT
SWAT
PUT UP YOUR HANDS!
017
DO IT!
WILMER MICHAELS, YOU'RE UNDER ARREST FOR MURDER, CONSPIRACY TO COMMIT MURDER, ASSAULT—THERE'LL BE MORE.
YOU HAVE THE RIGHT TO REMAIN SILENT...
WAKE UP, GRISSOM. YOU CAN'T POSSIBLY THINK HER CONFESSION WILL HOLD UP IN COURT.
I'M NOT A JUDGE. IT'S NOT MY PLACE TO SAY.
NOELLE LANSING WASN'T UNDER ARREST WHEN SHE SAID IT. WE HADN'T EVEN ACCUSED OR QUESTIONED HER.
AS I UNDERSTAND IT, A SPONTANEOUS ADMISSION AGAINST INTEREST IS PERFECTLY ACCEPTABLE. BY THE WAY, DID I HAPPEN TO MENTION YOU'RE UNDER ARREST?

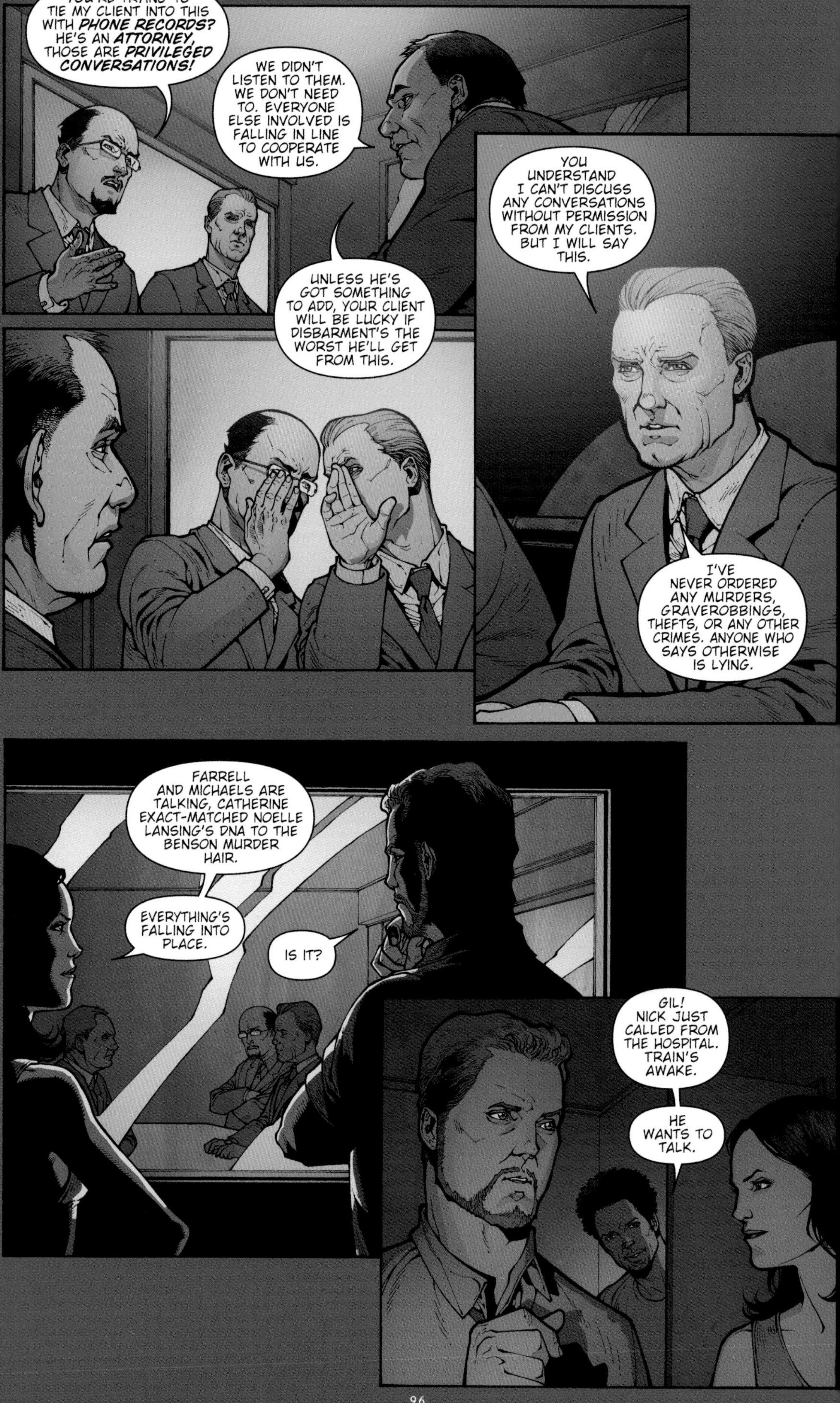

YOU'RE TRYING TO TIE MY CLIENT INTO THIS WITH *PHONE RECORDS?* HE'S AN *ATTORNEY,* THOSE ARE *PRIVILEGED CONVERSATIONS!*
WE DIDN'T LISTEN TO THEM. WE DON'T NEED TO. EVERYONE ELSE INVOLVED IS FALLING IN LINE TO COOPERATE WITH US.
UNLESS HE'S GOT SOMETHING TO ADD, YOUR CLIENT WILL BE LUCKY IF DISBARMENT'S THE WORST HE'LL GET FROM THIS.
YOU UNDERSTAND I CAN'T DISCUSS ANY CONVERSATIONS WITHOUT PERMISSION FROM MY CLIENTS. BUT I WILL SAY THIS.
I'VE NEVER ORDERED ANY MURDERS, GRAVEROBBINGS, THEFTS, OR ANY OTHER CRIMES. ANYONE WHO SAYS OTHERWISE IS LYING.
FARRELL AND MICHAELS ARE TALKING, CATHERINE EXACT-MATCHED NOELLE LANSING'S DNA TO THE BENSON MURDER HAIR.
EVERYTHING'S FALLING INTO PLACE.
IS IT?
GIL! NICK JUST CALLED FROM THE HOSPITAL. TRAIN'S AWAKE.
HE WANTS TO TALK.

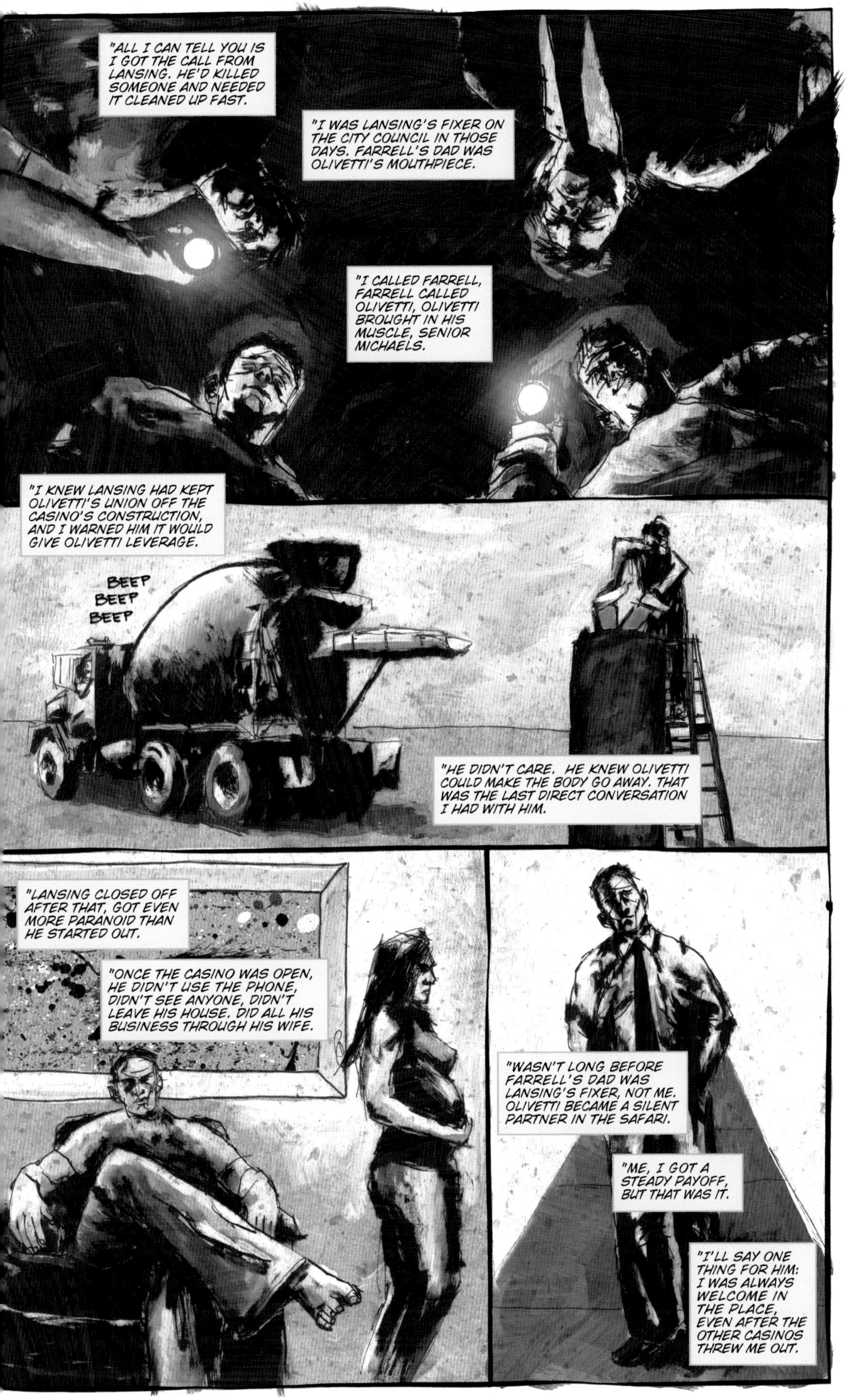
"ALL I CAN TELL YOU IS I GOT THE CALL FROM LANSING. HE'D KILLED SOMEONE AND NEEDED IT CLEANED UP FAST.
"I WAS LANSING'S FIXER ON THE CITY COUNCIL IN THOSE DAYS. FARRELL'S DAD WAS OLIVETTI'S MOUTHPIECE.
"I CALLED FARRELL, FARRELL CALLED OLIVETTI, OLIVETTI BROUGHT IN HIS MUSCLE, SENIOR MICHAELS.
"I KNEW LANSING HAD KEPT OLIVETTI'S UNION OFF THE CASINO'S CONSTRUCTION, AND I WARNED HIM IT WOULD GIVE OLIVETTI LEVERAGE.
BEEP BEEP BEEP
"HE DIDN'T CARE. HE KNEW OLIVETTI COULD MAKE THE BODY GO AWAY. THAT WAS THE LAST DIRECT CONVERSATION I HAD WITH HIM.
"LANSING CLOSED OFF AFTER THAT, GOT EVEN MORE PARANOID THAN HE STARTED OUT.
"ONCE THE CASINO WAS OPEN, HE DIDN'T USE THE PHONE, DIDN'T SEE ANYONE, DIDN'T LEAVE HIS HOUSE. DID ALL HIS BUSINESS THROUGH HIS WIFE.
"WASN'T LONG BEFORE FARRELL'S DAD WAS LANSING'S FIXER, NOT ME. OLIVETTI BECAME A SILENT PARTNER IN THE SAFARI.
"ME, I GOT A STEADY PAYOFF, BUT THAT WAS IT.
"I'LL SAY ONE THING FOR HIM: I WAS ALWAYS WELCOME IN THE PLACE, EVEN AFTER THE OTHER CASINOS THREW ME OUT.

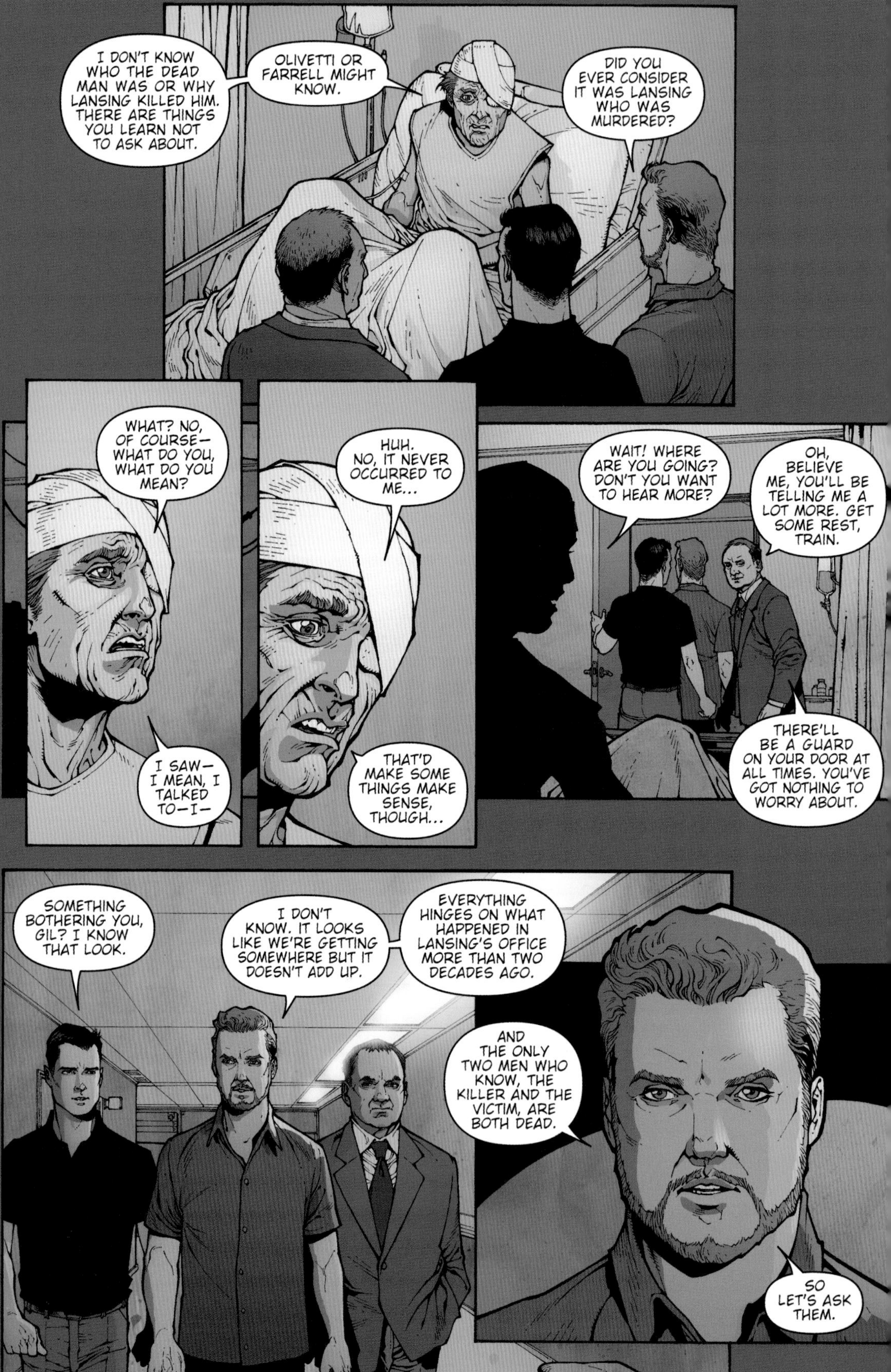
I DON'T KNOW WHO THE DEAD MAN WAS OR WHY LANSING KILLED HIM. THERE ARE THINGS YOU LEARN NOT TO ASK ABOUT.
OLIVETTI OR FARRELL MIGHT KNOW.
DID YOU EVER CONSIDER IT WAS LANSING WHO WAS MURDERED?
WHAT? NO, OF COURSE— WHAT DO YOU, WHAT DO YOU MEAN?
I SAW— I MEAN, I TALKED TO—I—
HUH. NO, IT NEVER OCCURRED TO ME...
THAT'D MAKE SOME THINGS MAKE SENSE, THOUGH...
WAIT! WHERE ARE YOU GOING? DON'T YOU WANT TO HEAR MORE?
OH, BELIEVE ME, YOU'LL BE TELLING ME A LOT MORE. GET SOME REST, TRAIN.
THERE'LL BE A GUARD ON YOUR DOOR AT ALL TIMES. YOU'VE GOT NOTHING TO WORRY ABOUT.
SOMETHING BOTHERING YOU, GIL? I KNOW THAT LOOK.
I DON'T KNOW. IT LOOKS LIKE WE'RE GETTING SOMEWHERE BUT IT DOESN'T ADD UP.
EVERYTHING HINGES ON WHAT HAPPENED IN LANSING'S OFFICE MORE THAN TWO DECADES AGO.
AND THE ONLY TWO MEN WHO KNOW, THE KILLER AND THE VICTIM, ARE BOTH DEAD.
SO LET'S ASK THEM.

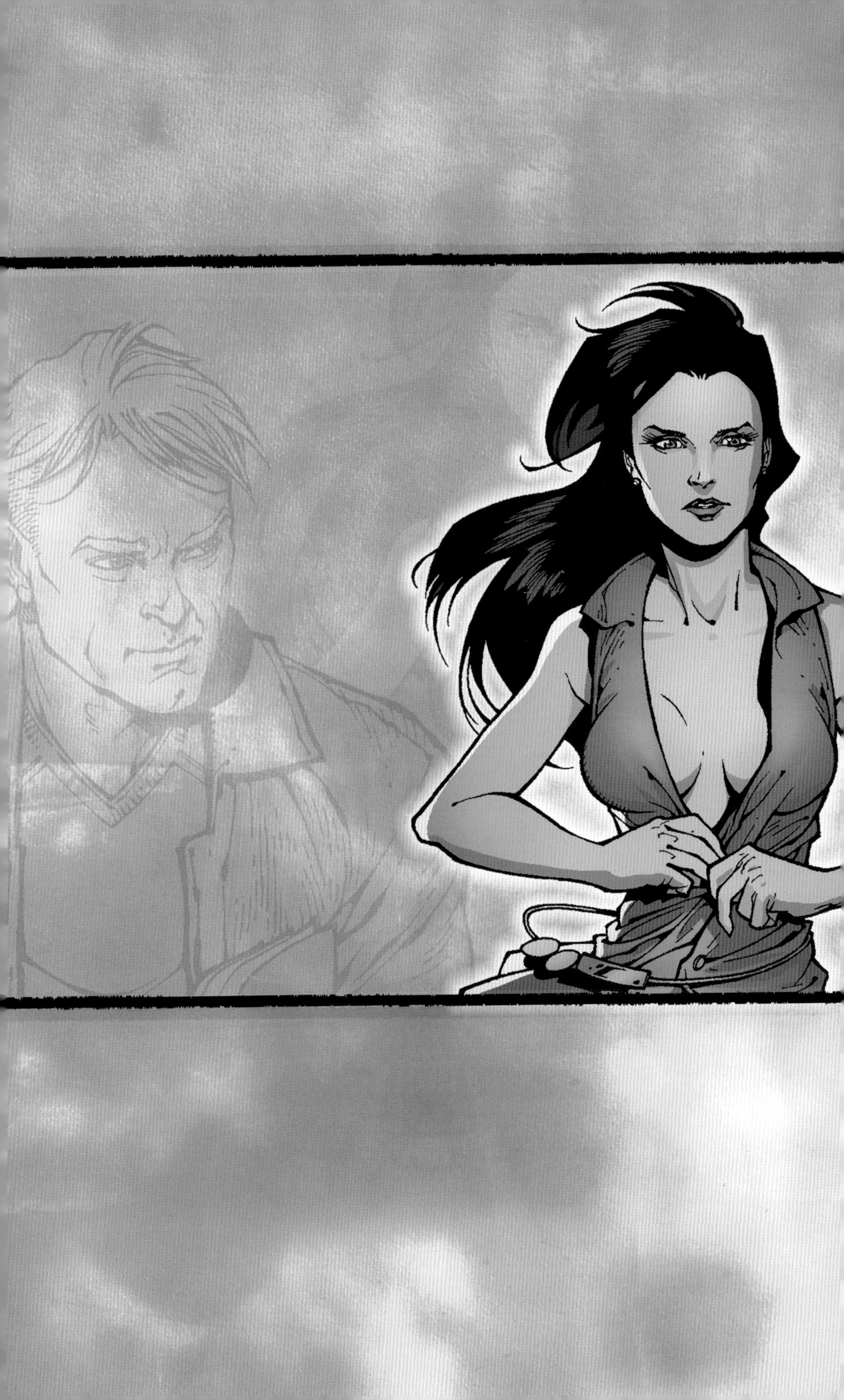

chapter five

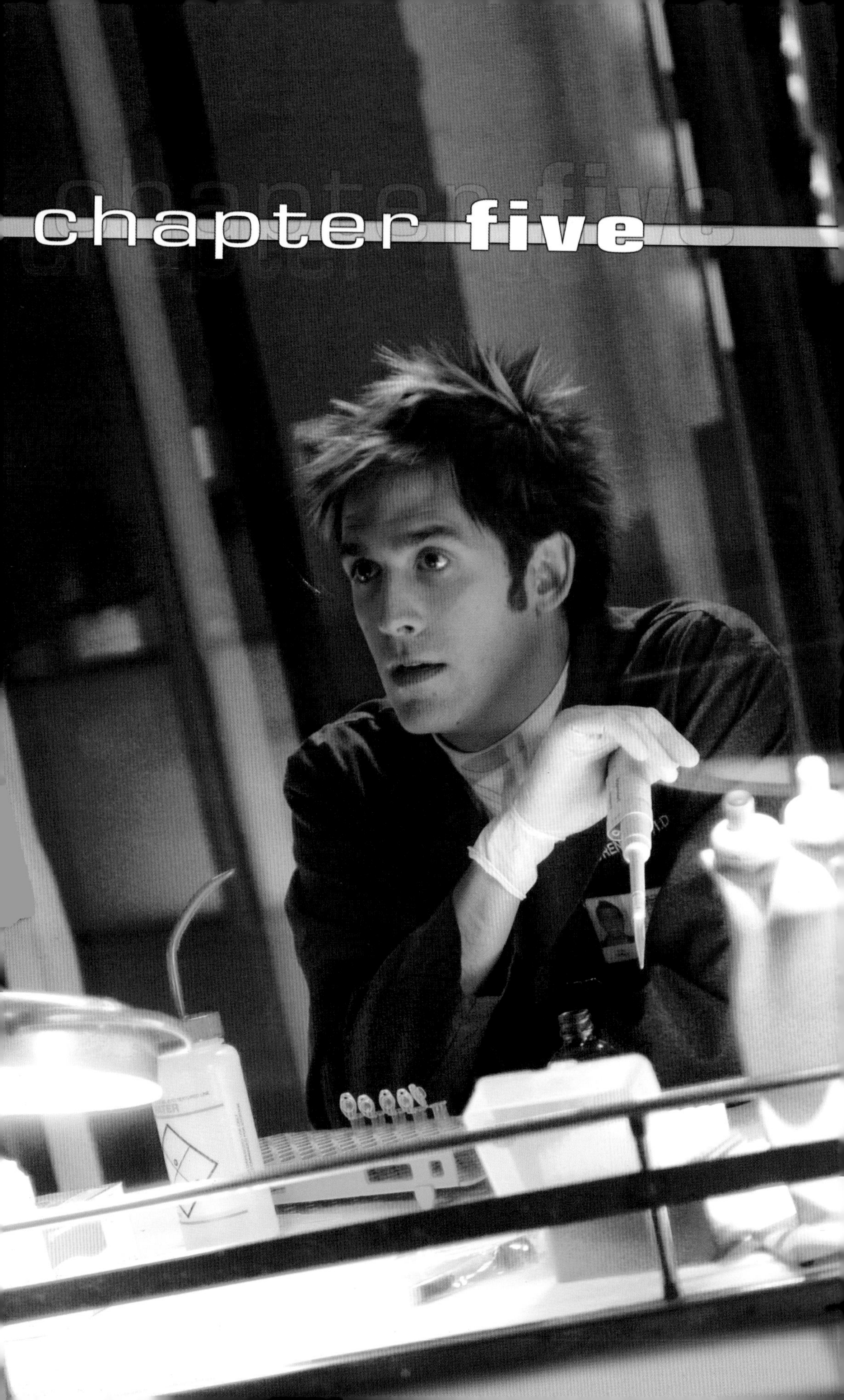

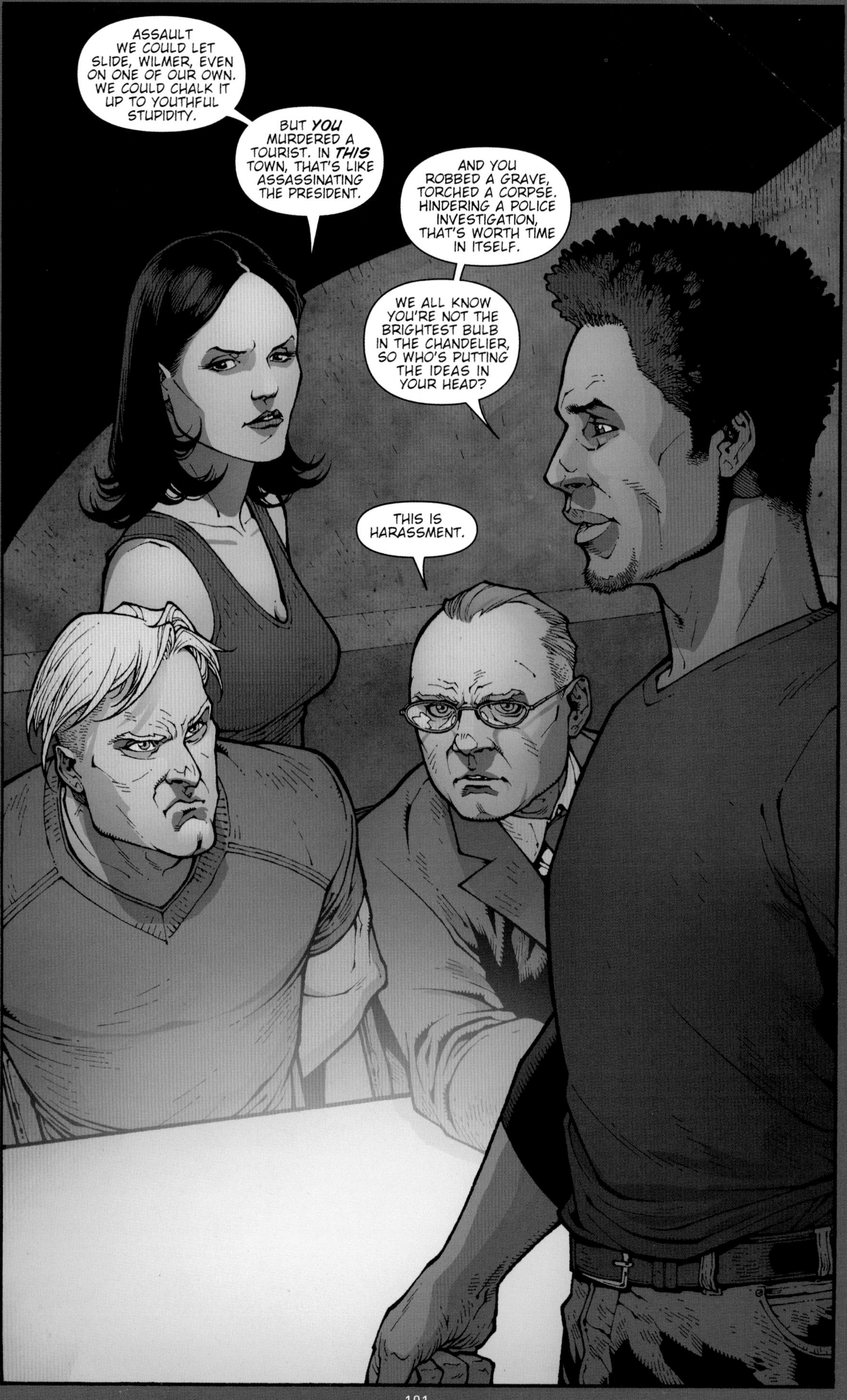
ASSAULT WE COULD LET SLIDE, WILMER, EVEN ON ONE OF OUR OWN. WE COULD CHALK IT UP TO YOUTHFUL STUPIDITY.
BUT YOU MURDERED A TOURIST. IN THIS TOWN, THAT'S LIKE ASSASSINATING THE PRESIDENT.
AND YOU ROBBED A GRAVE, TORCHED A CORPSE. HINDERING A POLICE INVESTIGATION, THAT'S WORTH TIME IN ITSELF.
WE ALL KNOW YOU'RE NOT THE BRIGHTEST BULB IN THE CHANDELIER, SO WHO'S PUTTING THE IDEAS IN YOUR HEAD?
THIS IS HARASSMENT.

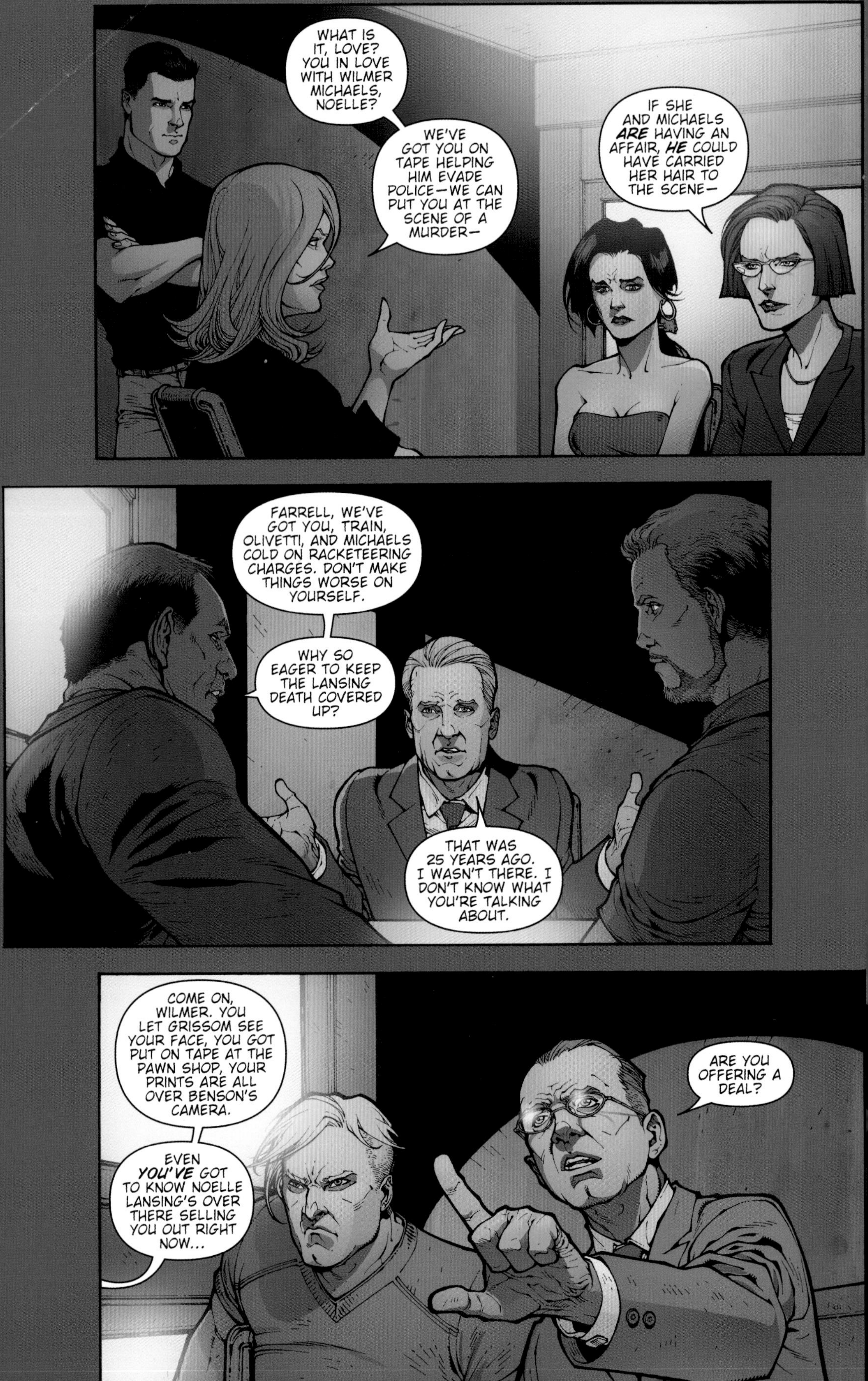
WHAT IS IT, LOVE? YOU IN LOVE WITH WILMER MICHAELS, NOELLE?
WE'VE GOT YOU ON TAPE HELPING HIM EVADE POLICE—WE CAN PUT YOU AT THE SCENE OF A MURDER—
IF SHE AND MICHAELS ***ARE*** HAVING AN AFFAIR, ***HE*** COULD HAVE CARRIED HER HAIR TO THE SCENE—
FARRELL, WE'VE GOT YOU, TRAIN, OLIVETTI, AND MICHAELS COLD ON RACKETEERING CHARGES. DON'T MAKE THINGS WORSE ON YOURSELF.
WHY SO EAGER TO KEEP THE LANSING DEATH COVERED UP?
THAT WAS 25 YEARS AGO. I WASN'T THERE. I DON'T KNOW WHAT YOU'RE TALKING ABOUT.
COME ON, WILMER. YOU LET GRISSOM SEE YOUR FACE, YOU GOT PUT ON TAPE AT THE PAWN SHOP, YOUR PRINTS ARE ALL OVER BENSON'S CAMERA.
EVEN ***YOU'VE*** GOT TO KNOW NOELLE LANSING'S OVER THERE SELLING YOU OUT RIGHT NOW...
ARE YOU OFFERING A DEAL?

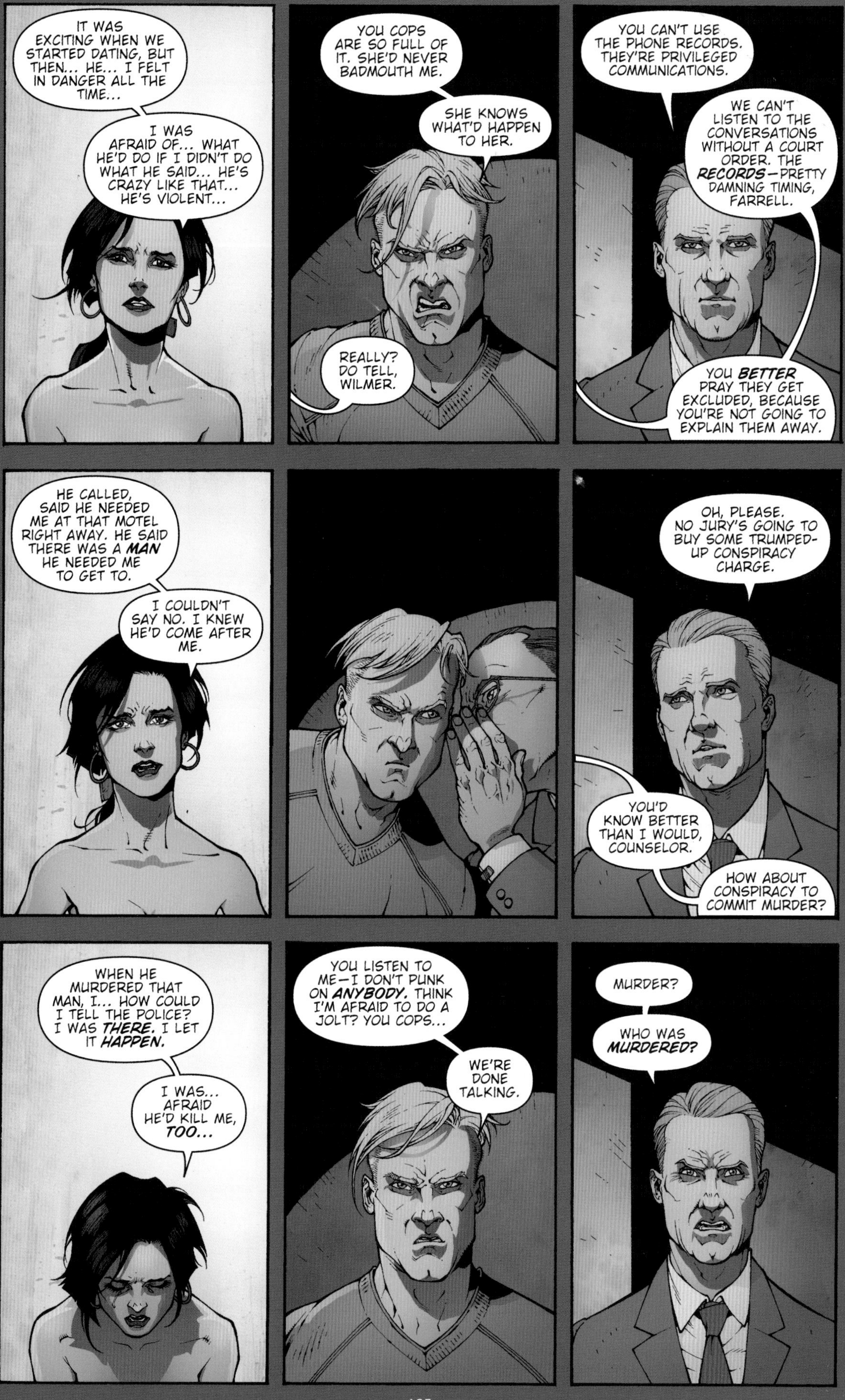
IT WAS EXCITING WHEN WE STARTED DATING, BUT THEN... HE... I FELT IN DANGER ALL THE TIME...
I WAS AFRAID OF... WHAT HE'D DO IF I DIDN'T DO WHAT HE SAID... HE'S CRAZY LIKE THAT... HE'S VIOLENT...
YOU COPS ARE SO FULL OF IT. SHE'D NEVER BADMOUTH ME.
SHE KNOWS WHAT'D HAPPEN TO HER.
REALLY? DO TELL, WILMER.
YOU CAN'T USE THE PHONE RECORDS. THEY'RE PRIVILEGED COMMUNICATIONS.
WE CAN'T LISTEN TO THE CONVERSATIONS WITHOUT A COURT ORDER. THE ***RECORDS***—PRETTY DAMNING TIMING, FARRELL.
YOU ***BETTER*** PRAY THEY GET EXCLUDED, BECAUSE YOU'RE NOT GOING TO EXPLAIN THEM AWAY.
HE CALLED, SAID HE NEEDED ME AT THAT MOTEL RIGHT AWAY. HE SAID THERE WAS A ***MAN*** HE NEEDED ME TO GET TO.
I COULDN'T SAY NO. I KNEW HE'D COME AFTER ME.
OH, PLEASE. NO JURY'S GOING TO BUY SOME TRUMPED-UP CONSPIRACY CHARGE.
YOU'D KNOW BETTER THAN I WOULD, COUNSELOR.
HOW ABOUT CONSPIRACY TO COMMIT MURDER?
WHEN HE MURDERED THAT MAN, I... HOW COULD I TELL THE POLICE? I WAS ***THERE.*** I LET IT ***HAPPEN.***
I WAS... AFRAID HE'D KILL ME, ***TOO...***
YOU LISTEN TO ME—I DON'T PUNK ON ***ANYBODY.*** THINK I'M AFRAID TO DO A JOLT? YOU COPS...
WE'RE DONE TALKING.
MURDER?
WHO WAS ***MURDERED?***

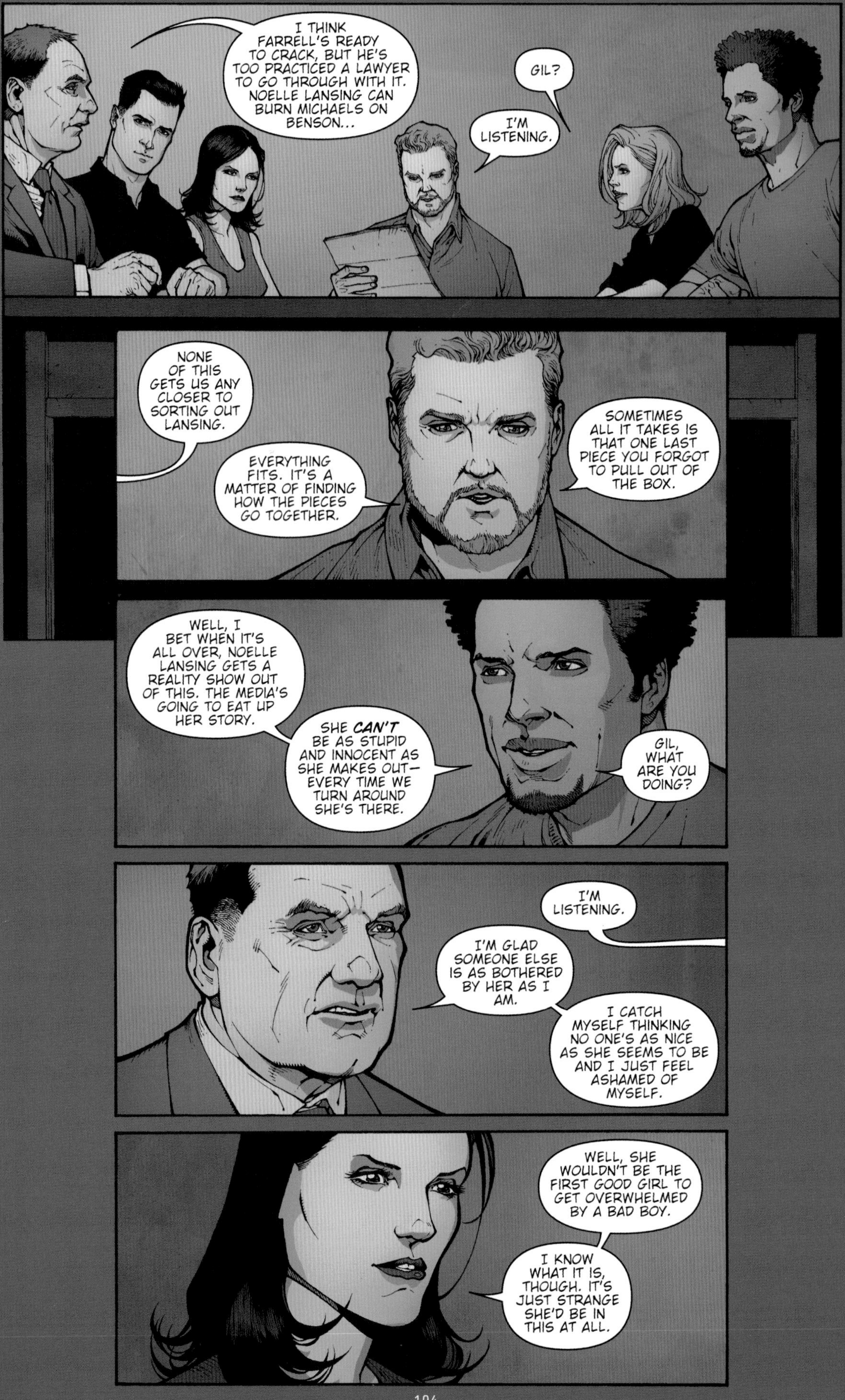
I THINK FARRELL'S READY TO CRACK, BUT HE'S TOO PRACTICED A LAWYER TO GO THROUGH WITH IT. NOELLE LANSING CAN BURN MICHAELS ON BENSON...
GIL?
I'M LISTENING.
NONE OF THIS GETS US ANY CLOSER TO SORTING OUT LANSING.
EVERYTHING FITS. IT'S A MATTER OF FINDING HOW THE PIECES GO TOGETHER.
SOMETIMES ALL IT TAKES IS THAT ONE LAST PIECE YOU FORGOT TO PULL OUT OF THE BOX.
WELL, I BET WHEN IT'S ALL OVER, NOELLE LANSING GETS A REALITY SHOW OUT OF THIS. THE MEDIA'S GOING TO EAT UP HER STORY.
SHE *CAN'T* BE AS STUPID AND INNOCENT AS SHE MAKES OUT— EVERY TIME WE TURN AROUND SHE'S THERE.
GIL, WHAT ARE YOU DOING?
I'M LISTENING.
I'M GLAD SOMEONE ELSE IS AS BOTHERED BY HER AS I AM.
I CATCH MYSELF THINKING NO ONE'S AS NICE AS SHE SEEMS TO BE AND I JUST FEEL ASHAMED OF MYSELF.
WELL, SHE WOULDN'T BE THE FIRST GOOD GIRL TO GET OVERWHELMED BY A BAD BOY.
I KNOW WHAT IT IS, THOUGH. IT'S JUST STRANGE SHE'D BE IN THIS AT ALL.

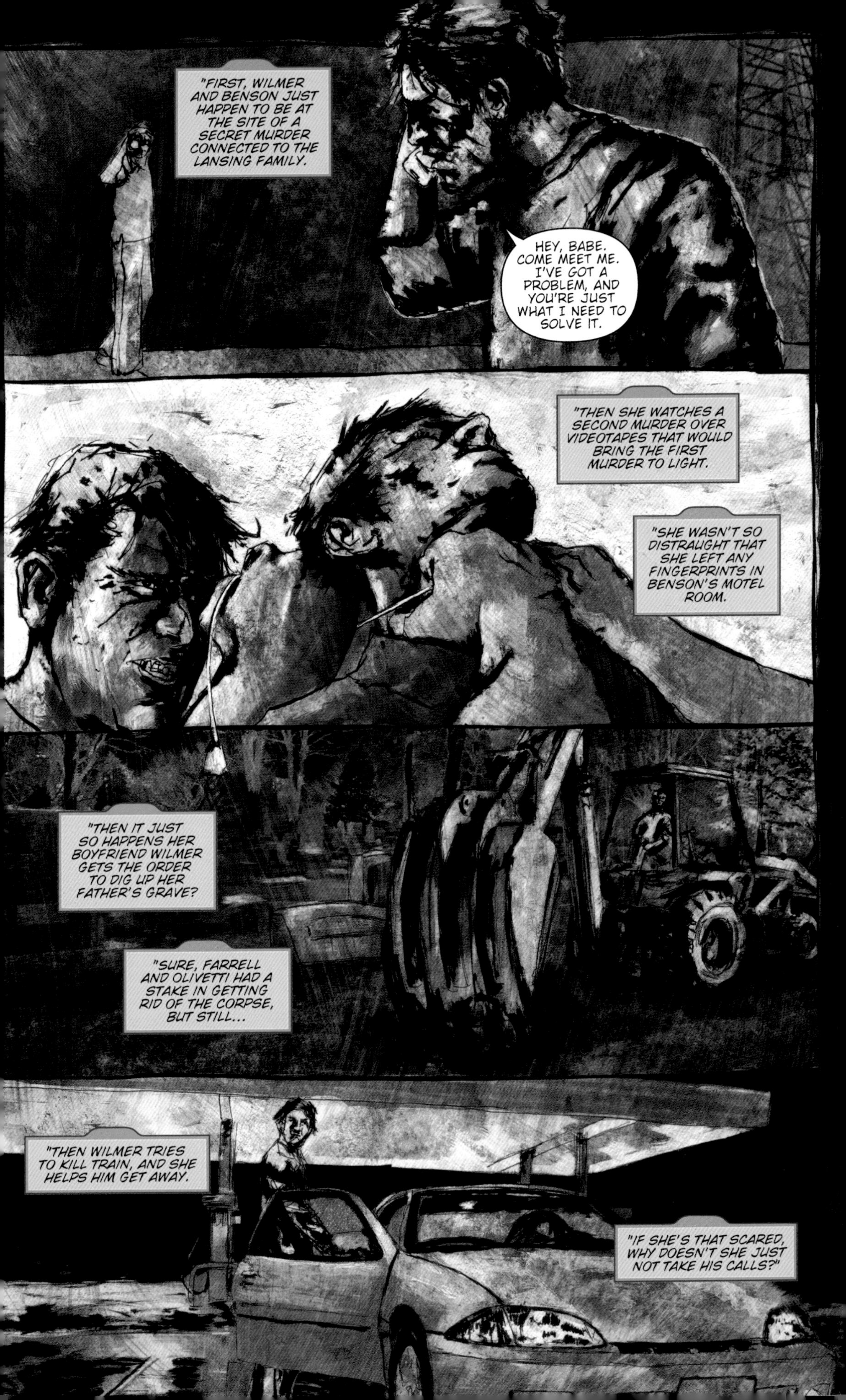
"FIRST, WILMER AND BENSON JUST HAPPEN TO BE AT THE SITE OF A SECRET MURDER CONNECTED TO THE LANSING FAMILY.
HEY, BABE. COME MEET ME. I'VE GOT A PROBLEM, AND YOU'RE JUST WHAT I NEED TO SOLVE IT.
"THEN SHE WATCHES A SECOND MURDER OVER VIDEOTAPES THAT WOULD BRING THE FIRST MURDER TO LIGHT.
"SHE WASN'T SO DISTRAUGHT THAT SHE LEFT ANY FINGERPRINTS IN BENSON'S MOTEL ROOM.
"THEN IT JUST SO HAPPENS HER BOYFRIEND WILMER GETS THE ORDER TO DIG UP HER FATHER'S GRAVE?
"SURE, FARRELL AND OLIVETTI HAD A STAKE IN GETTING RID OF THE CORPSE, BUT STILL...
"THEN WILMER TRIES TO KILL TRAIN, AND SHE HELPS HIM GET AWAY.
"IF SHE'S THAT SCARED, WHY DOESN'T SHE JUST NOT TAKE HIS CALLS?"

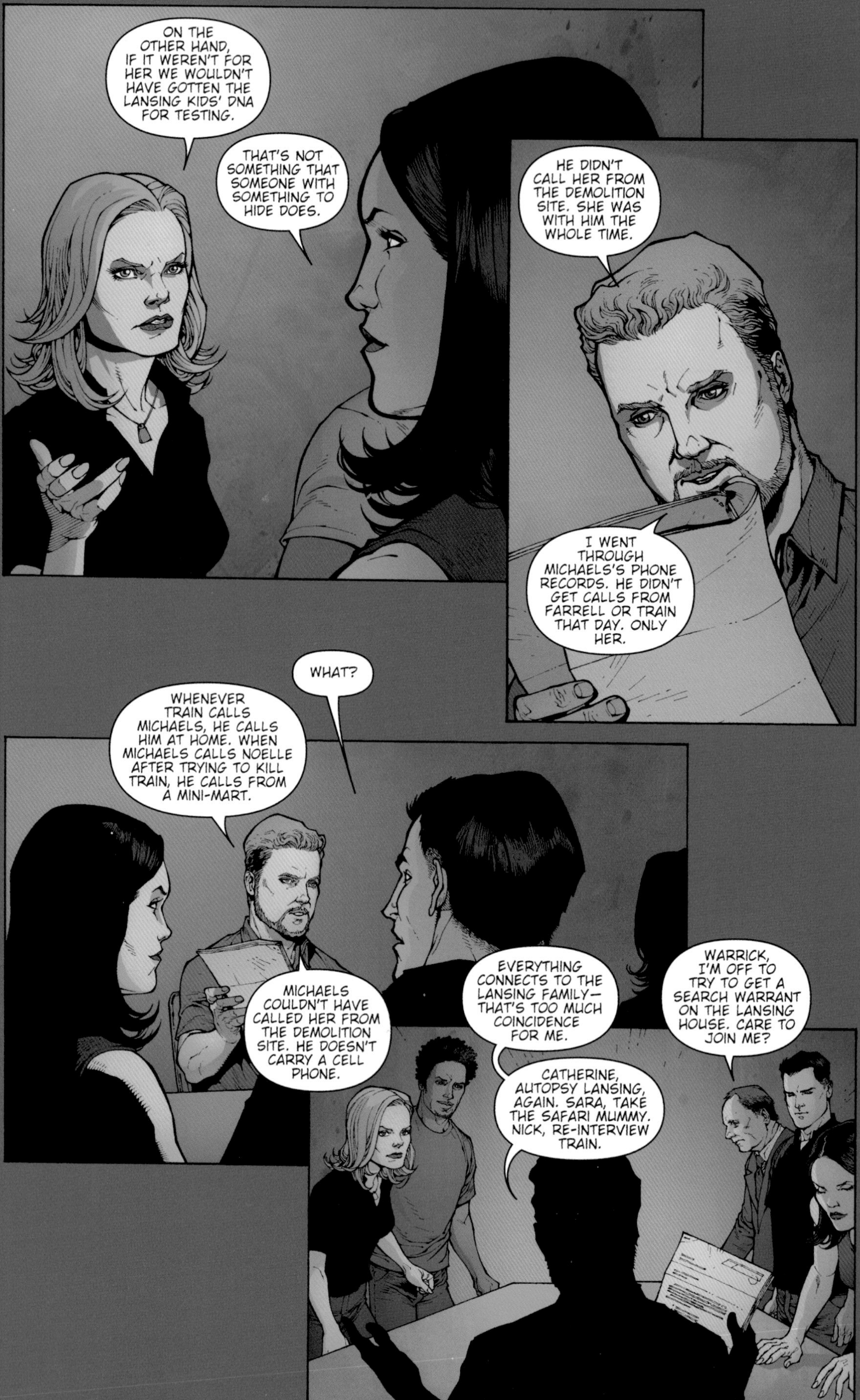
ON THE OTHER HAND, IF IT WEREN'T FOR HER WE WOULDN'T HAVE GOTTEN THE LANSING KIDS' DNA FOR TESTING.
THAT'S NOT SOMETHING THAT SOMEONE WITH SOMETHING TO HIDE DOES.
HE DIDN'T CALL HER FROM THE DEMOLITION SITE. SHE WAS WITH HIM THE WHOLE TIME.
I WENT THROUGH MICHAELS'S PHONE RECORDS. HE DIDN'T GET CALLS FROM FARRELL OR TRAIN THAT DAY. ONLY HER.
WHAT?
WHENEVER TRAIN CALLS MICHAELS, HE CALLS HIM AT HOME. WHEN MICHAELS CALLS NOELLE AFTER TRYING TO KILL TRAIN, HE CALLS FROM A MINI-MART.
MICHAELS COULDN'T HAVE CALLED HER FROM THE DEMOLITION SITE. HE DOESN'T CARRY A CELL PHONE.
EVERYTHING CONNECTS TO THE LANSING FAMILY— THAT'S TOO MUCH COINCIDENCE FOR ME.
CATHERINE, AUTOPSY LANSING, AGAIN. SARA, TAKE THE SAFARI MUMMY. NICK, RE-INTERVIEW TRAIN.
WARRICK, I'M OFF TO TRY TO GET A SEARCH WARRANT ON THE LANSING HOUSE. CARE TO JOIN ME?

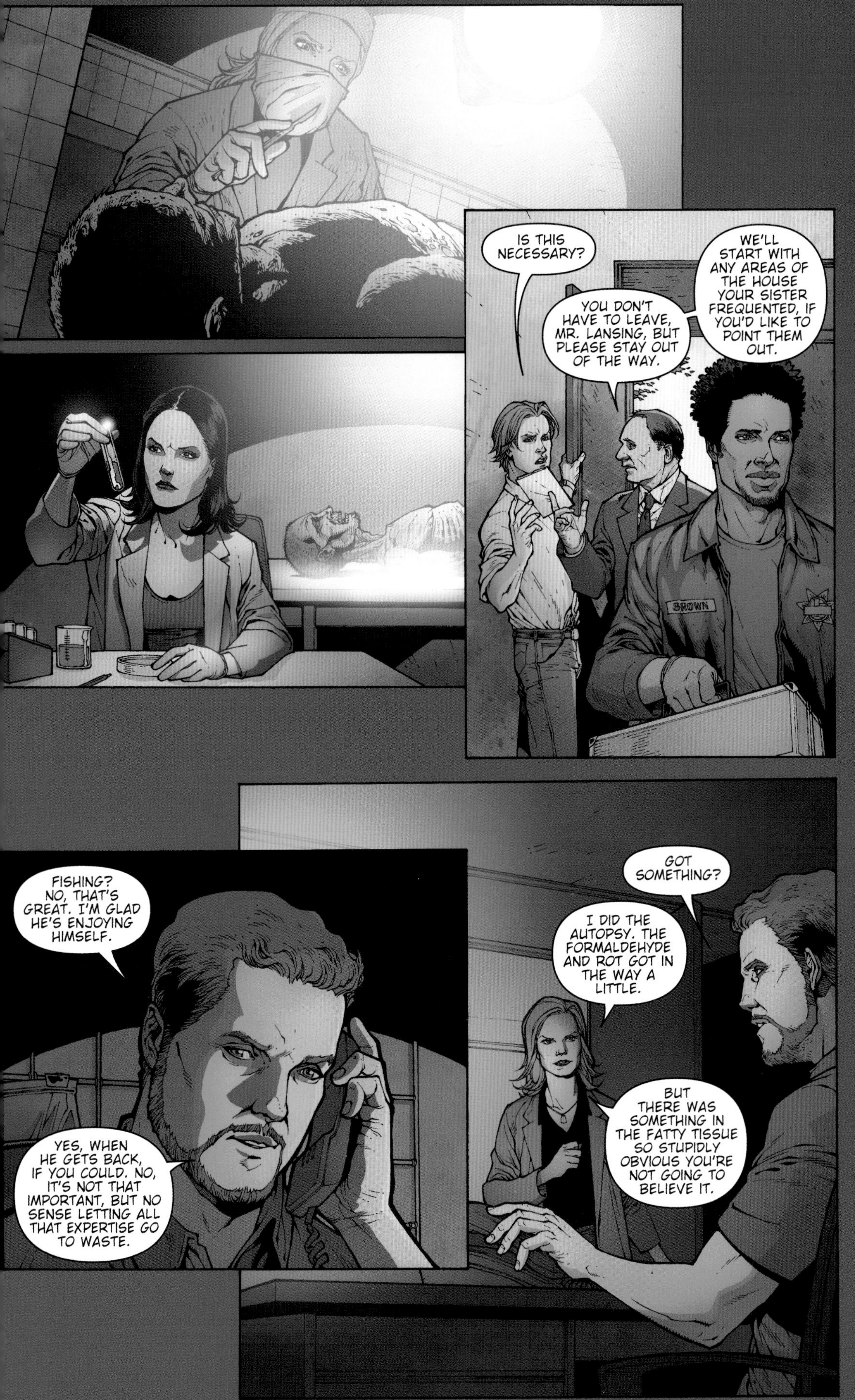

IS THIS NECESSARY?
YOU DON'T HAVE TO LEAVE, MR. LANSING, BUT PLEASE STAY OUT OF THE WAY.
WE'LL START WITH ANY AREAS OF THE HOUSE YOUR SISTER FREQUENTED, IF YOU'D LIKE TO POINT THEM OUT.
BROWN
FISHING? NO, THAT'S GREAT. I'M GLAD HE'S ENJOYING HIMSELF.
YES, WHEN HE GETS BACK, IF YOU COULD. NO, IT'S NOT THAT IMPORTANT, BUT NO SENSE LETTING ALL THAT EXPERTISE GO TO WASTE.
GOT SOMETHING?
I DID THE AUTOPSY. THE FORMALDEHYDE AND ROT GOT IN THE WAY A LITTLE.
BUT THERE WAS SOMETHING IN THE FATTY TISSUE SO STUPIDLY OBVIOUS YOU'RE NOT GOING TO BELIEVE IT.

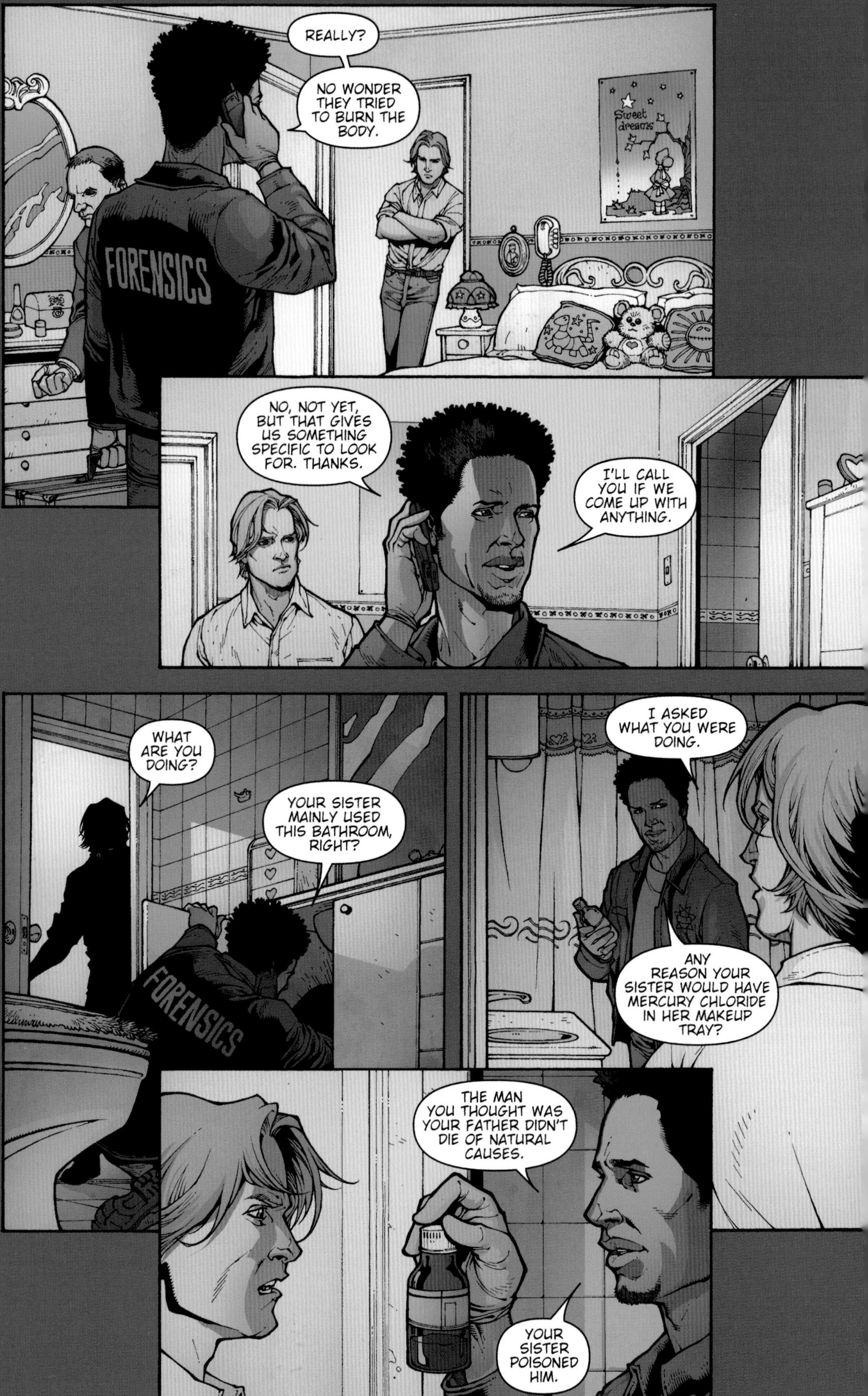
REALLY?
NO WONDER THEY TRIED TO BURN THE BODY.
FORENSICS
Sweet dreams
NO, NOT YET, BUT THAT GIVES US SOMETHING SPECIFIC TO LOOK FOR. THANKS.
I'LL CALL YOU IF WE COME UP WITH ANYTHING.
WHAT ARE YOU DOING?
YOUR SISTER MAINLY USED THIS BATHROOM, RIGHT?
FORENSICS
I ASKED WHAT YOU WERE DOING.
ANY REASON YOUR SISTER WOULD HAVE MERCURY CHLORIDE IN HER MAKEUP TRAY?
THE MAN YOU THOUGHT WAS YOUR FATHER DIDN'T DIE OF NATURAL CAUSES.
YOUR SISTER POISONED HIM.

DEREK...

OH, *DEREK*... DEREK *TRAI-AIN*...

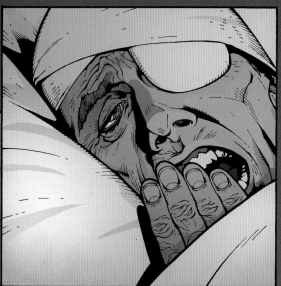

HELLO, DEREK.

WHAT ARE *YOU* DOING HERE?!

NURSE! NURSE!

AND AFTER I SAVED YOUR LIFE.

ALL I WAS GOING TO DO WAS SAVE YOUR LIFE AGAIN.

WHAT DO YOU MEAN?

I KNOW YOU'RE JUST A HARMLESS OLD GO-BETWEEN, BUT EVEN THEY CAN LIVE OUT THEIR TWILIGHT YEARS IN A PENITENTIARY.

I'LL MAKE YOU A DEAL. I'LL TELL YOU WHAT WE'VE GOT, AND THEN YOU TELL ME HOW YOU WANT TO SPEND THE REST OF YOUR LIFE. OKAY?

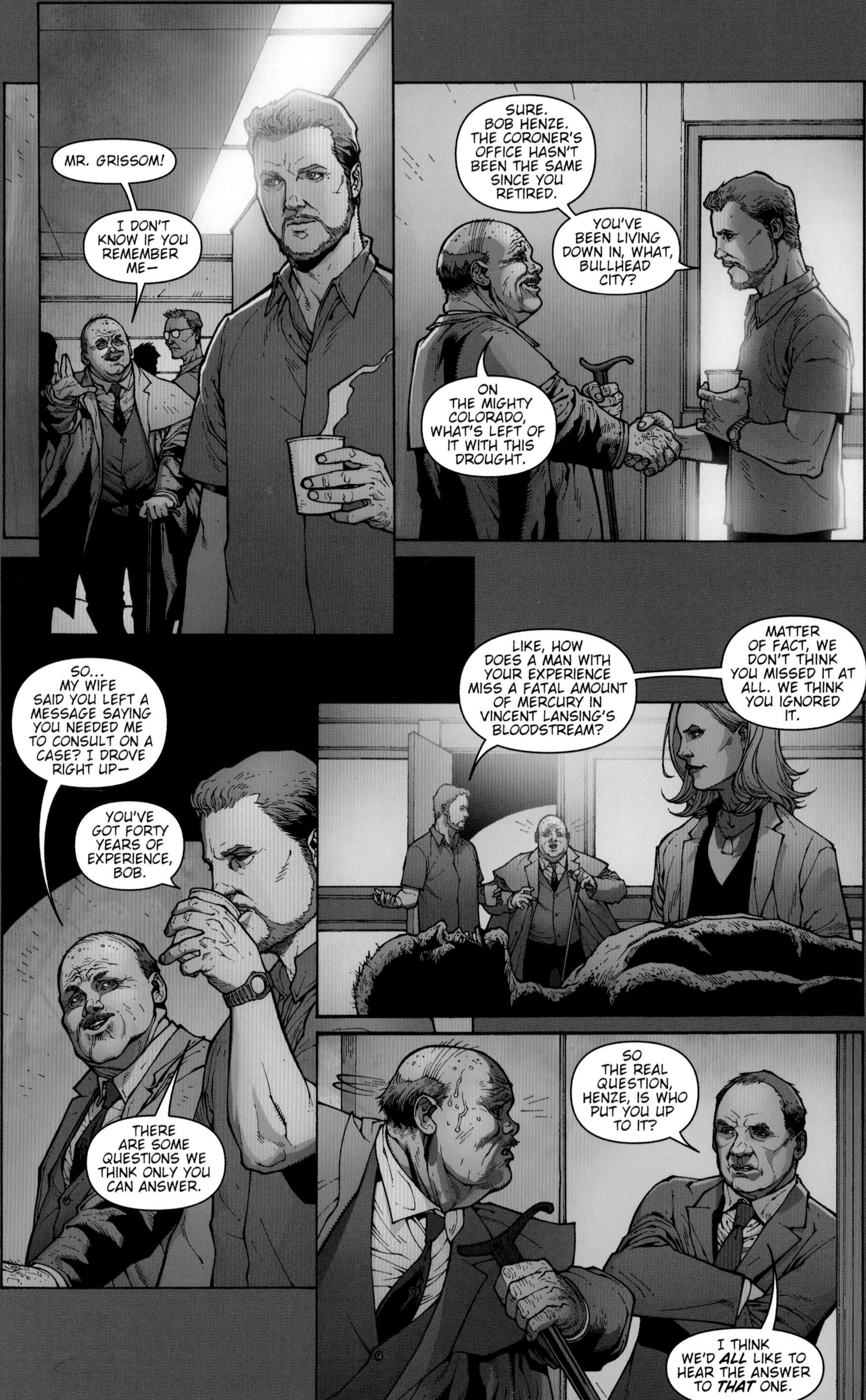
MR. GRISSOM!
I DON'T KNOW IF YOU REMEMBER ME—
SURE. BOB HENZE. THE CORONER'S OFFICE HASN'T BEEN THE SAME SINCE YOU RETIRED.
YOU'VE BEEN LIVING DOWN IN, WHAT, BULLHEAD CITY?
ON THE MIGHTY COLORADO, WHAT'S LEFT OF IT WITH THIS DROUGHT.
SO... MY WIFE SAID YOU LEFT A MESSAGE SAYING YOU NEEDED ME TO CONSULT ON A CASE? I DROVE RIGHT UP—
YOU'VE GOT FORTY YEARS OF EXPERIENCE, BOB.
THERE ARE SOME QUESTIONS WE THINK ONLY YOU CAN ANSWER.
LIKE, HOW DOES A MAN WITH YOUR EXPERIENCE MISS A FATAL AMOUNT OF MERCURY IN VINCENT LANSING'S BLOODSTREAM?
MATTER OF FACT, WE DON'T THINK YOU MISSED IT AT ALL. WE THINK YOU IGNORED IT.
SO THE REAL QUESTION, HENZE, IS WHO PUT YOU UP TO IT?
I THINK WE'D ***ALL*** LIKE TO HEAR THE ANSWER TO ***THAT*** ONE.

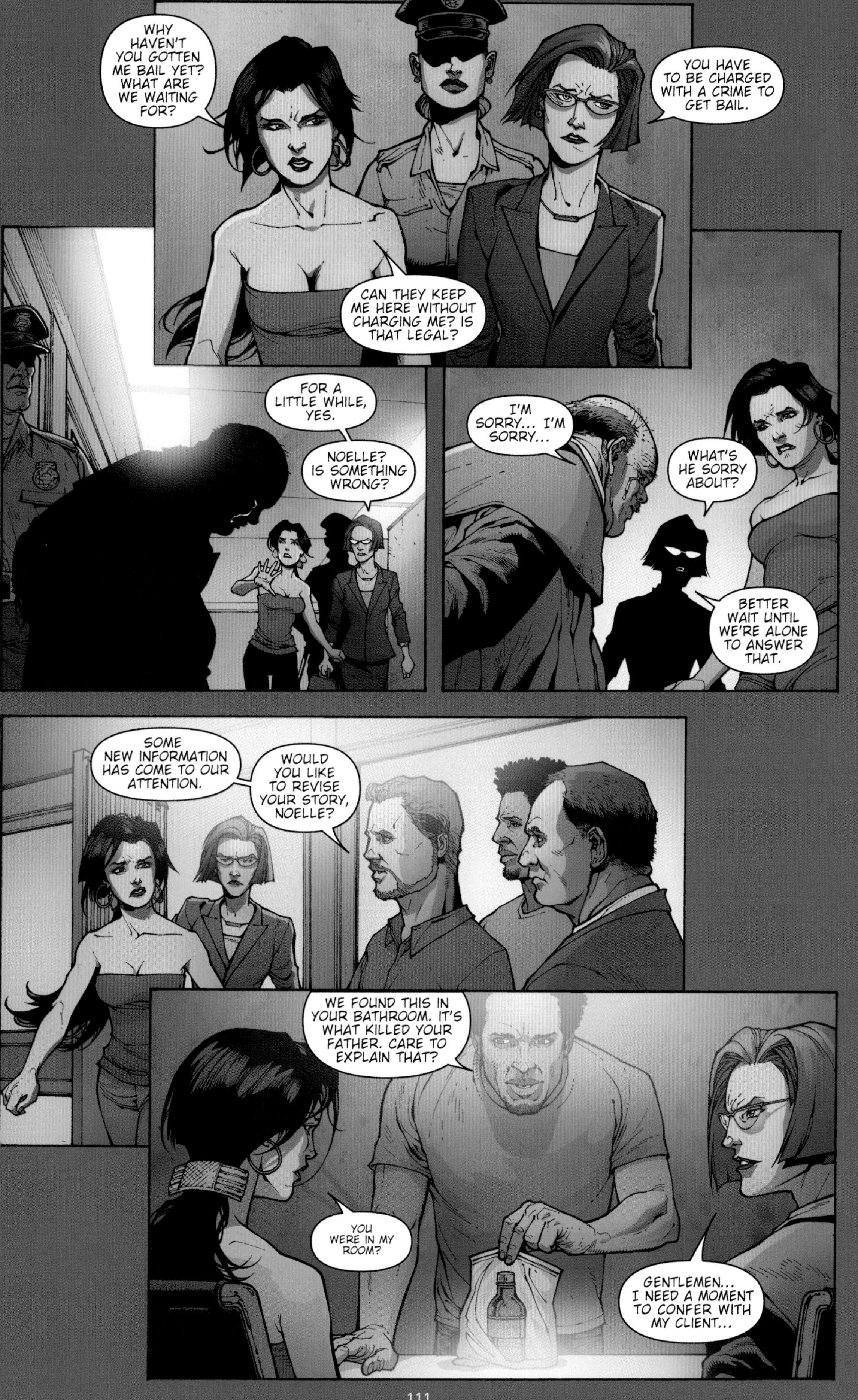
WHY HAVEN'T YOU GOTTEN ME BAIL YET? WHAT ARE WE WAITING FOR?
YOU HAVE TO BE CHARGED WITH A CRIME TO GET BAIL.
CAN THEY KEEP ME HERE WITHOUT CHARGING ME? IS THAT LEGAL?
FOR A LITTLE WHILE, YES.
NOELLE? IS SOMETHING WRONG?
I'M SORRY... I'M SORRY...
WHAT'S HE SORRY ABOUT?
BETTER WAIT UNTIL WE'RE ALONE TO ANSWER THAT.
SOME NEW INFORMATION HAS COME TO OUR ATTENTION.
WOULD YOU LIKE TO REVISE YOUR STORY, NOELLE?
WE FOUND THIS IN YOUR BATHROOM. IT'S WHAT KILLED YOUR FATHER. CARE TO EXPLAIN THAT?
YOU WERE IN MY ROOM?
GENTLEMEN... I NEED A MOMENT TO CONFER WITH MY CLIENT...

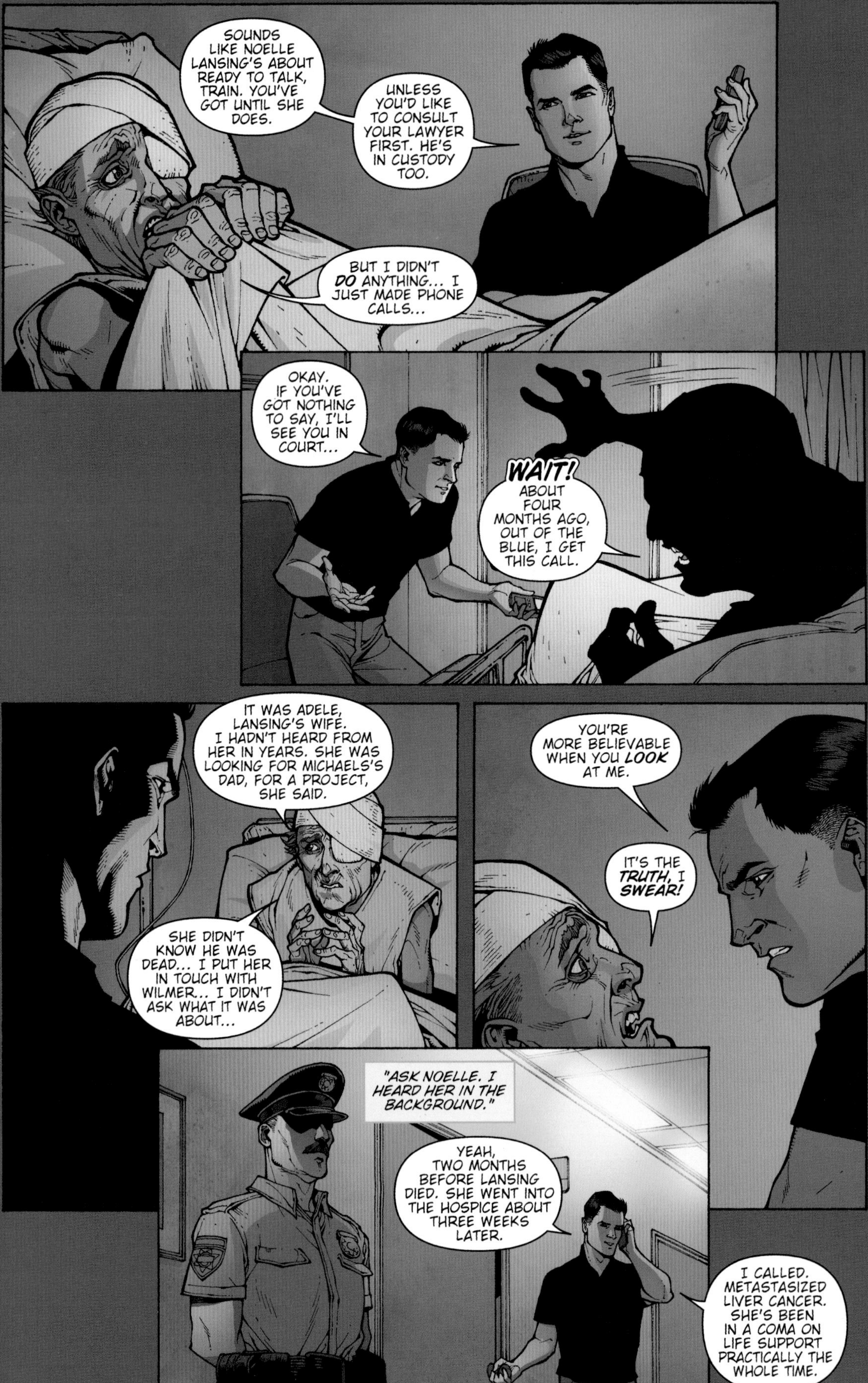
SOUNDS LIKE NOELLE LANSING'S ABOUT READY TO TALK, TRAIN. YOU'VE GOT UNTIL SHE DOES.
UNLESS YOU'D LIKE TO CONSULT YOUR LAWYER FIRST. HE'S IN CUSTODY TOO.
BUT I DIDN'T DO ANYTHING... I JUST MADE PHONE CALLS...
OKAY. IF YOU'VE GOT NOTHING TO SAY, I'LL SEE YOU IN COURT...
WAIT! ABOUT FOUR MONTHS AGO, OUT OF THE BLUE, I GET THIS CALL.
IT WAS ADELE, LANSING'S WIFE. I HADN'T HEARD FROM HER IN YEARS. SHE WAS LOOKING FOR MICHAELS'S DAD, FOR A PROJECT, SHE SAID.
SHE DIDN'T KNOW HE WAS DEAD... I PUT HER IN TOUCH WITH WILMER... I DIDN'T ASK WHAT IT WAS ABOUT...
YOU'RE MORE BELIEVABLE WHEN YOU LOOK AT ME.
IT'S THE TRUTH, I SWEAR!
"ASK NOELLE. I HEARD HER IN THE BACKGROUND."
YEAH, TWO MONTHS BEFORE LANSING DIED. SHE WENT INTO THE HOSPICE ABOUT THREE WEEKS LATER.
I CALLED. METASTASIZED LIVER CANCER. SHE'S BEEN IN A COMA ON LIFE SUPPORT PRACTICALLY THE WHOLE TIME.

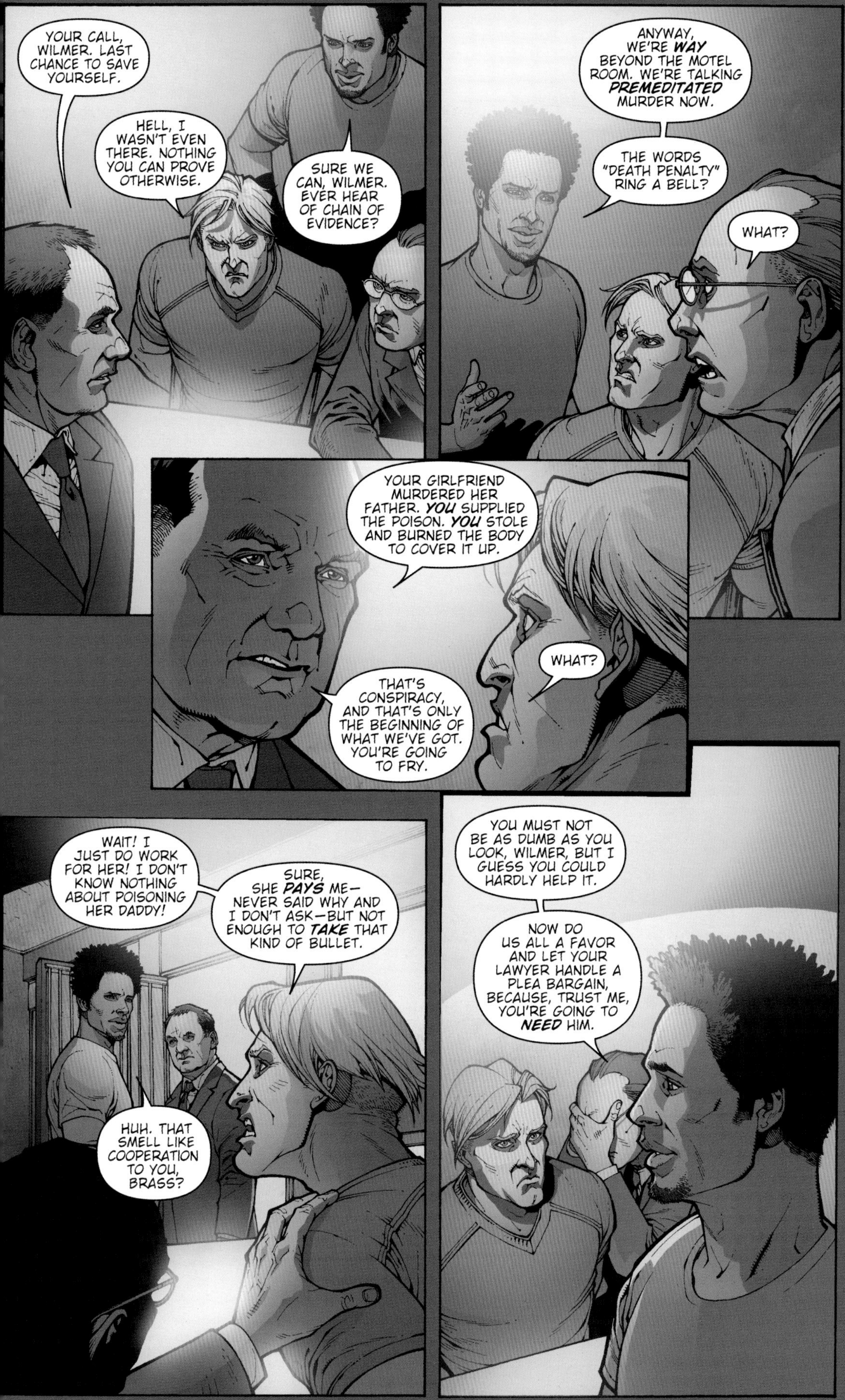
YOUR CALL, WILMER. LAST CHANCE TO SAVE YOURSELF.
HELL, I WASN'T EVEN THERE. NOTHING YOU CAN PROVE OTHERWISE.
SURE WE CAN, WILMER. EVER HEAR OF CHAIN OF EVIDENCE?
ANYWAY, WE'RE WAY BEYOND THE MOTEL ROOM. WE'RE TALKING PREMEDITATED MURDER NOW.
THE WORDS "DEATH PENALTY" RING A BELL?
WHAT?
YOUR GIRLFRIEND MURDERED HER FATHER. YOU SUPPLIED THE POISON. YOU STOLE AND BURNED THE BODY TO COVER IT UP.
WHAT?
THAT'S CONSPIRACY, AND THAT'S ONLY THE BEGINNING OF WHAT WE'VE GOT. YOU'RE GOING TO FRY.
WAIT! I JUST DO WORK FOR HER! I DON'T KNOW NOTHING ABOUT POISONING HER DADDY!
SURE, SHE PAYS ME—NEVER SAID WHY AND I DON'T ASK—BUT NOT ENOUGH TO TAKE THAT KIND OF BULLET.
HUH. THAT SMELL LIKE COOPERATION TO YOU, BRASS?
YOU MUST NOT BE AS DUMB AS YOU LOOK, WILMER, BUT I GUESS YOU COULD HARDLY HELP IT.
NOW DO US ALL A FAVOR AND LET YOUR LAWYER HANDLE A PLEA BARGAIN, BECAUSE, TRUST ME, YOU'RE GOING TO NEED HIM.

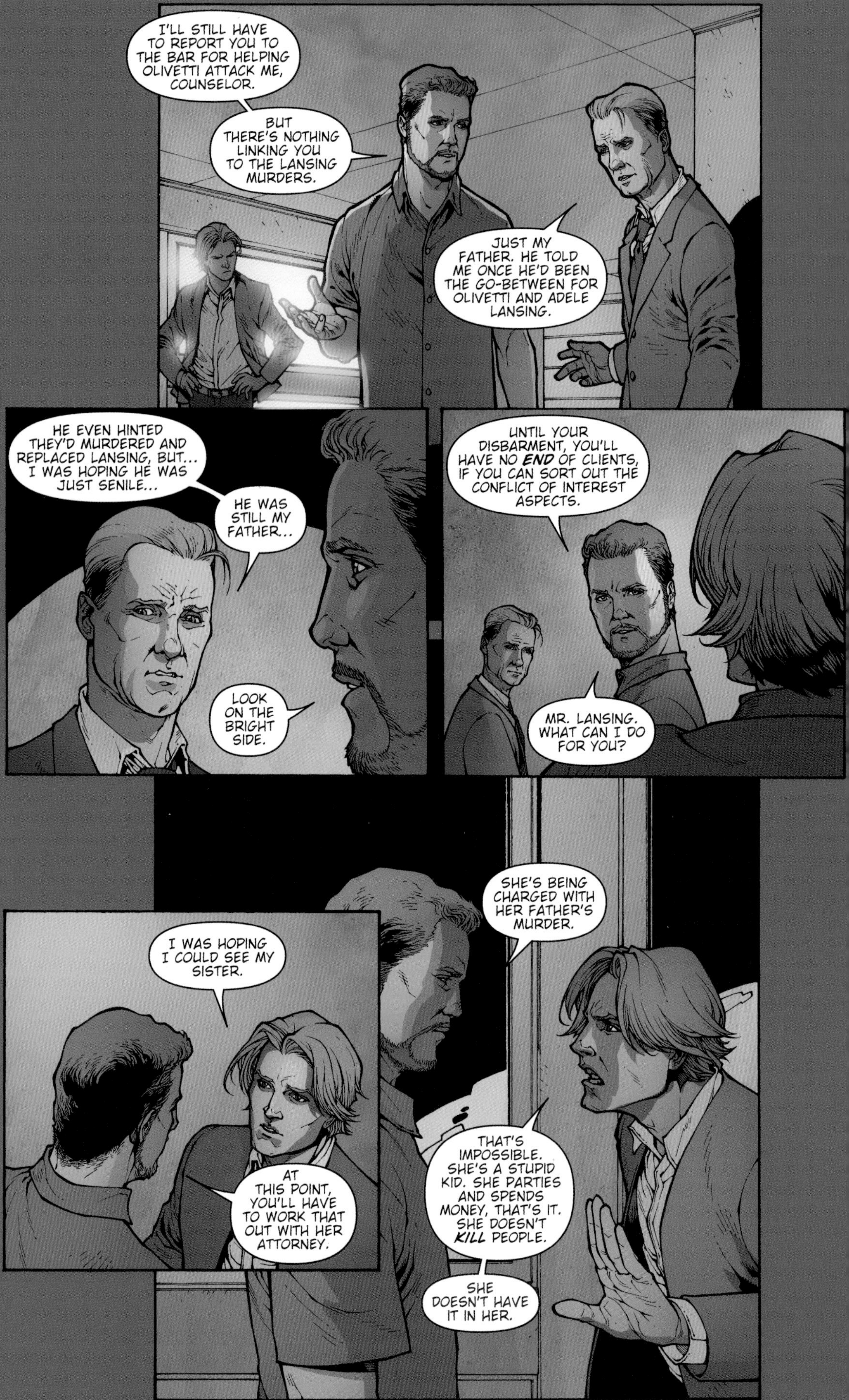
I'LL STILL HAVE TO REPORT YOU TO THE BAR FOR HELPING OLIVETTI ATTACK ME, COUNSELOR.
BUT THERE'S NOTHING LINKING YOU TO THE LANSING MURDERS.
JUST MY FATHER. HE TOLD ME ONCE HE'D BEEN THE GO-BETWEEN FOR OLIVETTI AND ADELE LANSING.
HE EVEN HINTED THEY'D MURDERED AND REPLACED LANSING, BUT... I WAS HOPING HE WAS JUST SENILE...
HE WAS STILL MY FATHER...
LOOK ON THE BRIGHT SIDE.
UNTIL YOUR DISBARMENT, YOU'LL HAVE NO END OF CLIENTS, IF YOU CAN SORT OUT THE CONFLICT OF INTEREST ASPECTS.
MR. LANSING. WHAT CAN I DO FOR YOU?
I WAS HOPING I COULD SEE MY SISTER.
AT THIS POINT, YOU'LL HAVE TO WORK THAT OUT WITH HER ATTORNEY.
SHE'S BEING CHARGED WITH HER FATHER'S MURDER.
THAT'S IMPOSSIBLE. SHE'S A STUPID KID. SHE PARTIES AND SPENDS MONEY, THAT'S IT. SHE DOESN'T KILL PEOPLE.
SHE DOESN'T HAVE IT IN HER.

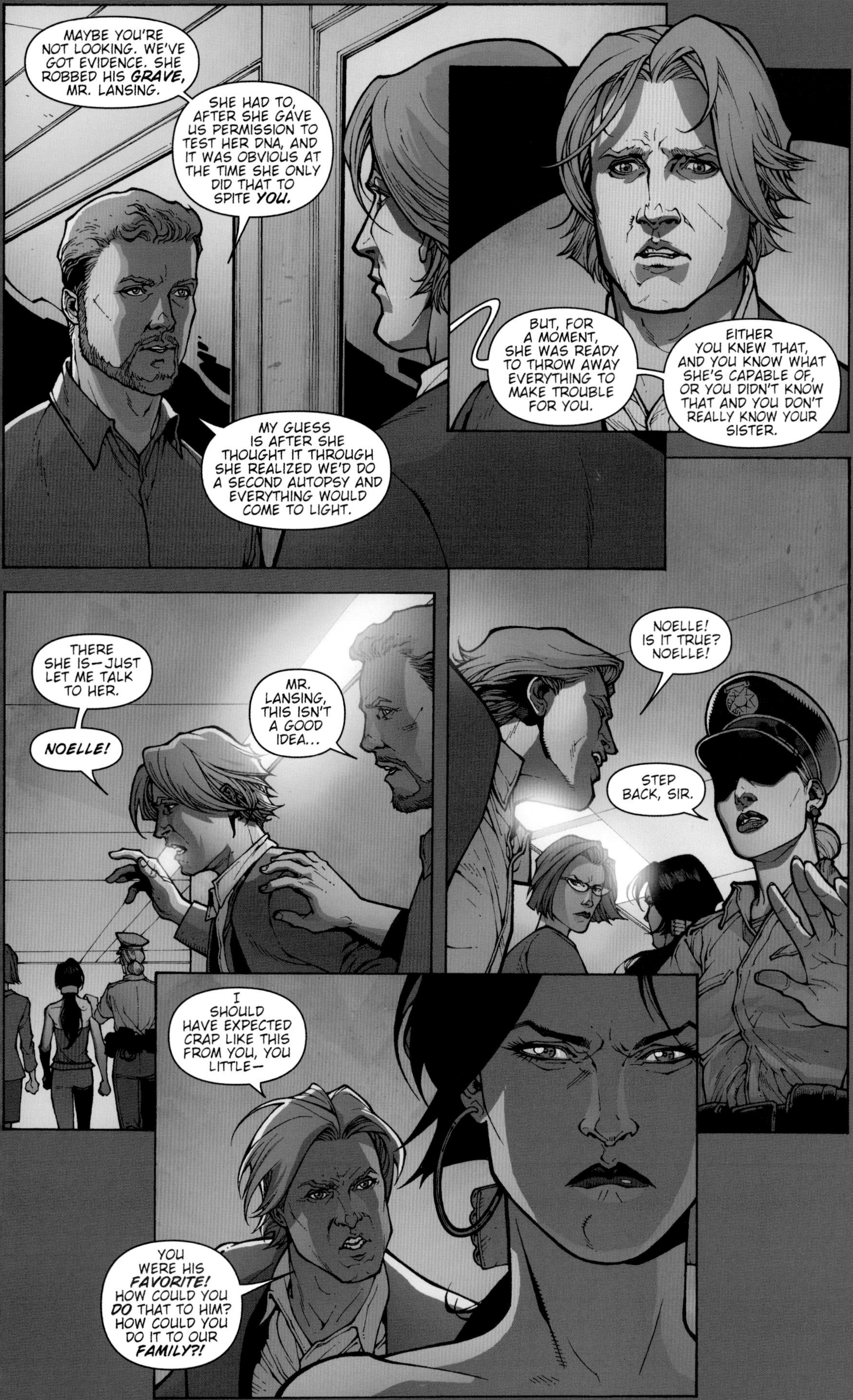

MAYBE YOU'RE NOT LOOKING. WE'VE GOT EVIDENCE. SHE ROBBED HIS GRAVE, MR. LANSING.
SHE HAD TO, AFTER SHE GAVE US PERMISSION TO TEST HER DNA, AND IT WAS OBVIOUS AT THE TIME SHE ONLY DID THAT TO SPITE YOU.
MY GUESS IS AFTER SHE THOUGHT IT THROUGH SHE REALIZED WE'D DO A SECOND AUTOPSY AND EVERYTHING WOULD COME TO LIGHT.
BUT, FOR A MOMENT, SHE WAS READY TO THROW AWAY EVERYTHING TO MAKE TROUBLE FOR YOU.
EITHER YOU KNEW THAT, AND YOU KNOW WHAT SHE'S CAPABLE OF, OR YOU DIDN'T KNOW THAT AND YOU DON'T REALLY KNOW YOUR SISTER.
THERE SHE IS—JUST LET ME TALK TO HER.
NOELLE!
MR. LANSING, THIS ISN'T A GOOD IDEA...
NOELLE! IS IT TRUE? NOELLE!
STEP BACK, SIR.
I SHOULD HAVE EXPECTED CRAP LIKE THIS FROM YOU, YOU LITTLE—
YOU WERE HIS FAVORITE! HOW COULD YOU DO THAT TO HIM? HOW COULD YOU DO IT TO OUR FAMILY?!

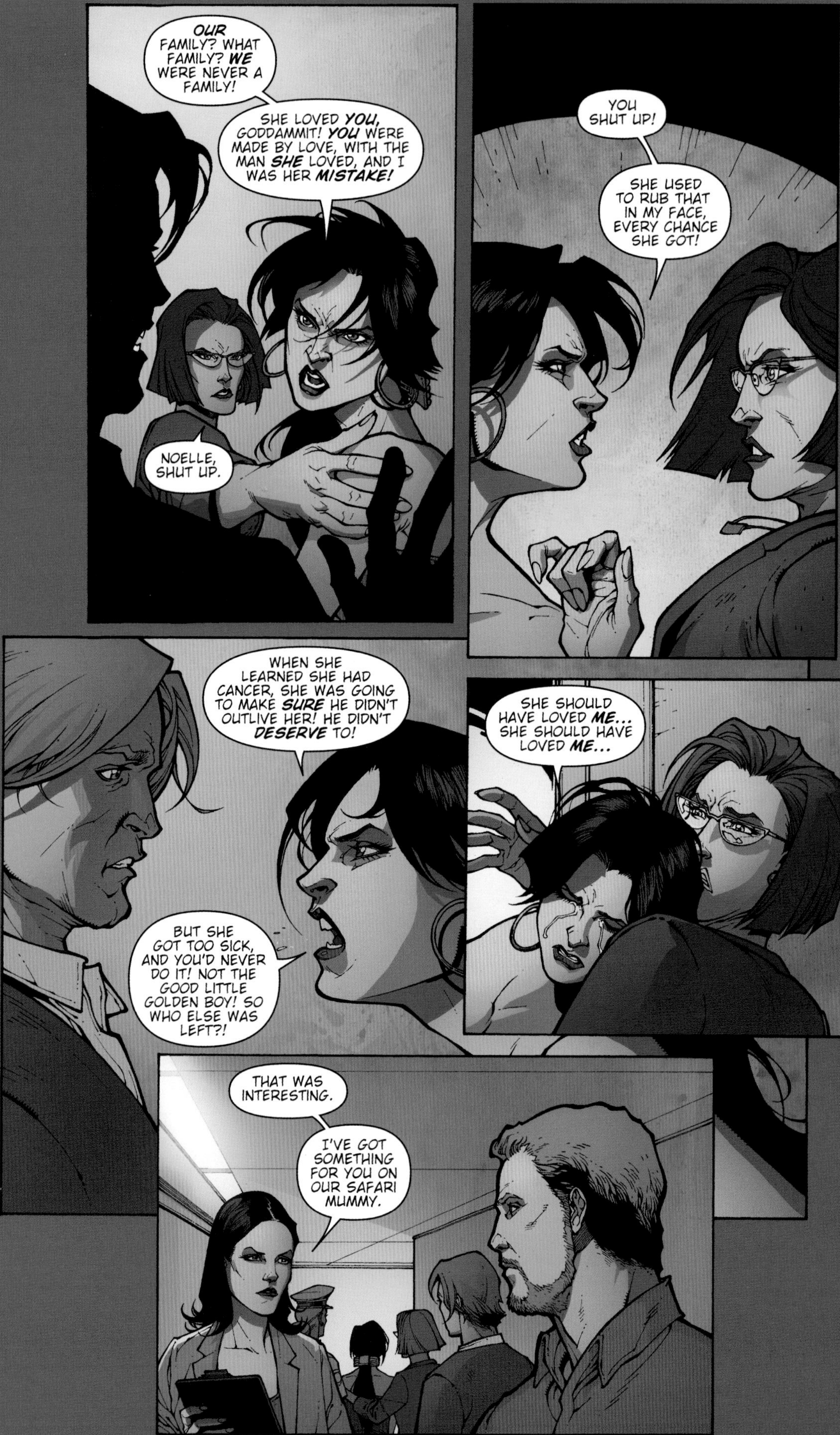
OUR FAMILY? WHAT FAMILY? WE WERE NEVER A FAMILY!
SHE LOVED YOU, GODDAMMIT! YOU WERE MADE BY LOVE, WITH THE MAN SHE LOVED, AND I WAS HER MISTAKE!
NOELLE, SHUT UP.
YOU SHUT UP!
SHE USED TO RUB THAT IN MY FACE, EVERY CHANCE SHE GOT!
WHEN SHE LEARNED SHE HAD CANCER, SHE WAS GOING TO MAKE SURE HE DIDN'T OUTLIVE HER! HE DIDN'T DESERVE TO!
BUT SHE GOT TOO SICK, AND YOU'D NEVER DO IT! NOT THE GOOD LITTLE GOLDEN BOY! SO WHO ELSE WAS LEFT?!
SHE SHOULD HAVE LOVED ME... SHE SHOULD HAVE LOVED ME...
THAT WAS INTERESTING.
I'VE GOT SOMETHING FOR YOU ON OUR SAFARI MUMMY.

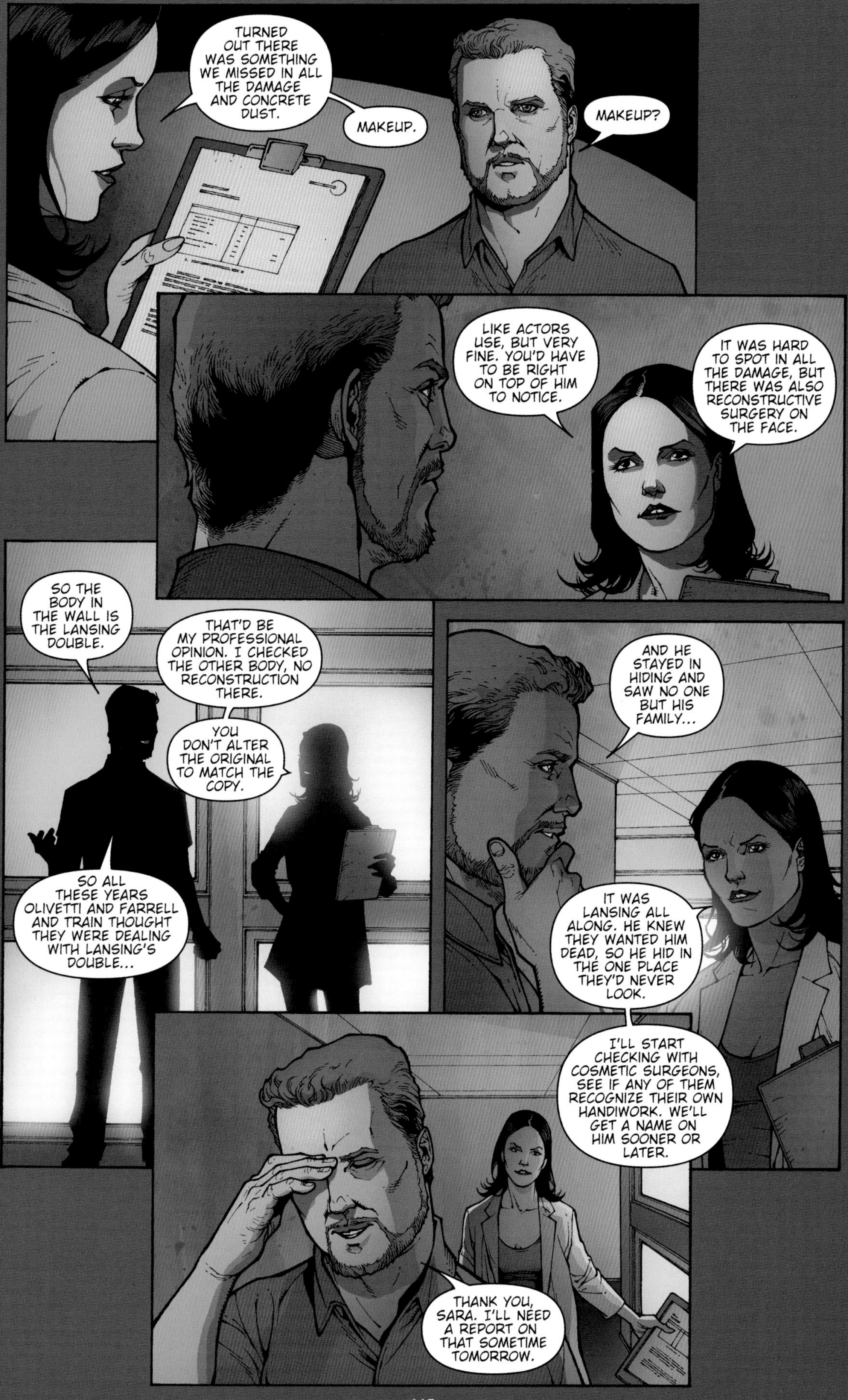
TURNED OUT THERE WAS SOMETHING WE MISSED IN ALL THE DAMAGE AND CONCRETE DUST.
MAKEUP.
MAKEUP?
LIKE ACTORS USE, BUT VERY FINE. YOU'D HAVE TO BE RIGHT ON TOP OF HIM TO NOTICE.
IT WAS HARD TO SPOT IN ALL THE DAMAGE, BUT THERE WAS ALSO RECONSTRUCTIVE SURGERY ON THE FACE.
SO THE BODY IN THE WALL IS THE LANSING DOUBLE.
THAT'D BE MY PROFESSIONAL OPINION. I CHECKED THE OTHER BODY, NO RECONSTRUCTION THERE.
YOU DON'T ALTER THE ORIGINAL TO MATCH THE COPY.
SO ALL THESE YEARS OLIVETTI AND FARRELL AND TRAIN THOUGHT THEY WERE DEALING WITH LANSING'S DOUBLE...
AND HE STAYED IN HIDING AND SAW NO ONE BUT HIS FAMILY...
IT WAS LANSING ALL ALONG. HE KNEW THEY WANTED HIM DEAD, SO HE HID IN THE ONE PLACE THEY'D NEVER LOOK.
I'LL START CHECKING WITH COSMETIC SURGEONS, SEE IF ANY OF THEM RECOGNIZE THEIR OWN HANDIWORK. WE'LL GET A NAME ON HIM SOONER OR LATER.
THANK YOU, SARA. I'LL NEED A REPORT ON THAT SOMETIME TOMORROW.

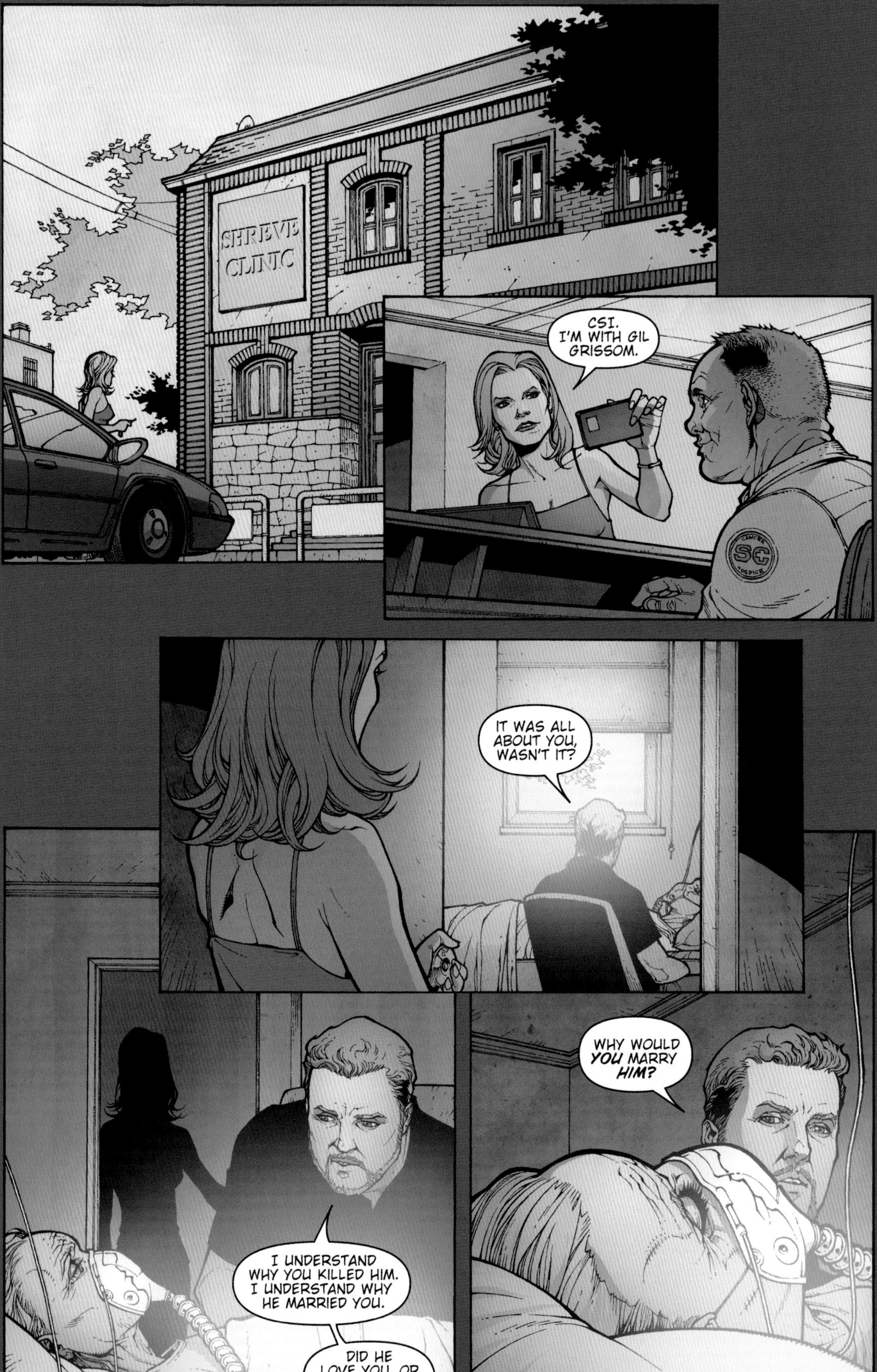
SHREVE CLINIC
CSI. I'M WITH GIL GRISSOM.
IT WAS ALL ABOUT YOU, WASN'T IT?
I UNDERSTAND WHY YOU KILLED HIM. I UNDERSTAND WHY HE MARRIED YOU.
DID HE LOVE YOU, OR DID HE BUY YOU OFF?
WHY WOULD *YOU* MARRY *HIM?*

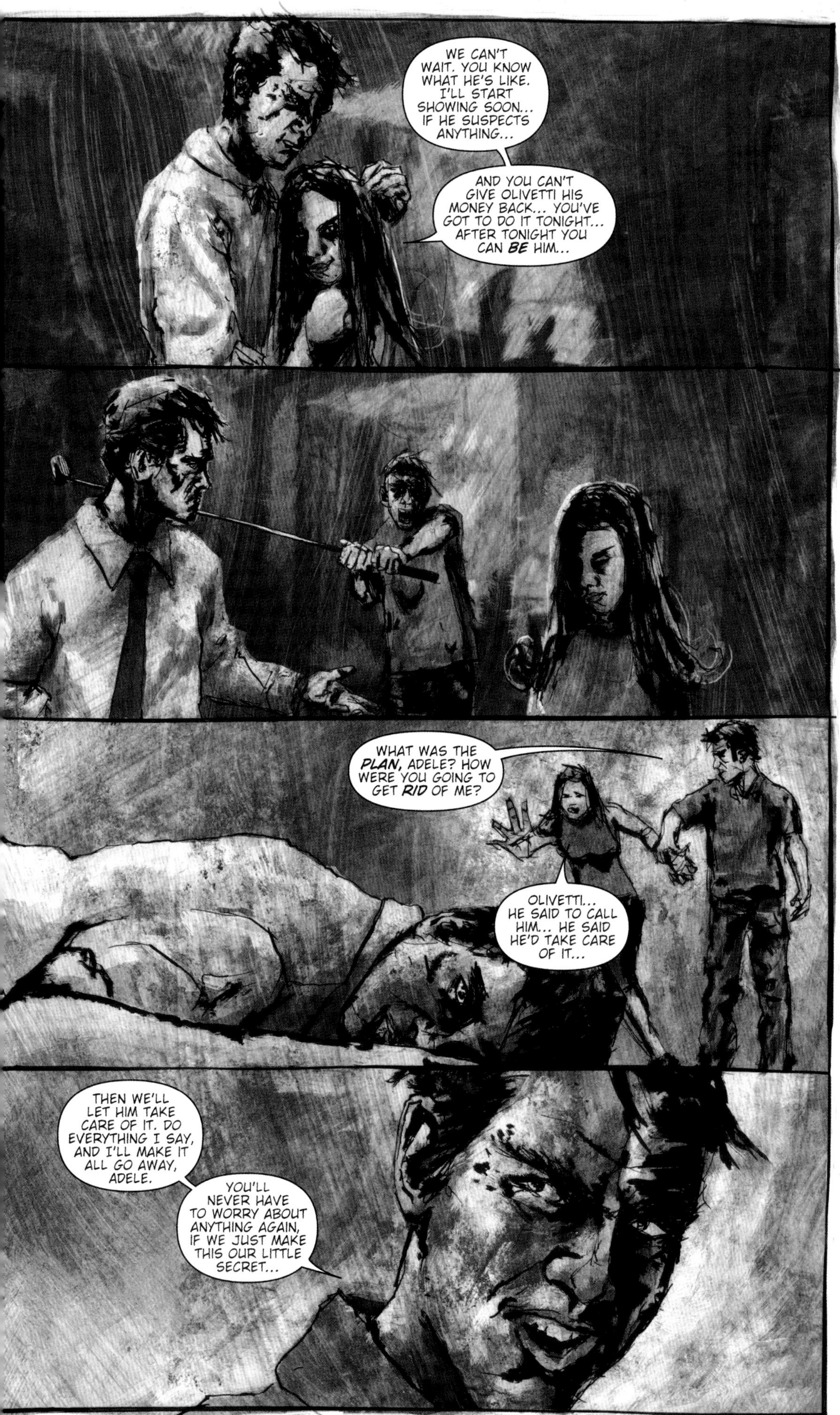

WE CAN'T WAIT. YOU KNOW WHAT HE'S LIKE. I'LL START SHOWING SOON... IF HE SUSPECTS ANYTHING...
AND YOU CAN'T GIVE OLIVETTI HIS MONEY BACK... YOU'VE GOT TO DO IT TONIGHT... AFTER TONIGHT YOU CAN **BE** HIM...
WHAT WAS THE **PLAN,** ADELE? HOW WERE YOU GOING TO GET **RID** OF ME?
OLIVETTI... HE SAID TO CALL HIM... HE SAID HE'D TAKE CARE OF IT...
THEN WE'LL LET HIM TAKE CARE OF IT. DO EVERYTHING I SAY, AND I'LL MAKE IT ALL GO AWAY, ADELE.
YOU'LL NEVER HAVE TO WORRY ABOUT ANYTHING AGAIN, IF WE JUST MAKE THIS OUR LITTLE SECRET...

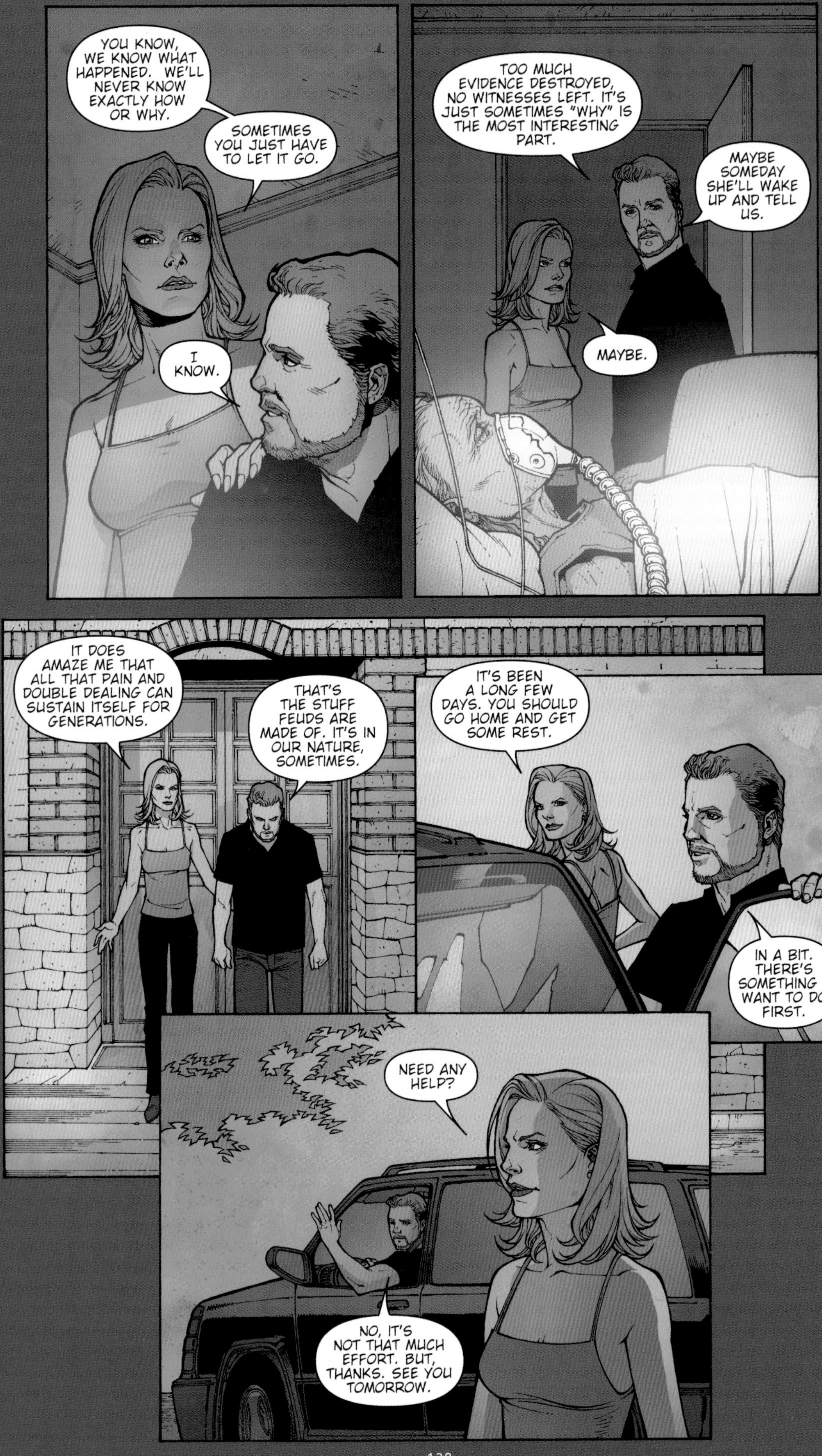
YOU KNOW, WE KNOW WHAT HAPPENED. WE'LL NEVER KNOW EXACTLY HOW OR WHY.
SOMETIMES YOU JUST HAVE TO LET IT GO.
I KNOW.
TOO MUCH EVIDENCE DESTROYED, NO WITNESSES LEFT. IT'S JUST SOMETIMES "WHY" IS THE MOST INTERESTING PART.
MAYBE SOMEDAY SHE'LL WAKE UP AND TELL US.
MAYBE.
IT DOES AMAZE ME THAT ALL THAT PAIN AND DOUBLE DEALING CAN SUSTAIN ITSELF FOR GENERATIONS.
THAT'S THE STUFF FEUDS ARE MADE OF. IT'S IN OUR NATURE, SOMETIMES.
IT'S BEEN A LONG FEW DAYS. YOU SHOULD GO HOME AND GET SOME REST.
IN A BIT. THERE'S SOMETHING I WANT TO DO FIRST.
NEED ANY HELP?
NO, IT'S NOT THAT MUCH EFFORT. BUT, THANKS. SEE YOU TOMORROW.

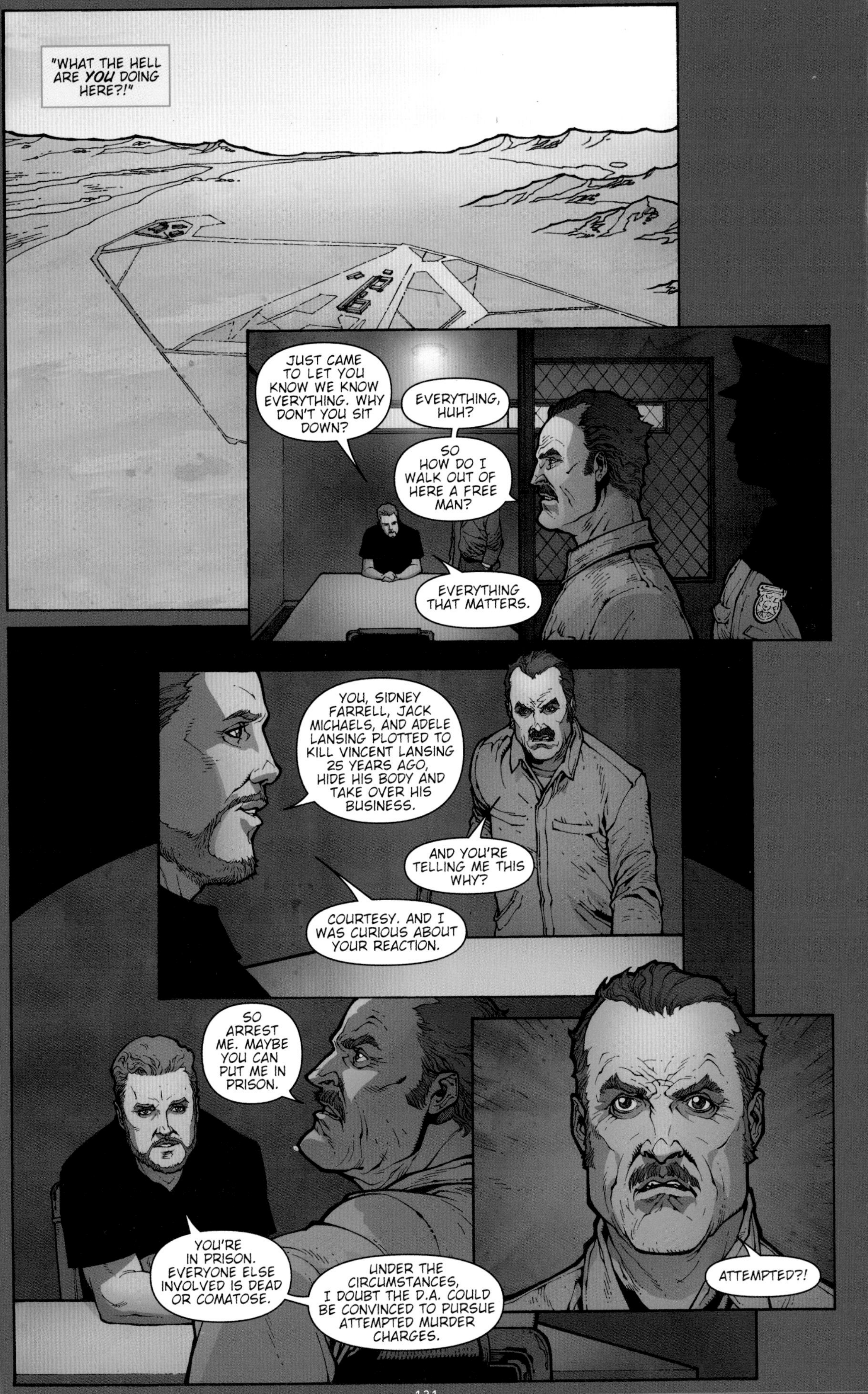
"WHAT THE HELL ARE YOU DOING HERE?!"
JUST CAME TO LET YOU KNOW WE KNOW EVERYTHING. WHY DON'T YOU SIT DOWN?
EVERYTHING, HUH?
SO HOW DO I WALK OUT OF HERE A FREE MAN?
EVERYTHING THAT MATTERS.
YOU, SIDNEY FARRELL, JACK MICHAELS, AND ADELE LANSING PLOTTED TO KILL VINCENT LANSING 25 YEARS AGO, HIDE HIS BODY AND TAKE OVER HIS BUSINESS.
AND YOU'RE TELLING ME THIS WHY?
COURTESY. AND I WAS CURIOUS ABOUT YOUR REACTION.
SO ARREST ME. MAYBE YOU CAN PUT ME IN PRISON.
YOU'RE IN PRISON. EVERYONE ELSE INVOLVED IS DEAD OR COMATOSE.
UNDER THE CIRCUMSTANCES, I DOUBT THE D.A. COULD BE CONVINCED TO PURSUE ATTEMPTED MURDER CHARGES.
ATTEMPTED?!

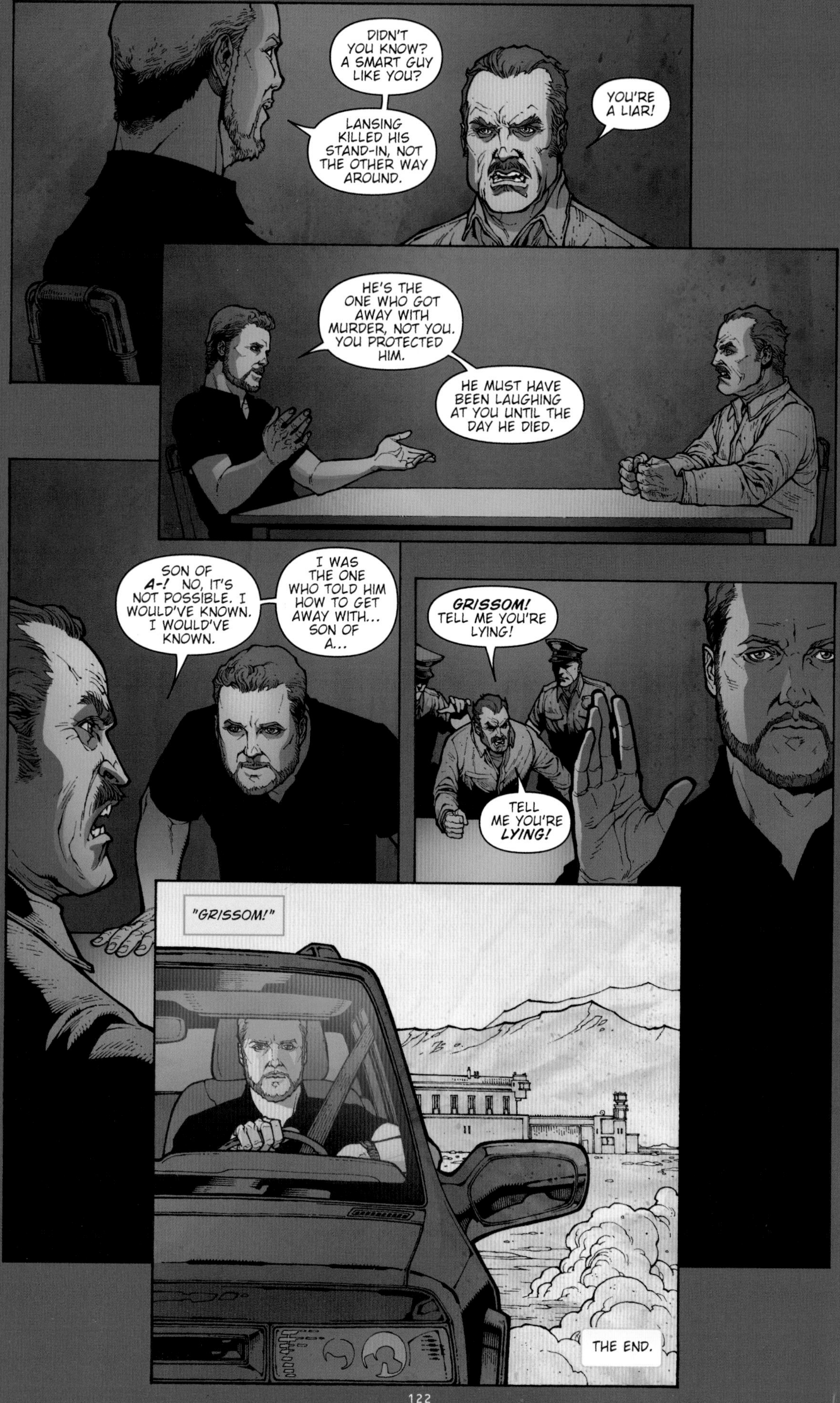
DIDN'T YOU KNOW? A SMART GUY LIKE YOU?
LANSING KILLED HIS STAND-IN, NOT THE OTHER WAY AROUND.
YOU'RE A LIAR!
HE'S THE ONE WHO GOT AWAY WITH MURDER, NOT YOU. YOU PROTECTED HIM.
HE MUST HAVE BEEN LAUGHING AT YOU UNTIL THE DAY HE DIED.
SON OF A-! NO, IT'S NOT POSSIBLE. I WOULD'VE KNOWN. I WOULD'VE KNOWN.
I WAS THE ONE WHO TOLD HIM HOW TO GET AWAY WITH... SON OF A...
GRISSOM! TELL ME YOU'RE LYING!
TELL ME YOU'RE LYING!
"GRISSOM!"
THE END.

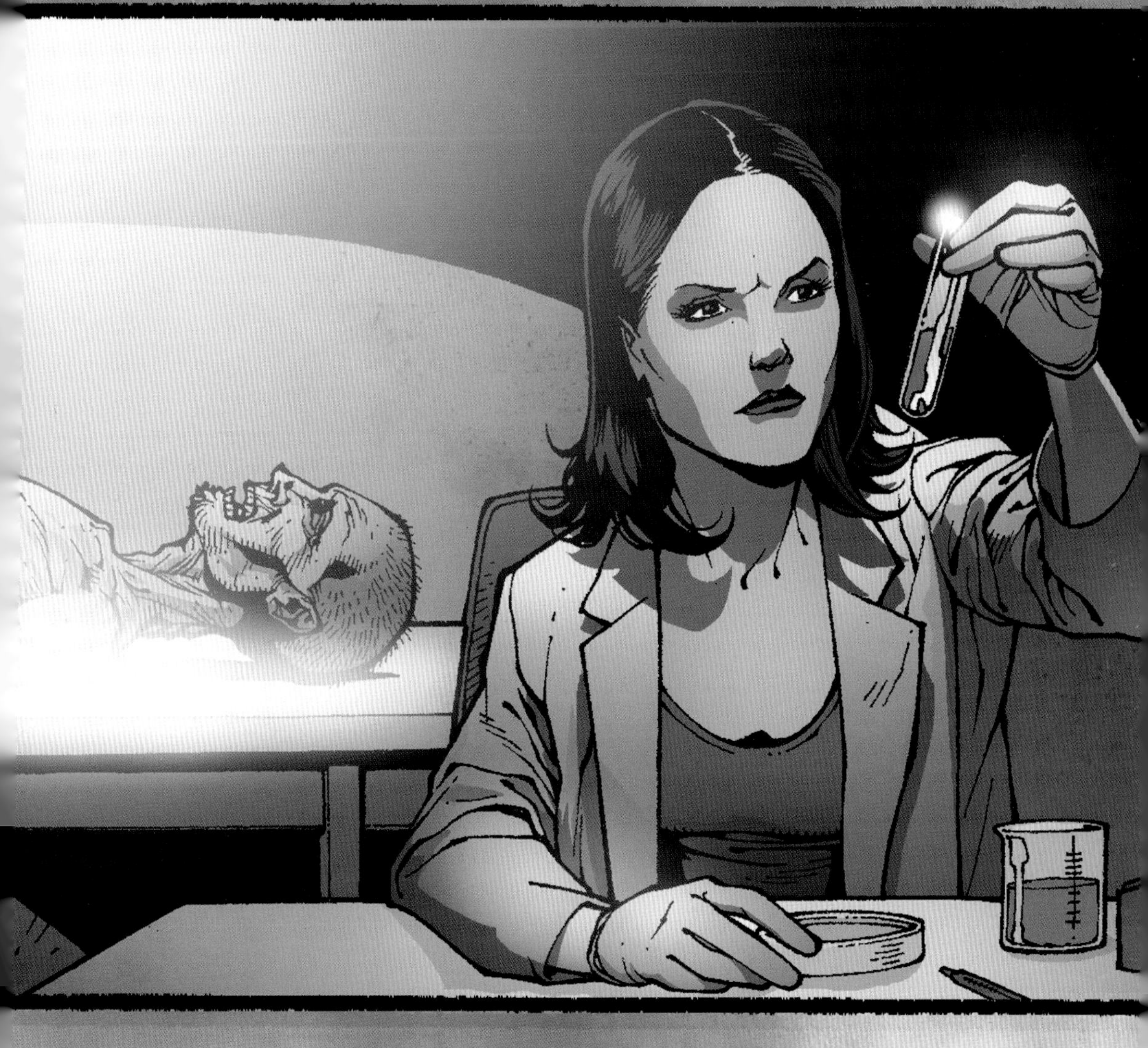

IDW

www.idwpublishing.com

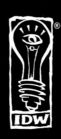